SECRET HABITS

Secret Habits

Catholic Literacy Education for Women in the Early Nineteenth Century

CAROL MATTINGLY

Southern Illinois University Press
Carbondale

Southern Illinois University Press
www.siupress.com

Copyright © 2016 by the Board of Trustees,
Southern Illinois University
All rights reserved
Printed in the United States of America

19 18 17 16   4 3 2 1

Cover illustration: View of Visitation Convent and Academy, Georgetown, Washington, D.C., 1829. Courtesy Georgetown Visitation Preparatory School.

Library of Congress Cataloging-in-Publication Data
Names: Mattingly, Carol, 1945– author.
Title: Secret habits : Catholic literacy education for women in the early nineteenth century / Carol Mattingly.
Description: Carbondale : Southern Illinois University Press, 2016. | Includes bibliographical references and index.
Identifiers: LCCN 2015046052| ISBN 9780809334926 (paperback) | ISBN 9780809334933 (e-book)
Subjects: LCSH: Women—Education—United States—History—19th century. | Literacy—United States—History—19th century. | Women in education—United States—History—19th century. | Catholic Church—Education—United States—History—19th century. | Catholic teachers—United States—History—19th century. | BISAC: LANGUAGE ARTS & DISCIPLINES / Literacy. | EDUCATION / History. | RELIGION / Christianity / Catholic.
Classification: LCC LC1752 .M336 2016 | DDC 370.82097309034—dc23 LC record available at http://lccn.loc.gov/2015046052

Printed on recycled paper. ♻

This paper meets the requirements of ANSI/NISO Z39.48-1992 (Permanence of Paper) ∞

For Mila and Kiernan

CONTENTS

Preface   ix

Acknowledgments   xiii

Chronology of Early Convent Schools and New England Proprietor Schools for Girls before 1840   xv

Introduction: Beyond the Protestant Literacy Myth   1

1. Literacy, Religion, and Schoolbooks   19

2. The Religious Nature of Early Women's Literacy   49

3. U.S.-Based Convents and the Literacy Experience   80

4. Literacy in Convent Schools of European-Based Congregations   131

5. Literacy, Benevolence, and the Paradox of Good Works   165

Conclusion   198

Appendixes

A. Chronological Index of the Earliest Catholic Women Religious Communities in the United States   207

B. Representative Academic Rules and Schedule   213

C. Schedule for Pupils from the Ursuline *Règlements*   218

Notes   219

Works Cited   235

Index   259

Gallery beginning on page 117

PREFACE

Convents and convent academies and schools were among the first U.S. schools to educate girls and young women, often providing excellent education in the South and frontier areas, instructing poor as well as wealthy young women, and creating the earliest U.S. normal schools. *Secret Habits: Catholic Literacy Education for Women in the Early Nineteenth Century* represents my effort to increase our understanding of women's literacy and rhetoric in the young United States by examining literacy practices in Catholic convents and their academies and schools, as well as their broader influences and repercussions. I do not take into account the numerous small private schools for Catholics (see Burns 1908), focusing instead on the networked schooling systems created by Catholic women religious, whose convents, academies, and schools became important sites of literacy for women. While such institutions proliferated exponentially throughout the nineteenth century and first half of the twentieth, this study concentrates primarily on the first four decades of the nineteenth century, as there is scant available information about women's literacy during this period. The U.S. Census provided no information on literacy before 1840, and nearly all studies examining literacy prior to that census are problematic in terms of women's literacy because they focus largely on records that rarely included women.

Recently scholars have examined numerous "literacies," such as financial literacy, workplace literacy, visual literacy, digital literacy, cultural literacy, and so on. For this study, I use the term "literacy" in the more traditional sense of reading and writing and examine other expected subject literacies for the early nineteenth-century student. While this work attempts to contribute to our understanding of women's literacy prior to 1840 by including Catholic convents and schools, records for literacy and education pertaining to the various convents and their schools during that period are not uniformly available. Nearly all early convents were subject to dire poverty in their initial decades. Members often taught and sewed for income, grew their own food, and cut wood to provide for heating in the winter; they had little time for recording their activities.

Complicating historical research further, Catholic women religious left few personal records, as community expectations required humility and self-effacement. As Carol K. Coburn and Martha Smith point out, "Special talents were to be hidden to avoid pride or any temptation to receive individual accolades for activities" (1999, 80). Breaching expectations for humility by calling attention to oneself and one's accomplishments would have created "a serious transgression of good convent manners" (Byrne 1986, 263). In addition, the records that did exist have been preserved unevenly, both because some individual convents maintained records more completely than others and because accidental destruction, such as fires, eliminated precious early records in others. For example, an 1849 fire destroyed the records of the Sisters of Charity of the Blessed Virgin Mary; another fire demolished many of the archival records for the Dominican Sisters of St. Rose.

A majority of the earliest U.S. convents and convent schools originated in the South. This is partly because of greater hostility to Catholics and Catholic institutions elsewhere, especially in the Northeast, and thus a larger Catholic population outside that area. While prejudice against Catholics was widespread, the Northeast was especially unfriendly to Catholics, most notably represented, perhaps, by the burning of the Ursuline convent in Charlestown, Massachusetts, in 1834 and subsequent press coverage and judicial actions. The greater number of Catholics in the South and the agricultural nature of the territory that had diminished earlier efforts at education joined to create a need for literacy efforts that sisters filled in increasingly large numbers.

The terms "nun" and "sister" to describe women religious have historical roots and contribute to the identity of individual communities, although increasingly they are used interchangeably. Nuns belong to congregations, make public vows, and usually lead a cloistered, contemplative life. Sisters are apostolic religious women who belong to a community, society, or company. I have tried to use the terms according to their technical meanings, "sister" for those in most U.S.-originated communities, according to their vows, and "nun" for those from European communities who established missions here, as they were most often cloistered originally, even if they lived without walls. Still, the terms do not always apply in this easy dichotomy. St. Vincent de Paul chose the term "sister" for his European

PREFACE

Daughters of Charity, as they were not to be cloistered but to serve the poor in their homes, hospitals, orphanages, and other places of need. The early Visitation religious in the United States followed the Visitandine rule for a cloistered community, but members did not take public vows and were not acknowledged by the papacy for some time. Most teaching groups eventually changed their rules to permit a greater participation in life outside their enclosure.

The introduction, "Beyond the Protestant Literacy Myth," questions many previous assumptions about women's literacy, complicating former beliefs by taking into account convents and convent schools. Much research on women's education has taken the New England proprietor schools as the standard against which to measure others, creating an incomplete portrait of women's literacy in the early nineteenth century. In contrast to common notions based primarily on northern Protestant schools, women were often encouraged and supported in their literacy efforts in Catholic areas, and because of the large numbers of women in convents and the numerous girls and young women they taught, women were likely more literate than men in some communities in the early United States.

Chapter 1, "Literacy, Religion, and Schoolbooks," examines how religious beliefs were incorporated into "public" or "common" schools by assessing the nature of the most popular texts used in those schools. Such schoolbooks, often written by Congregationalist ministers, presented Protestant writings and tenets, often denigrating Catholics and anything associated with their religion. Schoolbooks so fully incorporated Protestant ideas while demeaning Catholics that Catholic schools often struggled to obtain appropriate texts.

Chapter 2, "The Religious Nature of Early Women's Literacy," looks at the religious agenda of northeastern proprietor schools, especially of those usually deemed "pioneers" in women's education. Like the Catholic convents and their schools, the proprietor schools had a religious mission, focusing on training women as missionaries and teachers to further the Protestant cause and to counter the Catholic menace; they often gained support for their own schools by citing the dangers of Catholic schools.

Many U.S. Catholic women began convent communities for whom a major purpose was the education of girls and young women. Unlike similar European-based groups, who most often drew from a long tradition of educational services, these native groups found it necessary to create their own pedagogies and curricula. Chapter 3, "U.S.-Based Convents and the Literacy Experience," looks at literacy efforts among Catholic women religious communities originating in the United States, groups who found it necessary to create their own curricula and rules for their schools. Although these groups were influenced by European priests, and sometimes by European communities of women religious, they drew primarily on native women—who brought ideas and attitudes distinct from their European counterparts—for members and educators.

Chapter 4, "Literacy in Convent Schools of European-Based Congregations," addresses literacy efforts of those religious communities that originated in Europe but settled missionary communities in the United States. Members of these groups came to the United States with a sophisticated education and detailed rules and curricula for promoting literacy among girls and young women in their adopted country. Tied closely with the original European groups, these nuns initiated a typical European curriculum in their U.S. schools, adjusting to the expectations of their new society more slowly than their U.S. counterparts.

Prejudice against Catholics, and against Catholic convents and sisters in particular, created problems for the sisters, with attacks on their property and disdain for them personally. However, the sisters persisted in their mission to provide education for girls and young women; they also served their communities in numerous other ways, such as nursing during times of need and caring for orphans. Chapter 5, "Literacy, Benevolence, and the Paradox of Good Works," examines how Catholic women religious diminished prejudice through their acts of benevolence; it also reflects upon who was offered literacy and to what extent in this presumed Protestant nation and assesses the paradoxical actions of promoters of literacy and benevolent causes whose prejudices and attacks often seemed counter to their other ideals.

The conclusion highlights the contributions this study makes to our histories of women's literacy and rhetoric. It also suggests areas where more research might further our understanding of women and their historical roles.

ACKNOWLEDGMENTS

I am indebted to many whose support has contributed to this work. At the institutional level, the University of Louisville, through its internal research grants, has supported my travel to many archival locations. The Interlibrary Loan staff at the University of Louisville's Ekstrom Library has assisted me with professional, efficient, and always friendly and patient effort in locating difficult materials; Delinda Buie and staff in Rare Books at Ekstrom have been similarly cordial and helpful.

Over the years I have worked on this manuscript, I have been fortunate to meet and learn from many gracious individuals; for all of them I am grateful. The many kind persons I met in the numerous archives I visited not only assisted me with archival materials but also often helped me to understand their communities' histories. Many extended other kindnesses during my time at their locations. At the Archives of the Sisters of Loretto, Sisters Ann Francis Gleason and Aurelia Otterbach befriended me, offering companionship, support, and information about the sisters' history. Sister Kate Misbach also patiently helped me to navigate the archival material there. At the Sisters of Charity of Nazareth, a number of archivists assisted me with materials: Sister Anna Catherine Coon, Sister Bridgid Clifford, Ellen Clifford, Anna Powell, and Kathy Hertel-Baker. I am indebted to all of them, and especially to Anna Powell for discovering the handwritten manuals of Sister Columba Carroll. Sister Jane Behlmann, Sisters of St. Joseph of Carondelet, St. Louis Province archivist, assisted me during my research at those sisters' archives and offered numerous other courtesies during my stay there.

I am grateful to Sister Anne Francis Campbell, archivist for the Sisters of Charity of Our Lady of Mercy; to Carole Prietto, associate archivist, Daughters of Charity Province of St. Louise; and to Sister Betty Ann McNeil and Bonnie Weatherly at the Emmitsburg archives, who assisted me in the early years of this project when I was finding my way. McNeil and Weatherly also kindly read an early version of chapter 2, providing helpful suggestions.

ACKNOWLEDGMENTS

In addition, I wish to thank Sisters Frances Gimber, Mary Louise Gavan, and Carolyn Osiek, Society of the Sacred Heart, St. Louis; Sharon Knecht, archivist at the Oblate Sisters of Providence, who also responded to a portion of chapter 3; Sister Martha Jacobs, archivist, Louisville Ursuline Sisters; Elizabeth Johnson, Sisters of Mercy Archives, Mercy Heritage Center, North Carolina; Jenny Mayo, director of communication, Georgetown Visitation Preparatory School; Sister Joan Marie Aycock, archivist for the New Orleans Ursuline Sisters; and the staffs at Sisters of Mercy Archives, Cincinnati, and Ursuline Sisters of the Central Province.

David P. Miros, archivist at the Jesuit Midwest Archives, kindly helped me to understand the Jesuit relationship to the sisters' work, as did John Wm. Waide, university archivist, St. Louis University, and Leon Hooper at the Woodstock Theological Center Library, Georgetown University. Tricia T. Pyne at the Baltimore Sulpician Archives helped with similar understanding with regard to the Sulpicians. I am also grateful for the assistance of Wm. Kevin Cawley and his staff at the University of Notre Dame Archives and for that of Emilie G. Leumas, archivist, Archdiocese of New Orleans.

A number of friends and colleagues have read and responded to portions of this work, providing much-needed support during this lengthy process. My sincere appreciation goes to Lisa Arnold, Karen Chandler, Jo Ann Griffin, Benjamin Hufbauer, Vanessa Kraemer-Sohan, Samantha NeCamp, Annette Powell, Susan Ryan, and Elizabethada Wright. I am grateful, also, to two anonymous readers for Southern Illinois University Press. I want to express my appreciation, too, to Deborah Brandt, whose work and friendship have been inspirational to me, and to the numerous students I have been privileged to know over the years. I am always indebted to them for their intelligent insights and warmth.

Thanks go to Amanda Mottorn, account executive for Readex, for providing access to newly digitized historical materials; to Saundra Dockins, nurse anesthetist, and Kelsey Walsh, archivist, American Association of Nurse Anesthetists, for information regarding sisters' early anesthesia practices; and to Sister Ann Francis Gleason for helping me with French translation and Matthieu Dalle for assuring its accuracy.

Thank you, Kristine Priddy, for your support and insightful, excellent work as editor; Judy Verdich, for your help with images; and Julie Bush, for your careful copyediting that made this work so much better.

And, as always, I am grateful for the support of my loving daughters, Amy and Maggie.

CHRONOLOGY OF EARLY CONVENT SCHOOLS AND NEW ENGLAND PROPRIETOR SCHOOLS FOR GIRLS BEFORE 1840

The following chronology demonstrates the proliferation of convent academies that so frightened opponents of Catholicism. I recognize that graduates of the proprietor schools often became teachers; however, they rarely established academies and networked systems of education, their schools often one- or two-teacher elementary schools, and most taught only for a few years.

I have included Catholic sisters' orphan asylums in cases where no academy or day school was nearby, as the sisters educated orphans in a manner similar to those in their day schools. The chronology does not include the many private Catholic schools, which were oftentimes run by individual women. They usually were not as long-lived as the sisters' day schools and academies, and the ongoing literacy practices and teacher preparation of the convents were unavailable to them.

- 1727 Ursuline sisters establish convent and academy in New Orleans
- 1790 American Carmelite Sisters are established in Port Tobacco, Md.
- 1792 Sarah Pierce opens school in her home
- 1797 "Pious Ladies" open school in Philadelphia
- 1798 Sarah Pierce's school moves to building outside her home, renamed Litchfield School for Young Ladies
  Poor Clares open Georgetown Academy for girls, Georgetown, D.C.
- 1799 "Pious Ladies" move to Georgetown and open school
- 1802 "Pious Ladies," now Visitandines, open Visitation Academy, Georgetown

1803 The New Orleans Ursuline Academy becomes part of the United States after the Louisiana Purchase
1804 Four women calling themselves sisters, under the direction of Rev. Gabriel Richard, open St. Anne's school for girls in Detroit; the women were never formally recognized as a religious community
1806 Detroit "sisters" open second school in Detroit area.
1807 Emma Willard becomes head of Middlebury Academy, Vt.
1808 Elizabeth Seton opens school for girls in Baltimore
1809 Elizabeth Seton founds Sisters of Charity of St. Joseph in Emmitsburg, Md., and opens St. Joseph Academy for girls
1810 Emmitsburg Sisters of Charity begin free elementary school
1812 Sisters of Loretto founded in Loretto, Ky.; they open Loretto Academy
Sisters of Charity of Nazareth founded on grounds of St. Thomas Seminary near Bardstown, Ky.
Irish Ursulines establish convent and school for girls in New York that lasts only a few years
1814 Emma Willard opens Middlebury Female Seminary in Vermont
Emmitsburg Sisters of Charity establish St. Joseph Orphan Asylum, Philadelphia
Sisters of Charity of Nazareth open St. Thomas Academy
1816 Sisters of Loretto open boarding school in Calvary, Ky.
1817 Emmitsburg Sisters of Charity establish New York Orphan Asylum and Day School
Elizabeth Lange and Marie Balas begin free school for black children in Lange's home, Baltimore (this school will become St. Joseph Academy)
1818 Philippine Duchesne establishes Sisters of the Sacred Heart in St. Charles, Mo., opening school and academy
Sisters of Loretto open school and academy in Gethsemani, Ky.
Joseph Emerson opens Byfield Seminary for young girls
Free school for German Catholics opened in Philadelphia by Emmitsburg Sisters of Charity
1819 Nazareth Sisters of Charity open Bethlehem Academy, Bardstown, Ky.
1820 Emmitsburg Sisters of Charity open free school in New York
Irish Ursuline sisters establish convent and academy in Boston

Nazareth Sisters of Charity open St. Vincent Academy, Union County, Ky.

1821 Emma Willard opens Troy Female Seminary

Sisters of Loretto open school, Bethania, in Fairfield, Ky.

St. Mary's Asylum and Free School begun in Baltimore by Emmitsburg Sisters of Charity

Sisters of the Sacred Heart establish foundation in Grand Coteau, La.

1822 Dominican Sisters of St. Rose, Springfield, Ky., founded

Sisters of Charity of Nazareth move convent and academy to Nazareth, Ky., renaming their convent and academy Nazareth

1823 Catharine and Mary Beecher open small school in Hartford, Conn.; the school will become Hartford Female Seminary

Sisters of Loretto open convent and school, Mount Carmel, in Barrens, Perry Co., Mo.

Sisters of Loretto open Mount Carmel Academy, Breckinridge Co., Ky., later renamed Bethlehem Academy

Sisters of Loretto open school, Bethlehem Academy, in Perry Co., Mo.

Nazareth Sisters of Charity open St. Catherine Academy, White Sulphur, Ky.

1824 Zilpah Grant becomes principal of Adams Female Academy in Derry, N.H.

Sisters of Loretto open school, Mount Olivet, in Casey Co., Ky.

Sisters of the Sacred Heart establish school in Opeloussas, La.

St. John's School and Asylum, in Frederick, Md., opened by Emmitsburg Sisters of Charity

Nazareth Sisters of Charity open school in Vincennes, Ind. (Emmitsburg Sisters of Charity take over this school in 1838)

Academy of St. Mary Magdalen opened by Dominican Sisters of St. Rose in Springfield, Ky.

1825 Sisters of Loretto open convent and school in Bayou La Fourche, La.

St. Vincent's School and Asylum, in Washington, D.C., begun by Emmitsburg Sisters of Charity

Sisters of the Sacred Heart establish school and convent, St. Michael, in Baron (now Convent), La.

1826 Poor Clares open school in Cincinnati; the school lasts only a year or two because of difficulties with ecclesiastical superiors
1827 Sisters of the Sacred Heart establish convent and Young Ladies Academy in St. Louis
Ursuline Sisters move convent and academy from Boston to Charlestown, Mass. (Mount Benedict Academy); it is destroyed by a mob in 1834
Sarah Pierce's school incorporated as Litchfield Academy
1828 Zilpah Grant dismissed from Derry; founds Ipswich Female Seminary, Ipswich, Mass.
Mary Lyon begins teaching at Ipswich Female Seminary
Catharine Beecher moves Hartford school to new building
Sisters of St. Clare establish convent and academy in Pittsburgh
Emmitsburg Sisters of Charity open St. Mary's School and Asylum, Albany, N.Y.
Poor Clares open school in Pittsburgh
1829 Founding of Oblate Sisters of Providence, Baltimore, and St. Joseph Academy for African American girls
Sisters of Charity of Our Lady of Mercy established in Charleston, S.C., opening day school and academy for girls
Emmitsburg Sisters of Charity take charge of St. Peter's Asylum, Cincinnati
1830 Emmitsburg Sisters of Charity establish St. Peter's Academy, Wilmington, Del.
Emmitsburg Sisters of Charity open orphan asylum in New Orleans
Dominican Sisters open school in Somerset, Ohio
Sisters of Loretto open St. Joseph's School in Apple Creek, Mo.; the school is closed two years later
1831 Bethlehem Academy, Hardin Co., Ky., established by Sisters of Loretto
Carmelites open Female Academy in Baltimore
St. Mary's Academy, Somerset, Ohio, opened by Dominican Sisters
Presentation Academy, Louisville, opened by Nazareth Sisters of Charity

CHRONOLOGY

1832 Visitation sisters open Female Academy of the Visitation, Mobile, Ala.
Sisters of Loretto open St. Mary's in New Madrid, Mo. (closed 1837)
St. Michael's, in Fredericktown, Mo., opened by Sisters of Loretto (closed 1837)
Emmitsburg Sisters of Charity open St. Francis Xavier in Alexandria, Va.
St. Aloysius School and Asylum opened in Boston by Emmitsburg Sisters of Charity
Nazareth Sisters of Charity open St. Vincent orphanage in Louisville, Ky.

1833 Sisters of Charity of the Blessed Virgin Mary established in Philadelphia
Visitation sisters open convent and academy in Kaskaskia, Ill.
Sisters of Loretto establish boarding and day school in Lebanon, Ky.
Nazareth Sisters of Charity open St. Catherine's Academy, Lexington, Ky.
Les Dames de la Retraite open Young Ladies' French and English Academy, Philadelphia
Poor Clares open Seminary for Girls in Detroit

1834 Irish Ursulines open Young Ladies' Academy in Charleston, S.C.

1835 Catharine Beecher opens Western Female Institute (closed 1837)
Emmitsburg Sisters of Charity begin St. Paul's Asylum and School in Pittsburgh
Sisters of Charity of Our Lady of Mercy found free school for girls of color in Charleston, S.C.

1836 Sisters of St. Joseph of Carondelet open school and academy in Carondelet, Mo., and in Cahokia, Ill.
Emmitsburg Sisters of Charity open St. Peter's Academy in Cincinnati

1837 Mary Lyon opens Mount Holyoke Academy
Sisters of St. Joseph of Carondelet open school for deaf
Our Lady of Mount Carmel, Saint Genevieve, Mo., opened by Sisters of Loretto
Visitation Sisters open convent and academy in Baltimore

1838   Sisters of Charity of the Blessed Virgin Mary open academy for girls

Emmitsburg Sisters of Charity open St. Mary's Female Academy in Vincennes, Ind.

St. Mary's, in Pine Bluff, Ark., opened by Sisters of Loretto

Sisters of Loretto open St. Vincent's Academy in Cape Girardeau, Mo.

Nazareth Sisters of Charity open day school in New Albany, Ind.

1839   Sisters of Charity of Our Lady of Mercy open Our Lady of Mercy Academy, Charleston, S.C.

Les Dames de la Retraite open Female Academy in St. Augustine, Fla.

SECRET HABITS

Introduction: Beyond the Protestant Literacy Myth

Literacy historians have long credited the Protestant mandate to read Scripture for advances in literacy, with historians of American literacy pointing to New England Puritans as the model for the Protestant impetus to literacy. This belief is commonplace in our best histories. For example, Lawrence Stone identifies the "critical element" of mass literacy "not so much as Christianity as Protestantism" (1969, 77) and declares, "At the deepest psychological level, Tridentine Catholicism remained a culture of the image. It intensified the worship of saints, and indulged in ever more lavish embellishment of churches with paintings, glass and sculpture. By contrast, Protestantism was a culture of the book, of a literate society" (78). Similarly, Kenneth Lockridge claims that "it is possible to hold great respect for the Protestant impulse as the sole force powerful enough to work a transformation in the level of literacy" (1974, 45). Harvey Graff finds that Irish Catholics in nineteenth-century Canada had a lower literacy rate than Protestants because Irish Catholics' religion "importantly influenced their disadvantaged status" while "Protestantism provided a greater impetus to literacy than Catholicism—a link that historians should well expect" (1979, 58); and E. Jennifer Monaghan, in noting the complex "religious, social, political and economic base" influencing literacy, nonetheless assumes that "the [Protestant] religious motive was paramount" (2005, 32). The claim surfaces in numerous other texts related to literacy studies. In the most used history of rhetoric text in English departments, for example, Patricia Bizzell and Bruce Herzberg claim, "The spread of Protestant Christianity in the eighteenth and nineteenth century aided women's efforts to become better educated.... Protestantism encouraged women to be literate so that they could read the Bible" (2001, 987).[1]

This overarching, seemingly self-evident belief in Protestantism and firsthand experience with biblical texts as the primary promoter of literacy

INTRODUCTION

in America has overshadowed other important efforts at literacy, leading to an incomplete understanding of American literacy history. The Protestant narrative was created amid patriarchal and religious attitudes that have shaped how we see ourselves and the stories we continue to tell, obscuring other valid narratives and promoting prejudicial inaccuracies. In this introduction, I use Catholic literacy efforts as a test case to question some accepted assumptions about American literacy, including beliefs that Protestants valued literacy while Catholics did not and that women were always less literate than men. I suggest that competition among religions to attract and maintain members may have been more important in the sponsorship of literacy than religious beliefs per se.

The American Protestant grand narrative arises partly because historians have synecdochically focused on early colonies, primarily the New England colonies, to craft a narrative of literacy for all of America;[2] however, prior to English settlement, French, Spanish, and Portuguese conquerors and missionaries introduced themselves to the New World as sponsors of literacies from a European Catholic tradition. As Jamie Candelaria Greene (1994) has noted, the presentation of American literacy as an English (Protestant) enterprise demonstrates an ethnocentric bias. For example, members of the religious Franciscan order both accompanied the first Spanish conquistadores to the Americas and continued to immigrate with the purpose of educating and "civilizing" native inhabitants. Franciscans and other religious orders created schools for natives and for children of the invading armies and settlers, teaching in both Spanish and Latin languages throughout the Spanish-conquered Americas, including areas that would become part of the United States (Barth 1945, 50; Gallegos 1992, 26, 34; Burns 1908, 39–66). The primary purpose, of course, was to extend the Christian (Catholic) religion and Spanish/European culture, imposing "a foreign world view on the native population" (Gallegos 1992, 67).

Similarly, members of Catholic religious communities followed French explorers and settlers to the New World to spread French and Catholic culture. Jesuits had arrived in Quebec as early as 1610, and Ursuline sisters joined them in 1639, establishing the first schools for girls and young women in the Americas. Shortly after, Catholic women religious created convents and schools in Montreal, Three Rivers, and other French Canadian communities.[3] The Ursulines also settled a community of religious women in New Orleans in 1727, shortly after their arrival establishing a school for girls; the New Orleans school is the oldest extant school for girls in the United States. Like Protestant groups, Catholics saw the Americas as a place to extend their religious and cultural vision. During the colonial period, Catholics established early schools in what would become Arizona, California, Florida, Illinois, Louisiana, Maine, Maryland, Michigan, New Mexico, New York, Pennsylvania, and Wisconsin, some as early as the sixteenth century (Buetow 1970, 1–37; Burns 1908, 39–65).

An important aspect of the Protestant narrative hinges on the importance of literacy in conducting oneself as a Protestant. Protestants often differentiated themselves from "papists" by pointing to their personal involvement with Scripture. According to the narratives of most literacy historians, Protestants did not rely upon clergy as intermediaries but could interpret God's word themselves, especially through the reading of the vernacular Bible (as opposed to the Catholic emphasis on Latin, for example, or to the Catholic distrust of anyone but the clergy for interpreting the word). Because of this belief in the individual's ability, right, and duty to read Scripture, reading was promoted by Protestant leaders beginning with Martin Luther. This theory has become commonplace in literacy studies.[4]

However, Richard Gawthrop and Gerald Strauss have argued that while Luther called for general, basic reading and writing for both boys and girls, he "favoured the school as a specialized facility for preparing a professional cadre capable of assuming positions of leadership in church and state: pastors and preachers, theologians and church administrators, lawyers and bureaucrats, teachers, physicians" (1984, 32). And, "by the second half of the 1520s he no longer thought that this internal change [within the individual conscience] could be effected by means of private Bible study" (35). The common schools thus established rarely provided or taught the Bible, instead using catechisms "suitable for memorizing" (37) to promote respect, loyalty, and acceptable social conventions (38). According to Gawthrop and Strauss, education in reading and writing increased as citizens, "more alert to the importance of literacy as a precondition of keeping or raising one's place in society," demanded it (38). Gawthrop and Strauss conclude that "the facts as we can establish them do not substantiate the generally accepted notion—which no one has ever felt obliged to prove—of a causal link between the Lutheran Reformation of the sixteenth century and popular Bible reading" (41).[5]

We might consider such a trend for the New England colonies. The complexity suggested by other-than-religious literacy sponsors, such as commercial interests, encourages the exploration of alternatives to the dominant American literacy narrative. New England saw little growth in literacy levels during the first generations of settlers, when one might expect the Protestant fervor to be especially intense. And while leaders spoke often of a literate community who could read the Bible, they placed greatest emphasis on readying a future generation of professionals, especially a ministry to lead the people. Early schooling laws in New England, often cited as evidence of Protestant interest in literacy, established Latin grammar schools, where children were expected to learn Latin, perhaps Greek, writing, and numbers, not reading, as the presumption was that children would learn reading at home, an expectation that went largely unmet (Monaghan 2005, 31–43). Leaders' early schooling emphasis focused on preparation for scholarly and commercial careers suitable for a chosen people, not on Scripture reading. When the schools began to teach reading because children entering them were unable to read, those schools relied largely on moral primers and catechisms, often emphasizing rote memorization instead of reading.

An Alternative Narrative

The reification of Protestantism as the source and guardian of literacy in America originated within an exclusionary structure of power and prejudice, and the remnants of the stories thus created continue to eclipse alternative narratives. One such example includes narratives about Catholics' disinterest in or hostility to literacy. Harvey Graff suggests in *Legacies of Literacy* that "Catholicism has suffered a too negative, too unilaterally condemnatory press" on the subject of literacy promotion (1967, 135). He is accurate here. The accepted premise that morality and literacy were linked, along with bitter prejudice toward Catholics, helped establish the notion of Catholic antagonism toward literacy, ignoring the socioeconomic context that assured a less literate Catholic population. The illiterate nineteenth-century Irish Catholics whom Graff focuses on in his *Literacy Myth* derived from a long history of the types of oppression scholars have recently recognized as impeding literacy acquisition, including laws and social circumstances that precluded advancement in literacy. Before coming to North America, Graff's Irish had suffered from centuries of conquest in which they were divested of property and civil rights. Already forced into darkest poverty by years of domination and oppression, Irish Catholics were further disadvantaged by British penal laws beginning in the late seventeenth century. Commonly called "popery" laws, these codes assured continued economic, social, and literacy deprivation for Irish Catholics. The laws banished most Catholic clergy, who were often educators, and greatly limited the activities and influence of others. After centuries in which their lands were confiscated, Catholics were further barred from buying and restricted from inheriting land. They were prevented from practicing law, holding office, or participating in other civil activities. The laws constrained meaningful attendance at established schools and forbade Catholics from creating their own schools or sending their children abroad to be educated.[6]

Literacy historians have largely dismissed or omitted Catholic efforts at literacy in the New World, accepting the stories of Catholic disinterest and ignoring the persecution that continued throughout British American colonies. Once the British gained control of Nova Scotia, in what is known as the Great Expulsion, they deported more than 75 percent of the French Catholics there to a variety of locations, burned their homes, and confiscated their lands. Many perished during the harsh, forced exodus. Survivors were dispersed widely, with large numbers permanently separated from family. Such prejudicial treatment was pervasive throughout British-held areas, including the United States: in New England, the presumed cradle of literacy in America, Pope's Day, an annual celebration ridiculing Catholics, ended with burning the pope in effigy, and the annual Dudleian lecture, Harvard Divinity School's oldest endowment, required the speaker to rotate among four topics, one being an exposure of "the idolatry of the Romish Church, their tyranny, usurpations, damnable heresies, fatal errors, abominable superstitions, and other crying weaknesses" to demonstrate that "the Church of Rome is that mystical Babylon, that man of sin, that apostate church, spoken of in the New Testament" (qtd. in Silcox and Fisher 1934, 9).[7] Catholics were persecuted in all English colonies except Pennsylvania (Buetow 1970, 23–37). Many colonial charters specifically excluded "papists." In Maryland, where Catholics were initially most numerous, school attendance for Catholic children became quickly restricted, and other acts similar to the English Penal Laws were imposed. In most colonies, literacy was employed to teach children to hate Catholics:

> All types of reading matter were utilized by those who employed the printed word to shower calumny on Catholicism. Children whose primary instruction was from one of the primers in common use were accustomed to crude engravings of Protestant martyrs and to

sentiments placing Popery in alignment with heathenism and infidelity. Infant minds were shaped to believe that "to be a Catholic, was to be a false, cruel and bloody wretch," and that Popery included everything that was vicious and vile. (Billington 1938, 347)

Recent literacy studies affirm the complex circumstances that influence literacy acquisition and the difficulty in achieving literacy for groups who have been historically relegated to illiteracy and oppressed in other ways. To assume, then, that low literacy rates among North American Catholics resulted from their disinterest is too quick a judgment. Both the hedge schools in Ireland, for which a tremendously impoverished people paid from scant incomes and braved harsh penalties to educate their children, and U.S. Catholics' willingness to construct and operate their own schools—a financial burden in addition to state-mandated taxes they paid for public schools promoting an anti-Catholic curriculum—suggest that Catholics, too, accepted the literacy myth that schooling was an avenue that ensured an improved socioeconomic status.

If Protestants promoted literacy, a tool for converting and maintaining disciples, Catholics became no less intent on using literacy in countering the Protestant "heresy" and in furthering and maintaining Catholicism. Catholic religious communities had historically provided schools, but numerous additional Catholic religious orders were founded and proliferated quickly as part of the Counter-Reformation and Catholic Reformation. Ignatius Loyola's Jesuits, perhaps the best-known group, devoted themselves to teaching, but numerous other male groups, such as the Franciscans, the Sulpicians, and the Oratorians, were formed as well and took on teaching missions. Women, too, came to the cause, outnumbering men in religious communities greatly by the beginning of the eighteenth century. Angela Merici, for example, established the Ursuline sisters in Brescia, Italy, in 1535 with the explicit purpose of educating girls and young women; by the end of the seventeenth century, the community numbered "between ten thousand and twelve thousand Ursulines in some three hundred and twenty communities" across France alone (Rapley 1990, 48). The Ursulines represent just one of numerous communities of women religious involved with literacy. Supported often by the teaching congregations that had already created detailed guides for teachers and assisted by one another, these women's communities established comprehensive curricula for their students and guidelines for training members in becoming effective teachers;

INTRODUCTION

the women in these communities placed a lifelong emphasis on literacy for themselves and made their life's occupation the teaching of girls and other women. In addition, the church also encouraged women's confraternities, which included married women who continued earlier educational quests and became active in their communities. The request for teachers of girls on the part of both Catholic authorities and Catholic parents appears to have been very high and nearly always exceeded the ability of the communities to provide enough teachers for the demand, dispelling notions of Catholics' hostility to literacy (Rapley 1990, 86; *Glimpses* 1897, 73; Friess qtd. in Mannard 1989, 158).

"In the English colonies . . . Catholics existed through a century and a half as an insignificant minority in a state of practical outlawry" (Ellis 1969, 41), but after the U.S. Constitution established freedom of religion, the number of Catholics increased rapidly. The first U.S. Census, in 1790, accounted for a population of 3,929,214. In 1785, Bishop John Carroll had put the number of Catholics at 24,500 plus an unknown number in the French-speaking territory east of the Mississippi, gained during the French and Indian War ([1785] 1978, 152). John Tracy Ellis puts the total number at 35,000 (1969, 43). Using Ellis's figure, the Catholic population would still have been less than 1 percent of the total. By 1836, Simon Bruté reported a Catholic population of 1,010,000. Based on the 1840 census number of 17,069,453 for the overall population, the number demonstrates a Catholic population that had increased to nearly 6 percent of the total population and was increasing rapidly in the years between the time of the report and the 1840 census (Bruté [1836] 1978, 223).

After the establishment of religious freedom, U.S. Catholic women began founding religious communities in the young United States with the explicit purpose of educating girls and young women. For example, five U.S. teaching communities were founded in just a twenty-year period, between 1809 and 1829. The numbers of communities grew rapidly. They provided education for tens of thousands of young sisters within their communities and hundreds of thousands of girls and young women in their schools and academies; their schools increased so quickly and became so renowned that Protestant leaders became fearful of the sisters' power. For example, the Sisters of Charity of Nazareth, founded in 1812 near Bardstown, Kentucky, had built a stately academy at their motherhouse by 1818 that included 60 sisters with 60 boarders; they had opened three additional schools by 1825 (M. Spalding 1844, 234; Howlett 1906, 302). Similarly, the Sisters of Loretto, another central Kentucky community founded in 1812, numbered more than 100 members with more than 300 girls in eight schools by 1824. Both the convent membership and schools continued to grow at this rate well into the twentieth century.[8] The sisters provided the first free schools in many locations. European religious communities with a similar mission began arriving and creating schools as well.

As the Catholic population grew in the young United States, U.S. Catholic Church authorities expressed concern for providing literacy instruction to the growing Catholic population, including females. Numerous extant letters between male clergy and the leaders of women's convents attest to efforts to provide schools for girls in Catholic communities, often at the behest of parishioners. By 1829 the Council of Baltimore had proclaimed,

> Whereas very many youth of Catholic parents, especially among the poor, have been and still are, in many parts of this Province, exposed to great danger of losing their faith, and having their morals corrupted, from the want of proper teachers, to whom so important a trust can be safely confided; we judge it indispensably necessary to establish schools, in which youth may be nurtured in the principles of faith and morals, while they are instructed in literature. (qtd. in Silcox and Fisher 1934, 166)

Both Protestants and Catholics saw literacy as an important part of their efforts at converting and maintaining membership and of establishing cultural hegemony. But the unique structure for providing education among Catholics is especially important for our understanding of American women's literacy. The Catholic Church was both hierarchical and paternalistic. In fact, previous to and immediately after the Reformation, the male hierarchy repeatedly curbed religious women's activist efforts, insisting on a cloistered retirement in return for the communal living many sought. Eventually, however, church leaders gave formal recognition to and supported more fully the efforts of the religious communities of sisters who became educators, as they saw women's literacy as essential to the church's interests. The sisters lived apart from men, pursued often very high levels of education, and actively promoted literacy among the women and girls of their communities. The large numbers of literate American Catholic women in religious communities alone calls into question claims that women were always less literate than men, and their influence spread beyond their convent walls.

INTRODUCTION

Women's Literacy in French American Colonies

Ursuline nuns began arriving in the New World in 1639. The first Ursulines in Quebec were highly educated, professionally trained teachers. They taught American Indian girls and women as well as the children of French settlers. They learned to speak the languages of the Hurons and Algonquins, and Mother Mary of the Incarnation, one of the original group, composed French treatises for the sisters' educational institutions as well as "a sacred history in Algonquin, a dictionary in Algonquin, a catechism in Huron, another catechism and a prayer-book in Algonquin" (*Glimpses* 1897, 101, 77). The nuns took responsibility for educating a large number of female boarders, both French and Indian, as well as day students. Seminarists, the name given American Indian girls who boarded at the convent, numbered as many as eighty during some years of the first half of the eighteenth century, and the number of French children was even higher (41). The sisters and priests instructed large numbers of adult American Indians as well, both women and men.[9] These and other communities of women religious soon established additional communities in Canada.

The Ursuline Rule required women to teach "reading and grammar, the Christian doctrine and sacred history, practical arithmetic, penmanship and needlework" (*Glimpses* 1897, 74). According to the early nuns, they gave "religious instructions in three languages, French, Algonquin, and Huron"; taught seminarists to read, write, and sew; and taught children of French settlers "all that is necessary to fit them for the station in society to which they belong" (43). Letters written by both Indian and French students attest to the girls' facility in written language. Another community of Ursuline nuns was begun in what would become part of the United States, in New Orleans in 1727, just nine years after the city's founding. These women, too, had expected to work among the American Indians; however, their mission became primarily the evangelization of the African American population and the education of French women and girls, as well as some African American and American Indian girls.

These two communities of French religious throw into question assumptions made about women's education during the colonization of the North American continent, which are based primarily on the British influence: that women were less literate than men and that "popular culture of the time ridiculed anyone educating a woman" during "the seventeenth and most of the eighteenth century" (Gordon and Gordon 2003, 21). Evidence suggests, rather, that women were supported in literacy efforts in French Catholic communities and that women were often more literate than men.

Most scholars of literacy in colonial America and the early Republic determine literacy estimates primarily based on signatures on a variety of documents. Distance in time and scarcity of extant evidence in any other form have made signature rates an accepted form of evidence among scholars for determining literacy rates—not an ideal one but one of the few concrete measures available. Such methods have provided important information, such as Lockridge's 1974 study, based largely on signatures found on wills and deeds, and Lee Soltow and Edward Stevens's 1981 study based on records of Philadelphia merchant seamen and army enlistees. Such records more likely (or only, in the case of Soltow and Stevens) provide information about men or favor higher rates for them.

However, Allan Greer reports that signature rates on marriage registers in a number of early eighteenth-century French Canadian colonies—Riviere-du-Loup, Three Rivers, and Boucherville in Quebec Province, where the Ursulines taught women and girls—demonstrate that women signed marriage registers more often than men. Greer acknowledges but makes little of this finding, which runs counter to findings in the numerous Protestant communities generally studied—and which has led literacy scholars to assume women's literacy was always lower than that of men.[10] This information was not new to nineteenth-century Americans. For example, John Pinkerton's widely used 1804 *Modern Geography*, in describing the Canadian people, acknowledges but presents French Canadian women's literacy in a derogatory manner, despite the strong connection made between literacy and morality generally: "The French women in Canada can generally read and write, and are thus superior to the men; but both are sunk in ignorance and superstition and blindly devoted to their priests" (2:481–82).

In studying signatures on parish marriage records in eighteenth-century New Orleans, Emily Clark found results similar to Greer's. In marriage registers dated 1760–62, 72 percent of women signed marriage registers, as compared with 70 percent of men. At the time of the arrival of the Ursulines, 36 percent of women and 53 percent of men had signed parish registers (1998, 242). The Ursulines also supported a strong laywomen's confraternity in New Orleans. According to Clark, "A devout woman was one who prepared herself to propagate the faith by becoming schooled herself. . . . Given the importance of print and literacy in the advance of Protestantism, the good Catholic woman must also learn to read and write so that she met the enemy with an arsenal of equal strength" (216).

One might reasonably infer that the higher literacy rates for women in both cases resulted from the Ursulines' efforts at educating women and, equally important, that the approach Catholics took to education, at least in the seventeenth- and eighteenth-century American colonies, offered women opportunities for literacy equal to or superior to those for men and superior to that available for women in British colonies. Women's literacy was almost certainly higher than that indicated by signatures in Catholic settlements, as the often large numbers of literate Catholic nuns would not have signed legal documents, such as wills and marriage registers, upon which literacy estimates are most often based.

Ironically, the very hierarchical and patriarchal nature of the Catholic Church may have afforded greater literacy opportunities to many women. The church, reluctantly accepting women's active role in teaching initially, came to support the literacy efforts of religious women; women, however, were restricted to efforts among their own sex.[11] Because education in Catholic countries and communities was relegated largely to religious teaching orders rather than to state-sponsored schools, overall literacy rates may have been lower than those where state laws and general funds supported schools; yet, because the number of nuns in religious communities was often twice that in men's religious teaching communities, women often had more opportunities than men to become literate, especially when living close by convents or other schools staffed by nuns.

Women's Literacy in the Early Nineteenth-Century United States

Historians have long acknowledged the close relationship between religion and literacy in the American colonies, where leaders promoted widespread reading of Scripture. As scholars trace the development of education further, however, the religious focus diminishes, despite the continued role religion played in literacy efforts, especially those on behalf of girls and women. In examining literacy for women in the early nineteenth century, scholars have concentrated primarily on such northeastern figures as Emma Willard, Catharine Beecher, Zilpah Grant, and Mary Lyon, highlighting these "pioneers" for having fought for and established the earliest quality schools for girls and young women (Boas 1935; Button and Provenzo 1983; Cott 1977; Jacobi 2001; Kerber 1986; Norton 1980; Sizer 1964; Woody 1929);

INTRODUCTION

seldom have they acknowledged the Catholic convents, their academies, and schools as a major force to which Protestants responded in promoting stronger education for girls and women. In a *History of Education Quarterly* special issue (2001), a number of scholars reexamined the importance of the academy in the early United States, naming it the primary means of higher schooling in eighteenth- and nineteenth-century America (Beadie; Leslie; Tolley; Tolley and Beadie), one calling the academy "the only form of higher education available to women in the early republic" (Nash 2001, 241). Margaret A. Nash and more recently others, such as Mary Kelley, have disproved Thomas Woody's claim that girls' academies were inferior to boys' academies, demonstrating that "curricula at academies . . . exhibited little gender differentiation. Core subjects were the same for both sexes" (Kelley 2006, 247). Despite their excellent reappraisal of the academy movement, however, these scholars have given only a nod to Catholic convent academies, despite their prominent role in the early literacy movement. Only Mary J. Oates (1994) has addressed the Catholic academies during this period of renewed interest in the academies. Kim Tolley and Nancy Beadie acknowledged this omission in their introduction to the special issue reappraising the academy movement, calling for more research on both Catholic education and on academies "outside the northeast region of the United States" (2001, 223).

The degree to which proprietors of the eastern schools have been seen as both pioneers of and the standard for early women's education is demonstrated in such depictions of them as "celebrators of the Republic and of American values" (Conway 1974, 5), which assumes homogeneous (Protestant) American values, and in the representation of Jacob Mordecai's 1809 school in Warrenton, North Carolina, as the "first southern school on the northern model" (Norton 1980, 274). Mary Beth Norton not only discounts earlier southern convent academies but also assumes the northern schools were the standard by which to judge others. H. Warren Button and Eugene F. Provenzo call Sarah Pierce's Litchfield Female Academy "exceptional, since most of the first academies for girls and women were, like other academies, short-lived, transitory, and operated by men" (1983, 138), ignoring the numerous early permanent convent academies operated by women religious.

Several scholars have recently reexamined the role of women in the early Republic and antebellum periods. Most pertinent for my project, Mary Kelley, in *Learning to Stand and Speak: Women, Education, and Public Life in America's Republic* (2006), has recovered information about women's

INTRODUCTION

education in the antebellum United States, looking explicitly at the academies' influence for preparing girls for participation in civic society. Kelley's excellent study makes apparent the degree to which scholars continue to overlook Catholic schools. While her work contains information on some academies outside the Northeast, she includes no Catholic academies. Still, the multitude of archival sources found in her work provides new material and valuable context for girls' academies. While Kelley specifically examines women's influence on society outside the political realm, Rosemarie Zagarri's 2007 *Revolutionary Backlash: Women and Politics in the Early American Republic* looks at women's participation in political matters immediately after the Revolution. Zagarri finds that women's significant role in shaping the political landscape changed with later generations, who forgot or had never known about the political activities of their foremothers. Carolyn Eastman's *A Nation of Speechifiers: Making an American Republic after the Revolution* (2010) has also complicated the way scholars have looked at women in the early Republic by arguing that women helped to shape the new country by reimagining themselves as part of that public.

A number of excellent histories of individual Catholic women or religious communities, a few of which contain information on the educational policies of the sisters, have become available in recent volumes that take advantage of rich archival materials. Mary Ellen Doyle's *Pioneer Spirit: Catherine Spalding, Sister of Charity of Nazareth* (2006) provides the first full biography of Catherine Spalding, the cofounder and leader of the Sisters of Charity of Nazareth in their early years. Diane Batts Morrow's 2002 *Persons of Color and Religious at the Same Time: The Oblate Sisters of Providence, 1828–1860* explores the history of the Oblate Sisters of Providence and their negotiation of racial prejudice in the antebellum United States. Carol K. Coburn and Martha Smith's 1999 examination of the Sisters of St. Joseph of Carondelet, *Spirited Lives: How Nuns Shaped Catholic Culture and American Life, 1836–1920*, highlights these sisters' influence through their work in schools, orphanages, hospitals, and other benevolent institutions. Emily Clark's edited letters of Marie Hachard (1999) and her study of early Ursuline nuns in New Orleans (1997 and 1998) address the nuns' early years in New Orleans; her work provides good background for the period studied here. I celebrate these studies, for as Gerda Lerner has told us, "Women have lived with the effect of having been deprived of a usable past. . . . History as memory and history as a source of personal identity have presented women with a world in which people like ourselves were, with a few exceptions, invisible in all those activities valued highly as 'contributions' to civilization" (1997, 120).

Most studies of Catholic education celebrate individual teachers or subjects and have been done in-house by members of women religious communities. However, some scholars in rhetoric and composition have begun to address the importance of religious rhetorics and Catholic rhetoric and education in particular. Michael-John DePalma has studied Austin Phelps's rhetorical influences (2008; 2012), and Jeffrey Ringer has looked at the role of faith in inquiry (2013). Together, in *Mapping Christian Rhetorics: Connecting Conversations, Charting New Territories* (2015), they address the importance of religious and Christian rhetorics for a fuller understanding of rhetoric by assembling contributors' research on previously ignored Christian rhetorics. Cinthia Gannett and John Brereton's edited collection *Traditions of Eloquence* (2015) addresses the influence of the Jesuit rhetorical tradition in the United States, and Elizabethada Wright's 2013 "'God Sees Me': Surveillance and Oratorical Training at Nineteenth-Century St. Mary-of-the-Woods in Indiana" presents girls' speaking at the Sisters of Providence's St. Mary-of-the-Woods Academy as part of a system of surveillance that reassured observers of students' adherence to acceptable norms while simultaneously allowing them to breach those norms. My own 2006 article, "Uncovering Forgotten Habits: Anti-Catholic Rhetoric and Nineteenth-Century American Women's Literacy," examines the anti-Catholic rhetoric used by supporters of New England proprietor schools for women in early nineteenth-century America. Chapters in two edited collections also address the Catholic influence: in *Literacy, Economy, and Power: Writing Research Ten Years After*, edited by John Duffy, Julie Nelson Christoph, Eli Goldblatt, Nelson Graff, Rebecca S. Nowacek, and Bryan Trabold (2014), and in Cindi Gannett and John Brereton's collection mentioned above. Portions of these works contribute to *Secret Habits*.

Knowledge of Catholic literacy efforts places in doubt notions we have held about women's literacy in the early nineteenth-century United States because of the ways they influenced literacy among Protestant women. While historians of women's literacy have most often cited such women as Sarah Pierce, Mary Lyon, and Catharine Beecher as pioneers of American women's education, those women, in fact, garnered support for their operations largely by promoting fear of well-established Catholic convent academies. Catholics had begun building an impressive network of schools for girls in the early United States to provide an education in rural and

INTRODUCTION

frontier areas devoid of schools, and sometimes as an alternative to state-sponsored schools whose texts were virulently anti-Catholic and whose curriculum promoted Protestantism. The teachers in the Catholic schools, especially in the academies and seminaries, were highly educated, professionally trained members of religious communities. Sarah Josepha Hale's famous crusade for women's education came in part in response to successful and well-attended academies run by Catholic sisters. Hale claimed, "The only effective way to prevent the increase of conventual seminaries, is to found Protestant schools" (1834b, 520), as "the convents are now considered the best and most fashionable places of education . . . and there, in all human probability, many of the future wives, of the pious students of Lane Seminary, are now receiving their impressions" (1834a, 561). Similarly, Lyon and Pierce were supported in their advocacy of women's literacy by Protestant leaders, and their promotional and fund-raising materials relied on anti-Catholic rhetoric, insisting on the need for their own schools and teachers for young Protestant women and capitalizing on fear of a papist takeover related to Catholic sisters' schools and academies (Mattingly 2006). Catharine Beecher, daughter of the blatantly anti-Catholic Lyman Beecher and sister to authors of numerous popular anti-Catholic texts, sought support for her teacher-training schools by insisting on the need to counter the "papist" threat, especially in the West. Catholic women were supported in achieving their own literacy and that of other girls and women partly in response to European Reformation efforts toward literacy. As Catholic women successfully established convents and schools in the Americas, Protestant women's literacy accelerated to a significant degree in order to counter the alleged "popery" threat inherent in Catholic convents and convent schools.

The schools established by the Catholic sisters provide another counter to claims that "in the half-century after the American Revolution, the best-educated women were either self-taught or . . . tutored at home by teachers or relatives" and that "although institutions offering secondary education for girls were established, many were temporary, underfinanced, haphazard ventures that catered more to society's demands for an 'ornamental education' than to more useful basic literacy" (Gordon and Gordon 2003, 107). The Catholic convents, on the contrary, produced large numbers of highly literate teachers who then provided a useful literacy for other girls and women. Because of the large numbers of women in convents and the numerous girls and young women they taught, women were likely more literate than men in some communities in the early United States. For example, by 1838 five communities of Catholic women religious had settled in the frontier St. Louis vicinity, and in central Kentucky three permanent early U.S. convents were established between 1812 and 1822 within a fifteen-mile radius of one another. Literacy among women may have been especially high in such areas, but marriage records do not provide a source of evidence, as licensing in the United States became a responsibility of the civil government rather than the church, and women were not asked to sign registers.[12]

Catholic women's institutions were impressive, enduring structures; most are still in existence. They provided many of the earliest normal schools with carefully outlined professional guidelines for substantial curricula and effective teachers. The sisters often taught sewing and music, practical, important skills for nineteenth-century women but part of a larger, rigorous curriculum.[13] Because of their numbers, the sisters were often able to specialize, giving instruction in their area of expertise; many of these academies continue to educate young women today.

I question the notion of Protestantism's superior connection with literacy not to cast doubt on the importance of religion in promoting literacy, to propose the superiority of any other religion in doing so, or to imply that literacy was always a positive force. Nor do I wish to criticize the scholars I have mentioned, who are among our best researchers and are scholars I admire greatly. My purpose is to suggest that by reifying Protestantism's place in promoting literacy, even as we have begun to acknowledge other important influences to literacy, we have neglected sources of information and alternative readings that might provide a more complete narrative. The Protestant literacy myth, though flawed, remains so strong that it inhibits our ability to see patterns that run counter to that grand narrative.

In some sense we have hesitated to engage with religious literacy narratives, even though our grandest narrative about literacy remains based on the religious domination of the Puritans. We have comfortably constructed a tale about Puritans' initiation of "common" schools that appear democratic and inclusive, even though those schools have been in many ways extremely exclusionary. We have continued to reify a New England literacy supremacy and largely neglected narratives about areas outside New England, especially the South, for example.[14] As most early nineteenth-century Catholic convents and schools were built outside New England, they can contribute to our understanding of literacy in other less-studied regions. And, we should be reminded of the need to continue searching for

INTRODUCTION

groups whom our grand narratives obscure and to reexamine and question accepted narratives. In a culture that places heavy moral and social values on literacy, groups outside the grand narrative are often left with negative images of the heritage that helps to shape their identities.

As Graff notes, history provides a "much needed perspective . . . allow[ing] us to reach out for new, different, and even multiple understandings of ourselves." But "history mandates focusing and refocusing the lenses of time, place, and alternative spaces" (2010, 637–38). Refocusing the lens through which we see the American religious experience with literacy can help to achieve a more accurate history, especially important because although contemporary beliefs help to construct our narratives about the past, historical representations determine present and future narratives and identities as well. Generations have glorified the literacy accomplishments of the Puritan and Protestant, but it may be difficult for those on the margins of such stories to envision themselves within a tradition of excellent and successful literacy. For example, Jacqueline Jones Royster has pointed to the importance of identifying and understanding "resonant patterns of engagement with issues of authority, agency, privilege, and entitlement across time" for shaping her own administrative direction as well as for the intellectual identity and engagement of her women students of color (2000, 265). While Royster's students have been marginalized in different crucial ways from other marginalized groups, such identification and understanding is nonetheless important for all women and all groups whose heritage of literate and intellectual practices has remained largely untold or misrepresented. We have learned that in earlier centuries, women were always less literate than men and that Catholics cared little for or were hostile to literacy. We have learned that those in the South valued literacy far less than those in the North. But these are all inaccurate, simplistic, and incomplete narratives.

The factual discrepancies about Protestant countries in historical literacy studies also leave many questions unanswered. Why did some Protestant communities advance far more rapidly in literacy than others? Why did Sweden achieve high rates of literacy without institutional schooling? Why did New England Protestants promote writing and numeracy among men but not women, while Swedish Protestant officials saw to an equal effort among men and women? Many questions about early Protestant literacy practices remain. Perhaps these can be more readily understood as we become more inclusive in our narratives and move beyond the Protestant literacy myth.

INTRODUCTION

The Catholic Church depended primarily on religious communities of men and women for disseminating and promoting literacy. This approach differed from that of Protestants and appears to have created different results. The Catholic religious orders, numerous though they were both in number of communities and in distribution of members within the communities, appear to have been unable to impart literacy on as massive a scale as state-sponsored and mandated literacy. However, because women taught girls and young women while men taught boys and young men in Catholic communities, the greater number of women in convents appears to have provided equal or greater literacy opportunities for girls and women than that received by boys and men, at least in some places. Catholic sisters often followed a lifelong pursuit of literacy practices, many becoming highly educated, breaking expectations that women might devote brief periods of their lives to their own education and to that of others but largely relinquish such efforts at marriage.[15] Sarah Curtis notes, "Congregations were able to nurture an esprit de corps that provided religious teachers with a sense of professional identity, in marked contrast to the experience of many lay teachers, especially women" (2000, 64).

Much of this women's tradition of literacy and intellectual rigor—a tradition in which women excelled at creating community among peers and at successfully building magnificent convents and academies that provided welcoming, literate environments for succeeding generations—has been largely hidden from our narratives. In a culture where women are often taught to compete with one another for the attention of men and similarly learn that education and career are more important for men, such a tradition provides one positive alternative. There may be many others.

1.
Literacy, Religion, and Schoolbooks

Just as the beliefs and prejudices prevalent in their ancestral homeland persisted among British colonial inhabitants, anti-Catholic sentiment prevailed in the early schoolbooks they used in America.[1] Many English texts crossed the Atlantic and found favor among educators both because of inadequate publishing facilities in the early years of settlement and because of traditional social and religious affiliations. Even as American authors and publishers began producing schoolbooks, however, most of those texts reflected the overwhelmingly negative attitudes toward Catholics found in most British schoolbooks. Many authors believed the importance of their books to lie equally in providing knowledge and in guarding against encroaching religious beliefs they saw as a foreign threat.

By the nineteenth century, the connection between literacy and morality continued; some questioned the appropriateness of public education's supporting specific religious sects, but general Christian morals were a major focus of the curriculum and were so typical, in fact, that by 1837 Horace Mann "abandoned" the law and his state senate seat to become secretary of the Massachusetts Board of Education for "the larger sphere of mind and morals" (qtd. in Mann 1937, 82–83). Morality continued to be a major theme throughout his tenure, reflected most succinctly in his 1848 report. Mann explained the righteous and practical purpose of taxation for public education:

> Every man, not on the pauper list, is taxed for their support. But he is not taxed to support them as special religious institutions. He is taxed to support them as a *preventive* means against dishonesty, against fraud, and against violence; on the same principle that he is taxed to support criminal courts as a *punitive* means against the same offences. He is taxed to support schools, on the same principle that he is taxed

to support paupers; because a child without education is poorer and more wretched than a man without bread. He is taxed to support schools, on the same principle that he would be taxed to defend the nation against foreign invasion, or against rapine committed by a foreign foe; because the general prevalence of ignorance, superstition, and vice, will breed Goth and Vandal at home, more fatal to the public well-being, than any Goth or Vandal from abroad. ([1848] 1957, 103–4)

Although generally accepted moral tenets imbued all religions, many Protestants saw them as uniquely Protestant and continued to believe some religions to be foreign and dangerous; these beliefs continued to ground curricula and books in most schools. This chapter examines the anti-Catholic climate absorbed in the majority of homes and schools that promoted literacy by surveying the most popular books used in promoting literacy: the hornbook, primer, catechism, and speller in colonial North America and readers, geographies, grammars, and histories that became increasingly common in the nineteenth century. The texts demonstrate not only what children were imbibing as part of their learning but also the difficulty of the sisters and other Catholic educators in acquiring appropriate texts for their students. Finally, it discusses how Catholic educators responded to these overwhelmingly anti-Catholic texts as they sought more friendly ones for their own schools.

First Literacy Efforts in the Colonies

In the colonial period, no literacy focus was greater and no texts more prolific than those intended for religious and moral formation. Colonists followed the "ordinary road" to literacy that John Locke had identified as early as 1692, progressing through the "Horn-book, Primer, Psalter, Testament and Bible" (Monaghan 1988, 19). The hornbook, consisting most often of a single sheet of paper attached to a wooden frame and overlain with a thin piece of horn for protection, began the literacy process. The paper presented the alphabet, a few lines of syllables, the invocation "In the name of the Father, and of the Son, and of the Holy Ghost," and the Lord's Prayer. The hornbook was intended for instruction of the very young, with prayers making up by far the largest portion of the "book."

The first actual book children encountered on their road to literacy was most often the primer. The word for the ubiquitous primer is telling, as it referred to "the first in a series of readers, but, in an older sense, it may derive from the 'prime' hour for prayers, signaling a book of prayers that includes reading instruction" to provide access to religious and moral readings without clerical assistance (Carr, Carr, and Schultz 2005, 104). As Jean Ferguson Carr, Stephen L. Carr, and Lucille M. Schultz have noted, "Such primers are often characterized as slipping moral lessons into a pedagogical textbook"; however, "historically, the drive for literacy came second" (104–5). Clearly literacy did come second; only about one-third of the text was devoted to alphabetic and syllabic instruction (even verses included in this portion instructed in moral precepts) with the remainder of the text changing over time. Nearly all contained one of the popular catechisms, accounts of Protestant martyrs, prayers, and sometimes short moral stories. After students had learned the primer adequately, they moved to the psalter, or the Book of Psalms, then to the New Testament, and finally to the entire Bible. Such a process should not surprise us. As Harvey Graff has pointed out, "Morality and literacy . . . were to be taught together: literacy speeding and easing moral instruction, morality guiding and restraining the potentially dangerous uses of literacy" (1979, 26). But the process was intended to instruct specifically in the Protestant religion, and "for Indians, blacks, Jews, Catholics, Mormons, and people of other religious heritages, the culture of the public school was alien and its benefits questionable" (Dolan 1985, 267). In books intended for school use, such hostility surfaced in openly anti-Catholic diatribes.

Anti-Catholicism took numerous public and political forms, with Catholics officially denied suffrage and access to public office in most colonies, but much of the hostility came to bear on literacy. Laws were often designed to dissuade instruction and instructional leadership among Catholics. For example, a 1700 New York law, "An Act against Jesuits and Popish Priests," forced the departure of every "Jesuit and Seminary Priest, Missionary, or other spiritual or ecclesiastical Person, made, or ordained by any Authority, Power, or Jurisdiction, derived, challenged, or pretended from the Pope or See of Rome" ([1700] 1894, 429), punished remaining official representatives of the Catholic faith with imprisonment or death, penalized any who harbored such persons with fines (two hundred pounds) and time in the pillory, and rewarded those who disclosed the presence of Catholics officially aligned with the church (429–30). The New York law was more typical than atypical in the colonies. Such laws were significant with regard to literacy because the Jesuits and other Catholic clergy were most often the best educated members of and educators in Catholic communities. Maryland specifically outlawed sending children to Europe for education and prevented their instruction in the Catholic religion.

In this atmosphere, most early literacy efforts, promoted as a means of instilling and improving religious devotion, incorporated Protestant tenets and explicit anti-Catholic tirades. For example, in the best-known and most-used early primer, the *New-England Primer*, alphabetic and syllabic instruction make up only about one-third of the book. This early portion of the text is laden with generally accepted moral tenets. The remainder of the material changed over time, but it was far more specifically Protestant, often anti-Catholic. The primer contained a catechism, usually either the Westminster Shorter Catechism or John Cotton's *Milk for Babes*. If the catechisms included in the primer were not specifically anti-Catholic, the information did present Protestant tenets rather than Catholic ones. For example, a major objective of the text was to teach about the commandments and sacraments. The commandments presented were those ascribed to by Protestants and differed somewhat from those honored by Catholics. In addition, the books presented the two Protestant sacraments, baptism and the Eucharist, as opposed to the seven included in Catholic teachings. Young children usually learned the commandments and sacraments by rote; those for whom schools required a different recitation would have found the enumeration confusing, but other, more explicit reproaches of their religion ensued.

Following instruction about the commandments and sacraments in nearly every primer, students learned of John Rogers, "minister of the gospel in London" and "the first martyr in Queen Marie's reign." A short, one-paragraph biography of Rogers tells the reader that he was "burnt in Smithfield" and that "his wife with nine small children and one at her Breast, followed him to the Stake." This reference to Rogers and his persecution and death at the hands of Catholics was a staple in the catechisms included in the *New-England Primer*, despite the narrative's inconsistency with *Foxe's Book of Martyrs*.[2] Early primers also included John Rogers's "exhortation to his children," "writ a few days before his Death":

> Abhor that arrant Whore of Rome
> and all her Blasphemies;
> And Drink not of her cursed Cup,
> obey not her decrees.
>
> (*New-England Primer* 1795)

The primers served the primary purpose of this stage of literacy very well, providing a sound inculcation in accepted Protestant narratives and tenets. Students who advanced beyond the *New-England Primer* focused largely on psalters and scriptural texts accepted in the creed and finally on the Bible. The Bible was such a major component of formal instruction that its use would become a great contention between Protestants and Catholics in the nineteenth century, as Protestants insisted on use of the King James Bible in schools while Catholics sought permission to use their own translation, the Douay translation.[3]

COLONIAL SPELLERS

E. Jennifer Monaghan suggests that in the eighteenth century, two texts—spellers and catechisms—supplemented traditional literacy promoters. Early spellers were largely made up of religious matter, often incorporating catechisms, and continued in the vein of older literacy texts, such as primers. One of the earliest spellers, Benjamin Keach's 1695 *Instructions for Children; or, The Child's and Youth's Delight, Teaching an Easier Way to Spell and Read* TRUE ENGLISH, provides four pages of alphabetical letters and syllables. The remainder of the 160-page text consists of catechisms and precepts for youth. Henry Dixon's 1736 speller begins in a fashion similar to Keach's text; the initial short presentation of letters is followed by works "Collected from the Holy Scripture: And Placed under Distinct Heads, in Words of One Syllable" (6). Later chapters include words from Scripture in two, three, and four syllables, and so on.

Spellers often included words and their definitions, many related to the Catholic religion. For example, *Entich's New Spelling Dictionary, Teaching to Write and Pronounce the English Tongue*, defines "protestant" as "one who protests against popery" (Entich 1800, 300). Sometimes spellers provided calendars of important dates as well; Daniel Fenning's *Universal Spelling-Book*, includes the date 1527, explained as "Martin Luther confutes Popery" (1786, 108). Occasionally, miscellaneous information was included where we would expect straightforward efforts. In *The Secretary's Guide, or, Young Man's Companion*, for example, part 1 includes letters of the alphabet, their pronunciation, and syllables. Part 2, "Arithmetick Made Easie, &c," gives information about addition, subtraction, and multiplication but also a category titled "Of Religion," which provides the history of British religion, followed by this explanation: "Although some of the fore-going Particulars may seem to be foreign to the design of this Book, yet we presume it may be of some Service to inform our Youth of some few of the Customs and Usages of the Kingdom to which we belong, as also the Religious societies therein" (1729, 85). According to the guide, under the rule of Edward VI, "the superstitions of *Popery* were almost abolished." The narrative continues by explaining the "Five Hundred *Protestants* . . . burnt for their not conforming to *Popery*" during Queen Mary's reign (80) and adding, "The *Papists* are not now very Numerous in *England*. . . . They are generally very Zealous in their way, and very intent upon gaining Profehtes, for which reason it has been thought adviseable to put some Check to their Progress and yet they are allowed greater Freedom than any *Protestants* are allowed in *Roman Catholic* Countries" (80). While spellers, ostensibly nonreligious books, often contained anti-Catholic bias, catechisms provided an even greater opportunity to instruct children to abhor Catholicism, as their fundamental purpose was to provide religious instruction.

CATECHISMS

Although catechisms were included in primers, stand-alone catechisms also found popular use throughout the colonies, some of the earliest and most popular making the opposition between Catholics and Protestants explicit. For example, Benjamin Harris's 1685 *The Protestant Tutor for Children* begins with a question about the nature of Christianity and an answer that aligns Christianity with Protestantism: "The Christian Religion is commonly called the Protestant Religion in opposition to Popery" (1). The catechism contains forty-eight questions, most of which refer in some manner to the Catholic religion and attack the Catholic Church directly. For example, one question asks if the pope's power derives from Satan, with the answer that Satan does, indeed, provide the pope's power (9). Others, less explicit but nonetheless hostile to Catholicism, ask derogatory questions about the Virgin Mary and praying to relics and saints. Harris's catechism, like the early *New-England Primer* and many of the early catechisms, includes a short biography of John Rogers, a picture depicting his burning at the stake, and the "exhortation to his children" regarding the "Whore of Rome."

Congregationalist ministers, among the most powerful leaders of their communities as well as the most popular writers of schoolbooks, nearly always participated in anti-Catholic instruction similar to that found in the Westminster Confession but with even greater fervor. For example, Cotton Mather's very popular *The Fall of Babylon: A Short and Plain Catechism*,

Which Detects and Confutes the Principles of Popery (1707) presents a systemized instructional program to instill "the Truth" in Protestant children. In his introduction, "The Protestant Armed from the Tower of David," Mather tells his reader, "Behold in a few pages digested and comprized, the Substance of whole Volumns, written to carry on the Triumphs of our Holy Religion over Popery" (n.p.). Mather continues with a recommendation that the "Religious Householder" read questions to youth, ask their opinions, then read the answers, and thereby "lead them to, & fix them in, the Right Opinion." Exercises offered for guiding young people contain such questions and answers as these:

> Q. What is to be thought of the Popish Doctrine which **forbids marriage**, unto persons professing certain Characters of Religion?
> A. By the prohibition of MARRIAGE to persons professing Religion, it is most Evident that Popery is the very Apostasy foretold by the Spirit of Truth, to come upon the Christian Church in the Latter Days. And the Religious Orders, & Religious Houses, as they call them, among the Papists, which make Rash Vows of Continency, are most Evidently the Filthy Seminaries of Antichrist. . . . (15–16)
> Q. Is the Pope of Rome to be looked upon as **The Antichrist** whose coming & Reigning is foretold in the ancient Oracles?
> A. The Oracles of God foretold, the Ruling of an ANTICHRIST in the Christian Church. (16–17)

Mather's catechism claims on the title page to be "Intended particularly for the Service of Christians in MARYLAND, who may be in danger of POPISH DELUSIONS." Indeed, at the time of Mather's writing, Maryland was home to more Catholics than any other colony; however, such virulent anti-Catholicism was prevalent in Mather's other sermons and writings, and in those of other Protestant leaders, especially in New England but throughout the colonies. And Mather's catechism was popular throughout New England.

Similar catechisms were published throughout the eighteenth century. *A Protestant's Resolution*, published in 1746, presented twenty-four explicit errors of the Roman Catholic faith. Resembling previous catechisms, *A Protestant's Resolution* attacks the pope, claiming him to be "Antichrist, because none have more the Mark of Antichrist than he" (8). The text also calls the Catholic religion "superstitious, idolatrous, damnable, bloody, traiterous, blind, [and] blasphemous" (9) and suggests that "popist Priests, Jesuits, and others that die for Treason and Murder" get "their just Desserts that bring them to that Punishment" (25).

These attitudes were so pervasive in sermons and texts used for literacy purposes that they continued even after the founding of the new country and the ratification of the Constitution. Although the Constitution's First Amendment declares religious freedom, providing some legal protection for Catholics and initiating the way for open worship and education, in some ways the legal acceptance of all religions increased fear and intolerance. Resentment about freedoms given to Catholics angered many people, as had the Acts of Toleration in England, and led to increased social hostility in some areas.

Early Nineteenth Century: A Continued Heritage

John A. Nietz claims that textbooks demonstrate what was taught in the earliest U.S. schools because "teachers in the early days of our country were so meagerly trained and educated that they depended strongly on the textbooks for what to teach and how to teach" (1961, 1). An examination of books used in schools, then, provides some sense of the attitudes and subjects children were learning in schools and demonstrates that patterns of anti-Catholicism in schoolbooks continued well into the nineteenth century. As Ruth Miller Elson notes in her extensive study of nineteenth-century American schoolbooks, "No theme in these schoolbooks before 1870 is more universal than anti-Catholicism" (1964, 53). Such patterns continued in spellers, which "offer in the lists of words to be memorized many terms referring to Catholicism, such as 'nunnery, abbot, monastick, papist, papal.' Such words need not suggest condemnation of the religion they represent, but in the context of the textbooks it becomes clear that they are needed only to understand the literature of anti-Catholicism" (53). Such instruction became common as well in newly popular schoolbooks across a variety of subjects, including readers, geographies, histories, and grammars—texts that became common to curricula throughout the United States. They provided an ideal forum for authors to create a world view that supported Protestantism and denigrated other religions, especially Catholicism.

READERS

Nineteenth-century readers exhibit the pervasive religious nature of U.S. society and subsequent educational practices. They include excerpts from the Bible and other religious narratives; in many cases, biblical quotations account for the majority of examples. Such emphasis on biblical text is often accompanied by references offensive to Catholics. For example, in addition to biblical passages, early nineteenth-century readers offer speeches, essays, and excerpts from the writings of famous and influential authors, many critical of Catholics. Mary Tudor became a favorite target for criticism in juxtaposition with praise for British Reform aristocracy. Such examples are demonstrated by the two most popular texts used at the end of the eighteenth century and well into the nineteenth. Lindley Murray's popular readers came to dominate the market for readers until the McGuffey readers began to slowly dislodge them in the 1840s. Murray's *The English Reader*, first published in 1799, includes character sketches by Scottish philosopher David Hume, one effusively praising Queen Elizabeth, who was tolerant and "able to overcome all prejudices" (1800, 111), and another of Lady Jane Gray, "carefully educated in the principles of the Reformation" and whose "wisdom and virtue" helped her to remain constant, "a shining example to her sex" (33). Lady Jane is presented in contrast to the Catholic queen Mary I, who "seems to have been incapable of generosity or clemency" and whose "bigotted zeal, under colour of tender mercy to the prisoner's [Lady Jane's] soul, induced her to send priests, who molested her with perpetual disputation" to convert her to popery (35). Similarly, Caleb Bingham's widely used 1794 *The American Preceptor* presents Mary as having "few qualities either estimable or amiable. . . . Amidst the complication of vices which entered into her composition, obstinancy, bigotry, violence, cruelty, we scarcely find any virtue but sincerity; unless we add vigour of mind, a quality which seems inherent in her family" (33). Such readings invite discussion of Catholic abuses and praise of Protestants.

Similarly, stories by American authors in the readers often present disparaging impressions of all things Catholic as well. Bingham includes the "Narrative of the Captivity of Mrs. Jemima Howe, Taken by the Indians at Hinsdale, New-Hampshire, July 27, 1755." Mrs. Howe tells of the escape of her children to a well-known nunnery, a "school of superstition and bigotry" (184). The escape story offers early traits that appear in later convent escape narratives: children "imprisoned" in convents and released to their parents only under threat from the authorities and a daughter who has been brainwashed into the Catholic religion.

Some texts picked up the hostile rhetoric that had surfaced in response to the Quebec Act. Noah Webster's 1787 *An American Selection of Lessons in Reading and Speaking. Calculated to Improve the Minds and Refine the Tastes of Youth* was popular well into the nineteenth century and included for oratorical practice an excerpt from the First Continental Congress's protest against the Quebec Act, which expressed anger at the British "for extending the limits of Quebec, abolishing the English and restoring the French laws, whereby great numbers of British freemen are subjected to the latter, and establishing an absolute government and the Roman Catholic religion, throughout those vast regions that border on the westerly and northerly boundaries of the free, Protestant, English settlements" (243).

GEOGRAPHIES

Geographies and histories provide a particularly meaningful way to examine literacy's relationship to religion in the eighteenth and nineteenth centuries. The battle for whose story gets told and how that narrative is conveyed represents power, a struggle as old as humans. Control of history and geography texts was important in establishing a collective interpretation of a specific worldview and construction of geographic identities that placed the chosen religion in a positive light while doing so in an ostensibly objective manner, one seemingly free of ideological intent. In the most popular books, the Protestant narrative claimed control, and slurs against Catholics became abundant.

Geographies became a mainstay of nearly every school curriculum by the late eighteenth century and presented an opportunity for writers to promote positive perceptions of Protestant religion and culture while undermining those of Catholics. According to Martin Bruckner, "The demand for geography textbooks was so high" at the turn of the nineteenth century "that nearly a dozen . . . geographies survived beyond their second and third editions" (2006, 147). Bruckner claims that "only the Bible and Noah Webster's spelling books were more popular than geographies" in both urban and rural areas of the northern United States for more than three decades (148). "The geographical catechism echoes the sacred history of literacy instruction," notes Bruckner, the alphabetic literacy becoming "secularized and made worldly by the geography book's substitution of biblical history with geographical knowledge" (149). Indeed, the spirit of anti-Catholicism prevalent in catechisms surfaces in many of the most-used geography texts. In describing the people, the cultural background, and the dominant religion of each country, authors of geography schoolbooks seized opportunities to elevate Christian/Protestant countries as exemplary and to denigrate others, presenting the Catholic Church as keeping its members depraved, impoverished, and ignorant.

The man most often recognized as the first author of a U.S. geography text and as the "Father of American Geography," Congregationalist minister Jedidiah Morse,[4] was vehemently anti-Catholic. Morse wrote a best-selling series of geography texts beginning in 1784 that "lasted for several decades and reached more than twenty editions" (Bruckner 2006, 147). In his schoolbooks, Morse praises those from Protestant countries and excoriates others. He includes numerous examples, such as the following from his discussion of Poland: "Popery is the established religion of Poland, and few people are more bigotted in their way. There are, however, a very considerable number of protestants, who have sometimes been tolerated, and sometimes persecuted. In the year 1724, there was a public massacre of the protestants under the sanction of law. The popish clergy are said to be in general, illiterate bigots; and the monks the most profligate of mankind" (1784, 172). Of Portugal, another traditionally Catholic country, he writes, "The people are treacherous, ungrateful, and intemperate in their passion for revenge. Portugal is, at present, little less than a kingdom of priests, monks, and nuns, who entirely devour the substance of the country. The Popish religion is practiced here with all its religious superstitions, in the highest degree" (145). In contrast, Morse's descriptions of Protestant countries, such as England, offer praise for a people who "excel all the nations of the world" in cleanliness and whose "honor and integrity . . . are known in every part of the commercial world" (1801, 109).

Other geography schoolbook authors followed Morse's lead. They presented Catholics as superstitious, filthy, indolent, and vicious, claiming that church policy kept them so. *A Compend of Geography Containing a Concise Description of the Different Countries of the Earth* continued in this tradition of reviling European countries whose inhabitants had retained the Catholic faith. According to this text, in Spain "they live in wretched habitations and are distinguished by rags, dirt, filth, idleness and dishonesty. . . . The popular dances are voluptuous and indecent. Many persons beg in the day and rob at night" (Nichols 1809, 90). And in Italy, "the state of learning is very low. Even the nobility and gentry, especially the women, are illiterate." Italians "are voluptuous, amorous, and licentious. The populace are ignorant, credulous, and superstitious" (96). Under the section "European Islands," after a loving depiction of the English, the reader learns that the "Irish are intemperate and vicious; easily excited to acts of violence and difficultly restrained by law" (112). Such descriptions intertwine literacy with religion by encouraging Protestant children to learn and cultivate traditions similar to their role models in Protestant countries in order to rise or remain above those in backward Catholic countries. For Catholic children and their parents, however, such rhetoric presented serious problems.

The established attitudes about the Protestant-Catholic relationship continued among most of the best-selling geography texts of the early nineteenth century. In *A New System of Modern Geography*, Benjamin Davies reports that in the Netherlands, education is "neglected, as in most Catholic countries" (1813, 75), and the "universities, like those in other Catholic countries, little promote the progress of solid knowledge" (76). In Ireland, "the Catholics retain their nominal bishops and dignitaries, who subsist by the voluntary contributions of their votaries, but not withstanding the blind superstition and ignorance of the latter, Protestantism increases every year" (52). Another of the most popular geography schoolbook writers, Benjamin Workman, in *Elements of Geography*, relates that in Portugal, "the Roman Catholic religion is practiced here in its greatest degree of splendour and superstition" (1801, 132), and Italy is "inhabited by a race of people who are become degenerated by superstition and political slavery" (21).

Geographies often resembled catechetical texts, as does Nathaniel Dwight's *Short but Comprehensive System of the Geography of the World; by Way of Question and Answers*. Dwight uses a questioning approach to reinforce the typical depiction of European Catholic peoples: "The Portuguese are treacherous and unfaithful" (1795, 8) and "The greater part [of the Irish] are very ignorant and imperfectly civilized; impatient of injuries, implacable in their resentments, and vehement in all their affections" (38). Customs peculiar to Ireland include "funeral howling and presenting their corpses in the street to excite the charity of strangers, and their convivial meetings on Sundays, and dancing to bag-pipes, which are usually attended by quarreling" (39). But Dwight extends his disdain for Catholics to the Americas as well. He explains that people of Mexico "are divided into three classes, viz. whites, Indians and negroes. The whites are much like the inhabitants of Old Spain, only more effeminate and vicious" (201).

HISTORIES

Until the early nineteenth century, history was rarely a separate subject in school curricula but was instead usually included unsystematically in readers, geographies, or classical languages (Russell 1914, 314). While not as pervasive as readers and geographies in the early nineteenth century, history schoolbooks became increasingly popular as the century progressed.[5] George H. Callcott claims that for the nineteenth century, history "was not so much the search for social truths, because truths came first and were already known; its purpose was to illustrate the truths on which men had agreed" (1970, 177–78). History was to "strengthen men's convictions and, consequently, strengthen the fabric of society" (178). In *History in the United States*, he observes that in the early nineteenth century, "running through the works of virtually all of the great literary historians, through those of hundreds of local chroniclers, blatant in popular magazines, and in almost every schoolbook, the hatred of Roman Catholicism colored the sweep of history" (170).

Initially, histories of British writers gained popularity as textbooks in academies and colleges. Many of the British historians were blatantly anti-Catholic, and numerous popular American history schoolbook writers, for all levels of education, adopted information from and modeled their own texts on the British writers. Especially influential in this respect was David Hume's multivolume *History of England*. Hume's original historical works were used in upper levels of education, but excerpts were regularly included in readers at nearly all levels and incorporated into the history schoolbooks authored by American writers.

Hume's narratives regarding Catholics are inaccurate and sensational. For example, Hume dedicates more than twenty pages in *The History of England* to the 1641 Irish rebellion. He praises the "great colonies of British [who] had been carried over, and . . . intermixed with the Irish" to "cure them of that sloth and barbarism to which they had ever been subject" (1810, 5:395). Although Irish lands were seized and redistributed among these British planters without compensation to the Irish, Hume claims that the Irish received "a more than equal return . . . by [the British planters'] instructing the natives to tillage, building, manufactures, and all the civilized arts of life" (5:395). Hume presents the Irish rebellion in gory and sensational detail, referring to the "depraved nature" and "perverted religion" that encouraged the rebellion (5:401). He repeatedly describes the "enraged superstition" (5:397) and "inhuman barbarities" of the Irish Catholics (5:399) against the "feeble age of children, the tender sex of women," and depicts Protestant husbands and sons bidding final adieus to perishing loved ones (5:404). He claims that "all the tortures which wanton cruelty could devise, all the lingering pains of body, the anguish of mind, the agonies of despair, could not satiate revenge excited without injury derived from no cause" and that "after rapacity had fully exerted itself, cruelty, and the most barbarous that ever, in any nation, was known or heard of, began its operations in the universal massacre on the defenceless English" (5:401). Hume claims that the English who perished in the Irish rebellion numbered "by some computations . . . a hundred and fifty or two hundred thousands: by the most moderate, and probably the most reasonable account . . . forty thousand" (5:405). More recent historians put this number between four and twelve thousand, but Hume's numbers and descriptions were picked up repeatedly as accurate and used in readers and history schoolbooks. Although nearly half the population of Ireland was lost as a result of Oliver Cromwell and Henry Ireton's harsh 1651 repression of the Irish, Hume presents the brutal conquest in less than one page, acknowledging the English people's appreciation of Ireton's "vigilance, industry, capacity," and "strict execution of justice" (6:219).

Subsequent history schoolbooks narrated similar stories of Catholic atrocities in a seemingly objective manner, often including stories of the pope's diabolical nature. In his 1817 *Catechetical Compend of General History, Sacred and Profane*, Frederick W. Butler explains that the "general moral character" of the popes who "have flourished since the time of Luther" is "corrupt in the extreme; practising and tolerating all the vices, and the blackest crimes" (114). He also includes negative reference to Catholic peoples. With regard to South America, Butler asks these questions:

> Q. Was the papal religion planted here?
> A. Yes, with all its ignorance, and superstitions.
> Q. Does it continue there to this day?
> A. Yes, with all its degrading effects on the southern world.
> Q. To what may this be imputed?
> A. Entirely to the difference of character between the Papal and Protestant religions. (111)

Butler also promotes notions of illiteracy among Catholics:

> Q. Were the prayers of the papal church all written in Latin, for the different nations of Europe?
> A. Yes, and throughout the world.
> Q. How could they understand them?
> A. They were taught to believe that unnecessary. (95)

LITERACY, RELIGION, AND SCHOOLBOOKS

In the preface to a later edition, Butler prepares the reader by openly explaining his intent in writing the history:

> It has been my first object through the whole work to shew the influence and importance of religion—to contrast the pure religion of the Jews with the idolatry of the ages in which they maintained the purity of their church. To contrast particularly the religion of Christ and his apostles, with the religion of the Popes and Mahomet, and to shew that Martin Luther was the angel of the gospel for the age in which he lived, and will continue to be the angel of the gospel until the millennial day, through the medium of the heralds of the cross, in the protestant cause. (1819, iv)

Such religious commentary in history texts became commonplace.

Other disparaging narratives in history texts reinforce those found in readers and other schoolbooks. Charles Carpenter calls Joseph Emerson Worcester's *Elements of History, Ancient and Modern* "the first really comprehensive and ably written American school history" (1963, 199). In his *Elements*, Worcester continues depictions common in readers. For example, he narrates Queen Mary's "bigotry, moroseness, tyranny and cruelty" and her "unrelenting persecutions" of eminent Protestants (1826, 71–72). American historians also presented anti-French and anti-Catholic accounts of history in the United States. The ongoing hostility and battles for territory between the British and French and the French historical affiliation with North American Indians offered an especially ripe venue for distaste of Catholics. Emma Willard, famous for her pioneering efforts in women's education, presents the Ralle affair as "the Jesuits' or Ralle's war," excoriating Father Sebastien Ralle who "excite[d] their Indians' jealousies against the English" (1854, 103).

As books by American authors and publishers increasingly replaced those by British authors, they rarely differed greatly in their presentation of material. In fact, even while calling for more American schoolbooks, critics praised American authors' fidelity to British texts. Pleased that "our best books for schools, will soon cease to be the re-prints of English works," a reviewer of John Robinson's abridgment of Hume and Tobias Smollett's 1823 *The History of England from the Revolution to the Death of George the Second* commended the text's "faithfulness" to the original, suggesting that the prejudices of Hume—if prejudices they were—which, in the opinion of those whose political views differ from his, have influenced and falsified his account of the Commonwealth, and of the reigns of the last of the Stuarts, are still more prominent in this abridgement;—either because the sentiments of the author are necessarily stated in an abridgment with less periphrasis or qualifications, or because Mr. Robinson agrees in opinion with Hume, and is willing to just say what he thinks. ("Hume and Smollet [sic] Abridged" 1824, 1)

The text might be synthesized or changed in any number of ways, but prejudicial treatment based on religion and ethnicity prevailed.

GRAMMARS

Grammars also served as popular texts for school use and continued the tradition of moral and religious inculcation. In his *English Grammar*, leading textbook author Lindley Murray explained to readers, "In the course of this work, some examples will appear of erroneous translations from the Holy Scripture with respect to grammatical construction; but it may be proper to remark, that notwithstanding these verbal mistakes, the Bible, for the size of it, is the most accurate grammatical composition which we have in the English language" (1795, 103). But authors often went beyond general biblical quotation in grammars, many times focusing on religious propaganda and equating Christianity with civilization and morality. For example, one grammar claimed that "Christianity is the prevailing religion of the leading nations of the world" (qtd. in Elson 1964, 46), and Murray maintained, "There never was any system besides that of Christianity, which could effectively produce in the mind of man, the virtues I have hitherto been speaking of" (1795, 87). Such generalizations were common, the authors making it clear that Christianity equated with Protestantism.

Both grammars and their accompanying exercise books included examples offensive to Catholics. Murray's *English Grammar* (1817 and in all subsequent editions) includes the following example of perspicuity: "It has been said, that not only Jesuits equivocate" (1817, 121). Murray's *Key to the Exercises Adapted to Murray's English Grammar* includes similar examples from which students are to make the better grammatical choice between the following:

It has been said, that Jesuits can not only equivocate.

Or—Jesuits are not the only persons who can equivocate. (1810, 109)

Materials derogatory of Catholics and Catholic practices surfaced outside the actual instructional material of schoolbooks as well, such as in advertisements at the back of texts. For example, *The Young Gentleman and Lady's Monitor, and English Teacher's Assistant* carried the following ad in the book's back matter: "THE FRENCH CONVERT: Being a true relation of the happy Conversion of a noble French Lady, from the Errors and Superstitions of Popery, to the Reformed Religion, by Means of a Protestant Gardener, her servant, wherein is shewn, her great and unparalleled Sufferings, on the Account of her said Conversion: as also her wonderful Deliverance from two Assassins, hired by a Popish Priest to murder her" (1795, n.p.). Thus, texts often used every chance to assure that young students imbibed Protestantism and recognized the alien and dangerous nature of Catholicism.

Alternative Textbooks

The examples cited above represent the most popular texts in the colonies and early United States, the majority of them published in the Boston area by Congregationalists. Catholic bishops and priests repeatedly expressed disquiet about existing texts and a wish for alternate materials. As Bishop Francis Kenrick (who was working on a theological textbook of his own) explained, "At present we experience no small difficulty in providing the students with Class-books, and still greater difficulty in furnishing the missionaries with theological works which they might consult in a variety of contingencies" (1834). However, some alternative texts became available. J. A. Burns explains that "some of the first Catholic school-books published in this country were but new editions of commonly used text-books, revised and recast, more or less, to give them a Catholic tone" (1908, 161). Timothy Walch calls Philadelphia the center of early Catholic publishing, citing the 1785 *Spelling Primer for Children with a Catholic Catechism Annexed*, published by Catholic priest Robert Molyneux, and the 1786 *Roman Catholic Primer* by an unknown publisher; these were followed by Mathew Carey's publishing house at the turn of the century (1988, 270). The Sulpicians published a mathematics textbook in 1806 and a prayer and devotional manual two years later. They also worked with Baltimore publisher Fielding Lucas, who published geography and astronomy texts, probably written by a member of St. Mary's faculty, as well as other texts for the seminary (Donohue 1940, 65). But many Catholic texts were available only locally or, at best, regionally. As Ronald Zboray has discussed, economics and poor transportation systems limited widespread access to many books (1993).

Publishers in Baltimore, Philadelphia, and Detroit provided Catholic catechisms and other basic materials for use by U.S. Catholics. Catechisms were the most widely available texts for Catholic children, as they had been for Protestants; Francis J. Donohue suggests that because of its ready availability and relatively minor expense, the catechism "was practically indispensable for religious instruction, and could be used as a reading book and a speller as well" (1940, 66). The most widely accessible and popular early catechism for instruction of Catholic youth seems to have been *A Catechism, or Short Abridgement of Christian Doctrine Newly Revised for the Use of the Catholic Church in the United States of America*. Essentially a translation from the French Council of Trent authorization, the catechism was published in Georgetown and Baltimore in the second half of the eighteenth century and later printed in a variety of regions. The text, approximately forty pages, presented a basic question-and-answer format to instruct Catholics in fundamental church tenets about God, Jesus Christ, the sacraments, and so on. A full chapter was dedicated to explaining, in depth, the meaning behind the Apostles' Creed. Later editions of the catechism, adapted more clearly for American Catholics, responded implicitly to Protestant criticism of Catholic beliefs. The later catechism contained more prayers traditionally accepted within the church, outlined a suggested morning ritual of prayer and meditation, and increased instruction in dogma, with explanations behind church doctrine that Protestants found questionable or heretical. For example, the later catechism defines and explains purgatory. In answer to how we know purgatory exists, the text explains, "Because the scripture often teaches, that God will render to every man according to his works; and that nothing defiled can enter Heaven; and that some Christians *shall be saved, so as by fire.* Cor. iii.13" (1816, 23). And chapter 6 explains the sacrament of penance thus:

> Q. How do you prove that the priest has power to absolve sinners if they be truly penitent?
> A. From the words of Christ: whose sins you shall forgive they are forgiven them. St. John xx.23. (51)

Other subjects addressed by the catechism include the place of relics and saints:

> Catholics honour saints and angels as God's special friends and servants, but not with the honour which belongs to God.
>
> Q. And is it allowable to honour relics, crucifixes, and holy pictures? A. Yes, with an inferior and relative honour, as they relate to Christ and his saints and are memorial of them, [but] by no means [pray to them as] they have no life or sense to hear or help us. (38–39)

These later catechisms armed students with answers to questions and criticisms they might receive from Protestants. Although they clearly address Protestant challenges, the texts speak to criticisms with positive information related to church doctrine; no direct criticism of Protestants or the Protestant religion is included. *A Catechism, or Short Abridgement of Christian Doctrine* remained the most popular catechism among U.S. Catholics until the early 1820s, when priests and bishops began writing and editing catechisms for their dioceses. For example, Bishop John England compiled a catechism for his diocese in Charleston, South Carolina, as did Bishop Jean Baptiste David for the Bardstown diocese.

A reprint of the popular British text authored by Reverend Richard Challoner, *The Catholick Christian Instructed in the Sacraments, Sacrifice, Ceremonies, and Observances of the Church. By Way of Question and Answer* (originally published in 1737), provided an in-depth understanding of church doctrine. According to Burns, Molyneux reprinted the Challoner catechism for post-Revolution schools in the United States (1969, 138), but Mathew Carey clearly published the text as well, as letters to him request copies of the text. This catechism appears to address a more mature audience than that discussed above; however, in a letter to Carey, Joseph P. Mobberley requests seventy-five copies for use in three New York City Catholic free schools (1813). Donohue claims it was used as an advanced reading text (1940, 66). The text as a simple reprint ran 265 pages, but later editions included introductory materials by other authors and might run 300 pages or more in length. Challoner offers more complex explanations of dogma and addresses articles of doctrine under attack from Protestants more fully, drawing from numerous biblical sources. For example, Challoner expounds on why the Eucharist is so named and explains it as a form of thanksgiving, citing Matthew 26:27, Mark 14:23, Luke 22:9, and 1 Corinthians 11:24 ([1737] 1786, 27). He points to tradition and the Council of Nice to explain why the church requires priestly celibacy:

> Because she does not think it proper that they who by their office and functions ought to be wholly devoted to the service of God and the care of souls, should be diverted from these duties by the distractions of married life. 1 Cor. Vii. 32, 33. *He that is unmarried careth for the things that belong to the Lord, how he may please the Lord; but he that is married, careth for things that are of the world, how he may please his wife.* (168)

Challoner's catechism—and to a lesser degree later editions of the church-sponsored catechism for youth—provides authority for the church's position, presenting a straightforward explanation of Catholic doctrine. The widely used youth catechism initially made few changes from the original French version that had been designed for use where Catholicism was deeply entrenched and faced few challenges. Later American editions implicitly defended against Protestant attacks without explicitly condemning Protestant religions. Similarly, Challoner's catechism, a British text authored by a minority priest in a dangerously hostile country, does not openly attack the majority religion yet subtly counters criticisms. Both reprints represented their country of origin, and both found acceptance in the United States where any open hostility to Protestantism would have been unsafe; at the same time, the texts provided an alternative instruction for young people and adults alike in a nation dedicated at almost every level to promoting a Protestant religion and society.

By the 1820s, a catechism by the Irish reverend James P. Butler (originally published in 1775) began gaining popularity and would become the most popular catechism of the nineteenth century. Butler's catechism, originally intended for Irish catechumens, was similar to later editions of the eighteenth-century Council of Trent types translated from French. It, too, offers explanations of dogma most often criticized by Protestants. Originally imported in its original, the text was eventually printed in Philadelphia with additions by American clergy. Approximately seventy-five pages, the catechism explains the commandments as outlined by the Catholic Church, as well as the six precepts of church law, including tenets about the requirements for confession and the Eucharist. None of the catechisms offer direct criticism of Protestants.

ALTERNATE SUBJECT TEXTS

Texts for secular subjects remained a constant concern to American Catholic clergy, however. At the 1829 First Provincial Council in Baltimore, the bishops declared that

> since not infrequently, in the books generally used in the schools, much is found by which the principles of our faith are impugned, our dogma falsely expounded, and history perverted, by reason of which the minds of children are infused with errors to the most grievous peril of their souls, the application of some remedy for this great evil is demanded not only by our zeal for religion, and the right education of youth, but even by the very honor of these United States. (qtd. in Buetow 1970, 146–47)

When these texts were used in the school, the bishops decreed, all inaccuracies should be removed.

The disquiet surfaced at the local levels as well. The clergy associated with the sisters' academies expressed concern about the textbooks used in the academies. As late as 1828, Reverend Jean Baptiste David wrote to Reverend Simon Bruté about his concern regarding schoolbooks used at Nazareth Academy:

> I see by your prospectus that you teach history. I would like to know what author you follow. Here at the college they have introduced a resume of the universal history by a Protestant, and I believe, what is worse, give as a reason that there are not others. Even though it were so, I do not think there is any reason to put such a book in the hand of our students. I will never let it come into Nazareth.

David continued, "They speak to me of a geography by Murphy, a Catholic author, in which he has put in a little history. It is greatly praised. Mr. Badin has sent here a little dissertation on the Spanish Inquisition, which is an extract. It is excellent. Do you know this Geography? Do you know where I can obtain it?"

David refers to a text by Irishman John Murphy, published in Dublin. The text was not readily available in the United States, however, and is not extant in any of the school archives I examined. However, archives of Catholic male seminaries and colleges, as well as some girls' academies, have early copies of French historian Charles Rollin's histories and other

French texts. The French texts, though, were most likely used as resources for teachers in most girls' schools, or only at the upper level. More likely used in the convent academies was a history text in English found in the archives of some of these schools.[6] Written by William Grimshaw, an Irish immigrant to Philadelphia, the text revises Oliver Goldsmith's popular histories, seeking to remove the "confusion, indelicacy, and grammatical inaccuracy" (1819, vi) in Goldsmith's abridgments because

> the narrative should not be exhausted on the infidelity of a queen, or the erection of a scaffold; upon the protracted siege, or the counter-marching of an army: entertainment should be free from ribaldry, and praise should be held from the commission of enormity. When we have wearied the reader with the minute recital of a fictitious plot, we should look back, lest we have omitted the *Burning of London*: we should consider, that a story may be humorous yet offensive, and avoid recommending *intrigues* and *virtues* as deserving of a *throne*. (vii)

Goldsmith and Grimshaw, both Irish and neither Catholic, framed their works with a decidedly different tone. Goldsmith's texts, like Hume's, are sensational, often obscuring the primary historical significance of events with lengthy and detailed narratives of murder and intrigue. His texts are also blatantly anti-Catholic. For example, Goldsmith presents a protracted explanation of the Gunpowder Plot, detailing, at length, scandalous information and attributing the plot to the pope and to Catholics in general. Grimshaw, on the other hand, provides a far more sympathetic interpretation of the Gunpowder Plot, much more succinct than either Goldsmith's or that of most histories of England published in Boston. Presenting the event as "displaying, at once, the widest departure from moral virtue," he continues:

> Catesby, a man of respectable family, and Percy, a descendent of the house of Northumberland, were the projectors of a scheme, for restoring the Roman Catholicks to power; and formed the diabolical plan of blowing up the House of Parliament with gunpowder.... For this purpose, they engaged one Fawkes, an officer in the Spanish service. ... Happily, however, Providence averted, by a discovery, this dreadful blow; and the gunpowder and the matches were conveyed into the vault under the House of Lords. Here, Fawkes being seized, he made a full confession of his own guilt, and that of his associates, who met

the reward which their crime so highly merited. But let us not involve the Roman Catholick body in this horrid plot. It would be unjust. The king was well aware that they were unfairly implicated.... Whilst with one hand he punished the guilty, with the other he would support and protect the innocent. (1819, 126–27)

ALTERNATIVE GEOGRAPHIES

The most popular geography textbook providing a more favorable description of Catholics and Catholic countries was a version of William Guthrie's *New System of Modern Geography*, a British text first published in the United States in 1794. Guthrie had actually died in 1770, but the popularity of his geographies led to their reprint in Philadelphia, originally by Mathew Carey, who revised and reprinted Guthrie's world geography. Carey provided far more favorable descriptions of Catholic countries and peoples than did other popular American texts, such as those of Morse. Later, the publishers Johnson and Warner issued a Guthrie text titled *A New Geographical, Historical, and Commercial Grammar*. The Johnson and Warner text, also published in Philadelphia, lacked the sympathetic treatment given by Carey.

Catholic Mathew Carey became the leading publisher in Philadelphia, indeed of the entire country in the early nineteenth century, helping to unseat Boston as the center of publishing.[7] John Tebbel calls Carey the "prototype of the modern publisher" (1972, 56) and "the first publisher in a modern sense" (100) and credits him with creating a Catholic reading public (188). Carey published the first U.S. printing of the Catholic Douay Bible in 1790;[8] like other Catholic publishers, he concentrated primarily on Bibles, prayer books, and catechisms in his Catholic publications. However, he also revised and printed schoolbooks for use in the classroom. The Carey geography published under Guthrie's name was likely revised by Carey himself, as he was a prolific writer and editor, as well as an ardent Catholic.[9] In addition, in ongoing correspondence with Carey, Archbishop John Carroll discussed revisions to the Guthrie geography to correct the "geographical mistakes, & more so, historical inaccuracies & frequent misrepresentations." Carroll explained that he would suggest the revised geography's use in the academy at Georgetown (Carroll 1793).[10]

In the preface to the Carey edition of Guthrie's geography, the editor explains, "We have thought it requisite to enter into this explanation with respect to the European editions of this performance. The alterations and editions in the present one, are so numerous, that it better deserves the title of an original work than some mutilated transcripts of Guthrie that, under a different name, have been introduced to the world" (Guthrie 1794, 10). But the text continues in less hostile attitude toward Catholics. In his explanation of religion in England, for example, he explains,

> Many families in England still profess the Roman Catholic religion. The laws against its professors are dreadfully severe, but, as is usual in such cases, they defeat themselves, being seldom put into execution. Some of these laws have been lately repealed, much to the satisfaction of every liberal-minded man, though a vehement outcry was not long after excited against the measure by ignorance and bigotry. This was the pretext of the well known and fatal riots in London, in 1780, excited by the extraordinary fanatic, Lord George Gordon. (239)

Carey later references these riots following Parliamentary efforts to alleviate some of the oppressive laws against Catholics, explaining that the "summer of the year 1780 was distinguished by one of the most disgraceful exhibitions of bigotry that had ever appeared in any country" (335). In his presentation of Ireland, he depicts Cromwell and Ireton's brutal conquest of Ireland, noting that Ireland's population in 1641, before the conquest, was 1,466,000; in 1652, the population stood at 850,000. "So great a havoc, as the loss of almost one half of its population in eleven years, has hardly ever happened to any people, unless perhaps the Jews" (361).

The Johnson and Warner revision, while much less anti-Catholic than the original Guthrie, nonetheless contains disparaging passages about Catholics. In addressing the Americas, for example, the Johnson and Warner text explains Brazil's religion simply as follows: "The religion of Portugal, or the Roman-catholic, is established here. Six bishoprics have been successively founded under the archbishopric of Bahia, or St. Salvador, which was established in 1552" (Guthrie 1809, 423). And in Canada, "about nine-tenths of the inhabitants of these provinces are Roman Catholic, who enjoy, under the present government, the same rights and privileges as were granted them in 1772, by the act of parliament then passed. The rest of the people are protestants of various sects" (302). Yet, passages on England continue much of the anti-Catholic attitude found in other geographies: Mary, once "settled on the throne . . . proceeded like a female fury to re-establish popery" and married Spain's Philip II, who, like Mary, was an "unfeeling bigot to popery" (222).

LITERACY, RELIGION, AND SCHOOLBOOKS

REGIONAL INFLUENCES

Obtaining textbooks was especially difficult in areas removed from East Coast traffic. Such areas often received help from Mathew Carey, whose sophisticated transportation network permitted him to regularly send books and supplies to Kentucky and other frontier areas that would otherwise have had trouble obtaining such materials. But schoolbooks acceptable to Catholics sometimes became available through smaller local efforts; the most notable of these appeared in the Detroit area when Catholic priest Gabriel Richard brought a printing press to Detroit in 1809. Richard devoted most of his life to educational concerns in the Michigan territory, establishing schools and helping to found the University of Michigan. Concerned about the dearth of schoolbooks available in the area, he published "not less than nine books, all but one of which were intended for use in the schools Father Richard established in Detroit" (Greenly qtd. in Buetow 1970, 70). Most of these publications were in French; some were in English. The preface to Richard's first textbook, *The Child's Spelling Book or Michigan Instructor*, outlined his purpose and future intentions:

> The great scarcity of School Books in the Territory, is a sufficient apology for the appearance of the following pages. This small book . . . is intended to answer the purpose of introducing the Youth of this Territory, into the fundamental principles of Education. If it gains encouragement it will, perhaps be succeeded by another Part containing Spellings of a maturer kind, intermixed with useful Lessons in Reading: such as, Maxims, Proverbs, Fables, Moral Stories, & calculated to inspire the youthful mind, with a sense of strict propriety and virtue. At the request of several Gentlemen and Teachers of this City, it is sent to the Press:—and it is hoped that it may meet the approbation and liberal patronage of a generous public. (qtd. in Buetow 1970, 70)

According to Frank B. Woodford and Albert Hyma, Richard's press produced "fifty-two known imprints" (1958, 70). In addition to *The Child's Spelling Book*, the press printed prayer books as well as classical works. "Many of these books reflect the need as well as the influence of Richard," noted Woodford and Hyma; "they were intended for his pastoral use, for the instruction and elevation of the Catholic mind" (70). Burns claims Richard's texts "had a considerable circulation in Catholic schools in the West" (1969,

138). While important to early education in the Detroit region, the press was relatively short-lived and appears to have ended publication in 1816.

The Status of Schoolbooks by 1840

The anti-Catholic bias in schoolbooks passed unremarked publicly before the mid-nineteenth century. Although late eighteenth-century and early nineteenth-century periodicals abound with advertisements for schoolbooks, each bookseller listing his stock of books, surprisingly little discussion about their content surfaces. Most who addressed the issue of schoolbooks in the classroom called for uniformity in the books used in the schools or criticized parents who failed to provide schoolbooks for their children. Except in some free schools where a benevolent society might furnish free books for students, parents were expected to provide their children's schoolbooks.[11] These might be from a suggested list provided by the school, but often students used handed-down books or those their parents obtained most inexpensively. Rarely did children in the same classroom have identical editions of a book, often lacking even a commonly authored text.

Despite the concerns expressed at the 1829 First Provincial Council and by individual Catholic clergy, little official action was taken by the Catholic Church hierarchy to assure appropriate textbooks for Catholic schools. "The 'nonsectarian' textbooks continued ... to be generally of such bigoted nature that their use in Catholic schools was impossible. In brief, the Catholic textbooks situation, except in isolated instances, was no nearer solution by about 1840 than it had been at the beginning of the nineteenth century," noted Donohue (1940, 66). The nation as a whole seemed completely uninterested in textbook reform. Remarkably little discussion of schoolbooks surfaced in eighteenth-century and early nineteenth-century periodicals. The most common references to schoolbooks in such print concern the Bible, as it was commonly considered the most important text for use in schools. These mentions call the Bible the "best of all school-books" ("For the Gazette" 1801), praising its use. Similar references surface in missionary society reports, as they often provided accounts of the distribution of Bibles in foreign schools. One interesting series in the Boston newspaper *Religious Intelligencer* during 1817 details efforts to distribute Bibles in Irish schools. These reports catalog the opposition by numerous Irish priests to missionaries' efforts to distribute the Bible to schoolchildren, alongside reports of success in conjunction with the Hibernian Society and a few priests who welcomed Bible donations for their schools. The latter group, according to the missionaries, supported use of the Bibles in schools, even if those Bibles were "Lutheran" ("The Bible a New School Book for Roman Catholics" 1817). Missionary reports related to other countries also detailed the number of Bibles distributed at schools. Another article declaimed about "what the Bible can do for Catholics" if only the Catholic clergy would allow its use in their schools. (1833).

As Protestant ministers and newspapers regularly admonished Catholic clergy for keeping parishioners in ignorance and for not allowing them access to the Bible, Catholic newspapers occasionally refuted that claim. For example, the *New-York Truth Teller* reported a homily delivered by Bishop Edward Fenwick, who noted the many efforts to provide Bibles to schools in Ireland and other Catholic countries and suggested that critics visit one of the many Catholic bookstores to examine titles appropriate for intelligent readers. Fenwick also responded to criticism that Catholics objected to the use of the Bible in schools. According to Fenwick, "putting the Bible into the hands of young children, before they had been prepared for those sacred books," was "absurd" and "could diminish the respect which children should pay to the word of God" ("Sketch of the Catholic Lecture" 1831). Such arguments rarely surfaced outside Catholic publications, however. The major public conversation about schoolbooks as related to Catholics prior to 1840 surround the controversy over use of the Bible in schools and Catholics' lack of interest in schooling.

I have found no entries, either in Catholic or Protestant periodicals, that discuss the anti-Catholic bias in textbooks. As correspondence between Mathew Carey and Catholic bishops and priests suggests, Catholic clergy promoted the purchase of the Douay Bible and other Catholic books among their parishioners and for their schools and discussed among themselves the problematic nature of most available schoolbooks. They did not, however, make their objections public prior to 1840. Catholics made up a small, unpopular minority of the U.S. population in the early decades of the nineteenth century. Leaders focused on providing for the needs of members and avoided negative public attention. In most areas where Catholics settled, hostility was minimal; as is typical of many new immigrants, Catholic immigrants, especially the Irish, took on the most dangerous and dirty jobs, such as building canals and the early railroads. In addition, immigration to Canada after the Revolution, especially by loyalists, largely offset migration from European countries. Anger among Protestants began to increase in the 1840s and 1850s as large numbers of Catholic immigrants arrived onshore, increasing the typical fears about a foreign takeover and concern for employment. As the number of Catholics increased, they and their leaders became bolder in public refutations and demands for rights. For example, in the early 1840s, New York Catholics, led by Bishop John Hughes, led a challenge to the "non-sectarian" public school system, seeking funds for Catholic schools. The Baptists had made a similar unsuccessful challenge earlier, so chances for success on the part of Catholics were not good and, indeed, ended in failure, despite support from Governor William Seward. The controversy was lengthy and gained much publicity, both in New York and nationally. As Timothy Smith has pointed out, "It was not secularism but nondenominational Protestantism that won the day" (1967, 687).

The rapid increase in the Catholic population after 1840 fueled the mid-century nativist movement that created anger and violence toward Catholics across the country. By the end of the 1850s, Boston became the scene of a controversy similar to the earlier dispute in New York, when a Catholic student at a public school, Thomas Whall, refused to recite the Protestant version of the Ten Commandments. Whall had followed the directions of the Reverend Bernardine Wiget, who had called upon the boys in his Sunday school to refuse to recite Protestant prayers and instead say their own Catholic prayers. When Whall repeatedly refused to recite the King James Bible version of the Ten Commandments, an assistant principal beat the boy's hands until they bled, insisting that he would "whip him till he yields if it takes the whole forenoon" (qtd. in McGreevey 2003, 8). The controversy resulted in a major exodus of Catholics from the public schools and hardened animosity among Catholics and Protestants, leading to greater impetus for Catholics to build their own schools. However, before 1840, Catholics and their leaders kept a very low profile.

Congregationalist Influences on Schoolbooks

Schoolbooks served an important purpose. They not only instructed children in literacy and general knowledge but also instilled a specific belief system. Popular schoolbooks were problematic for Catholics, as their prejudicial content placed Catholics in a precariously unsympathetic position and made their use untenable for Catholic schools. Pennsylvania had historically been far more accepting of Quakers, Catholics, and other minorities than other parts of the country, and eventually Philadelphia became a major center for textbook publishing, providing some more favorable schoolbooks for Catholics. However, most early schoolbooks were printed or authored in New England, which was led by powerful religious leaders who greatly influenced both the churchgoing public and the educational processes. Massachusetts and Connecticut state laws had mandated an established religion until the 1830s. The religious leaders were often the best educated in their community, and the best-known schoolbook writers publishing from Boston and New Haven were Congregationalist ministers, closely associated with one another, nearly all extremely intolerant of any who diverged from their theological principles—and especially biased against Catholics.

Colonial catechisms and other early texts were written by such staunch religious personalities as Cotton Mather or imported from England. However, as the United States began to produce other subject schoolbooks, New England and its religious leaders remained powerful in their writing and publishing.[12] The "Father of American Geography," Congregational clergyman Jedidiah Morse, found his most permanent position outside schoolbook writing in the pulpit of the First Congregational Church of Charlestown, Massachusetts, where the infamous burning of the Ursuline convent occurred. Staunchly orthodox, he fought every moderating inclination in the church, opposing the appointment of any but the most conformist to the Hollis Chair of Divinity at Harvard and forcing the more tolerant Unitarians from the Congregational Church. He helped to found the New England Tract Society and the American Bible Society, purveyors of a wealth of anti-Catholic pamphlets and books. Morse was close friends with other anti-Catholic Congregationalist leaders, such as minister and president of Yale Timothy Dwight. Dwight became president of Yale in 1795 and turned the school from a religiously moderate institution toward Calvinism. He was religious mentor to Lyman Beecher. Timothy Dwight's brother, Nathaniel Dwight, authored *A Short but Comprehensive System of the Geography of the World*, cited above, which saw thirty-eight editions between 1805 and 1814. Worldcat reports eighty-two editions of his various geographies prior to 1817. Grandsons of Jonathan Edwards, the Dwight brothers became leaders in the Congregational Church, Timothy himself a "faithful and earnest preacher" (Harris 1930) in the church. Timothy Dwight published *Open Convents; or, Nunneries and Popish Seminaries, Dangerous to the Morals, and Degrading to the Character of a Republican Community* (1836), an attack on Catholic institutions, especially convents and convent academies.

Other important figures in geography include William C. Woodbridge, a licensed Congregationalist minister, who studied theology under Timothy

Dwight and attended Princeton Theological Seminary. Woodbridge became powerful among educators, editing the *American Journal of Education*. He married Lucy Ann Reed, who had taught in Catharine Beecher's Hartford school, and joined with Emma Willard to author some of his most popular geographies. Thus, the Congregationalist leaders in New England had a major influence on educational progress in the colonies and early United States, shaping attitudes and beliefs and contributing greatly to a collective consciousness that equated Protestantism with republicanism, progress, goodness, and a righteous history, in contrast with Catholicism.

Schoolbooks represent one area in which Catholic convent schools differed from Protestant schools. Most of the women's proprietor schools in the Northeast would have been very comfortable with the texts outlined above. In fact, Goldsmith's histories are listed as texts for Catharine and Mary Beecher's Connecticut school in an 1824 ad (reproduced in Tolley 1996, 135). As we will see in chapters 3 and 4, teachers in Catholic convents and girls' schools often created their own materials for instruction or, in the case of European-originated communities, sometimes transcribed their French books into manuscripts for students. Eventually, Catholic presses would supply textbooks for the many parochial schools across the country, and some sisters became important authors of these texts. But prior to 1840, schoolbooks appropriate for their schools remained a concern for Catholic educators, a concern they expressed among themselves but avoided making public.

2.

The Religious Nature of Early Women's Literacy

⊢――⊣

Although seldom acknowledged, religious missionary zeal is inextricably intertwined with the history of women's literacy in the United States. Many scholars, following Linda Kerber, have credited the advancement in women's education in the early Republic to the interest in mothers' preparing and educating future citizens, but the most potent portion of that training was the transmitting of appropriate religious and moral convictions. Preparation for citizenship and the afterlife required, many believed, strong inculcation in or conversion to accepted religious truths and moral tenets. Catholic convent academies, because they were taught by Catholic sisters, were clearly marked as religious. However, early women's proprietor schools, such as those of Emma Willard, Catharine Beecher, Mary Lyon, Zilpah Grant, and Sarah Pierce, all of whom were heavily influenced by Calvinist ministers, were deeply committed to the extension of a specific religious agenda.[1]

Much anti-Catholic sentiment focused on Catholic sisters' convents and academies. Charges made against the sisters engendered fear of their proliferating schools and propelled support for Protestant schools and academies for women to counter their advance, anti-Catholic sentiment and rhetoric often acting as the most successful social and economic influences behind the growth of the proprietor schools. Despite the animosity toward Catholic convents and academies, however, the sisters' schools, among the most prestigious in the country, were heavily patronized by Protestants, including leading national figures.

Better girls' academies generally taught reading, writing, spelling, and grammar, with some math, history, and usually geography in the earliest years. By the 1820s, many began including additional subjects, such as elocution, rhetoric, modern languages, and a variety of sciences. Most also taught what have variously been called practical, vocational, or ornamental skills.

Such subjects nearly always included sewing and needlework of various types, music, and often drawing, sometimes dancing. This was generally true in the most respected schools, whether Catholic or Protestant. Most also held public commencements or examinations at the end of the school year, usually attended by local, sometimes national, dignitaries, who often questioned students in a display of their learning. Students read their written compositions and often performed musical or dramatic numbers.

Although taught by Catholic sisters, most Catholic academies focused far less on religion than did the New England proprietor schools. All the proprietor schools mentioned above claimed as their primary purpose providing a strong religious and moral foundation for women. Even Emma Willard, who is generally seen as less focused on religious conversion than the other eastern proponents of women's education, consistently identified religious and moral instruction as primary. In her 1819 address before the New York Legislature, for example, she assured them, "A regular attention to religious duties would, of course be required of the pupils by the laws of the institution. The trustees would be careful to appoint no instructors, who would not teach religion and morality, both by their example, and by leading the minds of the pupils to perceive, that these constitute the true end of all education" ([1819] 1918, 18).

Religious conversion remained the chief goal of the other proprietors. A major purpose of Sarah Pierce was the promotion of her religious agenda. Emily Noyes Vanderpoel and Elizabeth C. Barney Buel call her "emphatically the pioneer in the cause of female education in our country" (1903, 312). Commenting on Pierce's religious mission, Vanderpoel and Buel claim,

> She taught religion as she did science, practically; and openly placed before the young mind, the fear of God as a better motive than the shrine of applause, the love of Christ a stronger impulse, than the flatteries of the world. . . . In times of declension, her lamp was always trimmed & burning. In times of revival she was prepared to check the impulse of enthusiasm. Her religious instruction to her pupils, her calls upon them for repentance, faith and a holy life were as numerous, as pungent, and as practical, when all around her was religiously cold, as when under the excitement of a powerful revival. (312)

Pierce wrote plays based on Scripture for her students to perform. She also authored texts for them to better serve her purpose. She wrote her brother James, "I have at last completed a history in question and answer for the

THE RELIGIOUS NATURE OF EARLY WOMEN'S LITERACY

use of schools, beginning at the creation & reaching to the Destruction of Jerusalem by Titus. The intention of the work, is to unite Sacred & Profane history with moral instruction & designed for the use of schools" (qtd. in Vanderpoel and Buel 1903, 312). Theodore Sizer and his colleagues found that

> religious education permeated every aspect of life at the Litchfield Female Academy. Formal religious instruction was given in classes on sacred history and in the weekly religious lectures by local clergymen, such as Lyman Beecher who conducted the lectures from 1810 to 1824. Christian dogma was also infused into the study of all other subjects in the curriculum. The school rules required students to attend church all day on Sunday and the pupils were encouraged to take part in church benevolent and Bible-study groups. The school rules also required students to be present at the daily family prayers, which were observed in all the boarding homes each morning and evening. (1993, 56)

Other proprietors followed in similar fashion. Catharine Beecher had attended Pierce's school as a student and assistant teacher between 1810 and 1818, and her family boarded students from the academy. At her Hartford seminary in 1826, Beecher "did not concentrate on scholarly accomplishments but sought the conversion of her students" (Sklar 1973, 64); she referred to her institution as "my little church in school" (68). Later, in speeches on educating women to be teachers, Beecher called for taking women "possessed of missionary zeal," offering further training, and sending them "to the most ignorant portions of our land, to raise up schools, to instruct in morals and piety, and to teach the domestic arts and virtues" (1846, 50).

Grant's and Lyon's schools were also fashioned according to their evangelical mission; both were passionate orthodox Congregationalists. Grant had "gained the consent of her employers to occupy one seventh of the pupils' time and energy in the study of the Scriptures" when teaching at Derry, New Hampshire (Stow 1887, 147; see also Lyon to friend, 1824, qtd. in Lansing 35). According to Sarah D. Locke Stow, Grant and Lyon "concurred in an arrangement, which secured the Bible's being studied more in a year than any other book" (1887, 147). Yet Grant's "persistent efforts toward a Calvinist salvation of souls" so alarmed trustees at the Adams Academy in Derry that they confronted her about spending too much time on religious instruction; in the summer of 1826 they asked Grant for an exact accounting of time spent weekly on religion (Green 1979, 55).

Elizabeth Alden Green suggests "that all four young women [teachers at Derry] felt God was with them" (1979, 55) but that the amount of time spent on religion was minimal; however, much evidence suggests a major emphasis on religious conversion. Green also reports that while Mary Lyon, one of the teachers at the academy, reported "one hour and eleven minutes of class time, and two hours in private conversation with students" on religious beliefs per week, she also explains that "less than a week after Mary Lyon had given her account for the trustees of the week's religious instruction . . . she was writing about the prospects of more conversions in the school" (55). Green also claims that "Zilpah Grant's battle with the Adams Academy trustees" finally led the two toward a future together, resulting in their collaboration at the Ipswich Academy (55). The collaboration was based largely on their belief in the importance of students' religious conversion.

Both Grant and Lyon equated their schools' success with students' conversion to their Christian ideal. Their letters and recorded reflections are filled with regrets and rejoicings, depending on students' successful conversions. Early in their correspondence, Grant wrote Lyon of her concern for students: "Stupidity still generally prevails in school. Within the last two weeks, one of my pupils in the family has evidently experienced the stirrings of the Spirit, & she thinks that she trusts in Christ for salvation. Another in this family has very serious impressions, but does not realize her lost state" (1820). Similarly, in 1832, Lyon wrote to Grant, "How few have been the hopeful conversions the present year! I was forcibly reminded of this to-day, when I inquired who had made a public profession of religion" (qtd. in Hitchcock 1851, 87). In happier times, she wrote her mother in 1834, "The religious state of our school was favorable last term. About twenty indulged some hope of having been born again" (qtd. in Hitchcock 1851, 115).

Later, at Mount Holyoke, "Miss Lyon and her fellow-teachers felt that there should be a revival in the school each year" (Lyon and Lansing 1937, 262), and according to Stow, Lyon converted more than a quarter of her students there (1887, 22). "Miss Lyon was prone to regard the success of her efforts to create the school as sealing a covenant with God for the advancement of His Kingdom," Thomas Woody noted (1929, 362).

Catholic Convents and Academies as Danger

These New England women operated in an atmosphere that nurtured their commitment to a messianic mission in promotion of Calvinist beliefs. They pursued careers amid an environment that saw danger in Catholic educational institutions and a need to provide girls and young women with the necessary foundation to meet and accept their God while resisting papal heresies. They were assisted by a cultural attitude toward women's sexualized and gendered relationships to men that fueled animosity toward convents and convent academies. Fears and anger among opponents of Catholic convents and academies centered on issues of women's convent lives, as Catholic sisters resided in celibacy, without authority of husbands or fathers, often taking on nontraditional authoritative roles, such as administrators of schools, hospitals, and orphanages.

Amanda Porterfield has demonstrated the "Puritans' deliberate confusion of marriage as a trope of grace" (1992, 4), greatly altering the traditional imagery of the soul's marriage to Christ by placing it in a domestic context (3) and, thus, reversing the prior order that had deemed marriage acceptable but had preferred celibacy. While Catholics continued to honor celibacy, Puritans came to see it as suspect. In addition, the secrecy engendered by the hidden spaces behind convent walls and the confessional lent itself to alarming charges.

Anti-Catholic newspaper editors and the Protestant and American tract societies seized upon the notion of nominally celibate but, in reality, lascivious priests amid young, vulnerable women to create narratives of fear. For example, in "Rome's Substitute for Marriage," the Reverend J. Q. A. Henry presents the typical argument:

> The theory of a celibate priesthood is, that a woman must obey her confessor in everything he commands; that she will never be called to account for any action which she has performed to please her priest. These fair penitents are required to answer questions of the most revolting character, and yet it is denied that the Roman Catholic priests are dissolute. We charge that every one of them is compelled by his oath to pollute the minds and hearts of the mothers, wives and daughters. (n.d., 2)[2]

Henry insists upon the impossibility of purity among priests—the unrealistic expectations regarding celibacy—and the subsequent inability of women to remain pure under their influence: "No man or woman can take such thoughts into their mind without being polluted by them; hence the absence of surprise at the moral degradation of nations under the yoke of Rome" (2).

THE RELIGIOUS NATURE OF EARLY WOMEN'S LITERACY

The system, according to the author, was dangerous to all that American citizens held dear, constituting "the sewer of our American life" because "as confessor, he possesses the secrets of a woman's soul" (4). Accordingly, priests had access afforded no other: "A young woman will confess to a priest what she would never venture to tell her mother or acknowledge to her husband" (4). Authors nearly always expanded the dangers of confessional secrecy to convent academies and the defilement of young women there.

The stories incorporated into such reports are specifically about young women's initial purity and their subsequent violation in convent academies. These arguments, surfacing throughout the century, are perhaps most comprehensively distilled by ex-priest Charles Chiniquy, who relates the story of a young academy student. "Before I was seventeen years old," the student began, "God knows that His angels are not more pure than I was; but the chaplain of the Nunnery where my parents had sent me for my education, though approaching old age, put to me, in the confessional, a question that at first I did not understand, but, unfortunately, he had put the same questions to one of my young class-mates, who made fun of them in my presence, and explained them to me" (n.d., 18). According to Chiniquy, the corruption of the young and pure is clearly seen in the account of a young academy student, who explains that questions put to young women are "of such a polluting character that I fear neither the blood of Christ nor all the fires of hell will ever be able to blot them from my memory" (19). Specifics are sparse, however, appropriate for nineteenth-century norms, but also allowing for easy accusations difficult to refute. The narratives are filled with such phrases as "unmentionable things" (14) and events "simply surpassingly horrible—unmentionable, things which I hope you will never request me to reveal to you, for they are too monstrous to be repeated, even in the confessional, by a woman to a man" (19–20).

Such sentiments gained most notoriety in the early century in popular novels that swept the country, publications such as *Awful Disclosures, by Maria Monk, of the Hotel Dieu Nunnery of Montreal* (1836) and other convent "escape" novels. *Awful Disclosures*, a fictitious exposé of a Sisters of Charity Canadian convent,[3] was attributed to Maria Monk but apparently written primarily by and certainly promoted by Congregationalist ministers;[4] it became, according to Jenny Franchot, the best-selling American book of the nineteenth century prior to *Uncle Tom's Cabin* (1994, 154). *Awful Disclosures* tells of forced prostitution and imprisoned nuns, as well as murders—both of infants born to nuns as a result of illicit sexual activities and of nuns who refused to cooperate in the corrupt activities of the convent. Other popular novels added to the anti-Catholic, anti-convent rhetoric. Following in the wake of Monk's popular reception, numerous other "exposures," as well as Monk's own *Further Disclosures*, presented additional details of licentious and cruel "nunneries" and supposedly exposed the goings-on at such places as "Nuns' Islands," where pregnant nuns were said to be hidden in basements close to "vaults excavated to hide the 'unfortunate fruits of their love'" (Partridge 1839, 118) and where younger nuns were taken soon after their entrance into the convent for procedures, conducted by priests, to sever "the channels of nourishment leading from [the] right side to [the] breast" (121), "intended to prevent the supply of nourishment to their infant offspring" (118).

Such discourse supplemented other attacks on the "anti-Christian" and "anti-domestic" lives of the sisters. Because of their reclusive lifestyle, charges of licentiousness and unnaturalness were easily made by reframing their quiet, contemplative lives for prurient interest. Even those making less prurient claims questioned the convent life. For example, *New York Herald* editor James Gordon Bennett charged that celibacy was unnatural and could result in insanity: "To be shut up in a convent, and restricted from the happiness of a husband, is enough to drive any woman out of her senses" (qtd. in Mannard 1986, 309). Their lives behind closed doors permitted a fascination with the secrets enclosed there, and because Protestants rarely came into contact with sisters, the charges against them were readily believed. Every attempt was made to dissuade Protestant parents from sending their girls to Catholic schools. If the dire warnings were insufficient, authors used guilt, with such portraits as that of "an unhappy father deserted in his old age by two daughters, who had been taught that it was a meritorious act, and one which would secure their salvation, to bury themselves in the living death of a cloister, while, by thus trampling on every filial duty, they brought down their parent's grey hairs with sorrow to the grave" ("The School Girl in France" 1844, 286).

Thus, anti-Catholic sentiment often broke into open acts of aggression directed toward Catholic sisters, who had begun opening schools and academies, often with a majority of Protestant girls and young women in their boarding schools. The hostility seems to have stemmed partly from fear that Catholic women might be educating future wives and mothers of the Republic. If, as Kerber and others have suggested, a primary role for women had become that of educators and molders of future citizens, Catholic sisters' educating a large number of those wives and mothers, especially those expected to become mothers of the Republic's leaders, would not do.

THE RELIGIOUS NATURE OF EARLY WOMEN'S LITERACY

The burning of the Charlestown Ursuline convent and academy near Boston in 1834 is probably the best-known attack on a convent, instigated in significant measure by Congregationalist ministers associated with the New England proprietor schools credited as the pioneers of women's education. Stanley Schultz calls Lyman Beecher the "leader of the anti-Catholic evangelicals"; Beecher's incendiary sermons in the days immediately prior to the convent's burning are generally acknowledged, but many other Congregationalist ministers had waged war against the convent from its inception. The Reverend Joseph Emerson, himself an early educator and mentor of girls and young women, most notably Mary Lyon and Zilpah Grant for our purposes, railed against popery and, in particular, the Charlestown Ursuline convent and academy, to his Massachusetts audiences. His brother Ralph writes of Joseph Emerson's carefully planned Boston lectures and their strong effect on the young. According to Ralph Emerson, "The very sorceress of Rome was seen before us, riding on her 'scarlet-colored beast,' full of names of blasphemy" (1834, 331).

The sermon draws primarily from the books of Daniel and Revelation to demonstrate the biblical beast to be the Roman beast and to show the mystical Babylon now represented in popery. Drawing from Joseph Emerson's notes, his brother Ralph outlined the repetitive emphasis on these connections but then turned specifically to his brother's attention to the Charlestown convent:

> Let us not even look toward a nunnery, except with emotions of horror.
> A nunnery in Charlestown!—the most dreadful sight that these eyes have ever looked upon.
> A nunnery in Charlestown!—It is the flag of Babylon on the very altar of the first great burnt offering in the cause of our freedom. (1834, 334)

Emerson concludes with a rousing indictment of the pope and convent as the greatest dangers to all that is dear to early nineteenth-century Americans:

> Let our Samsons beware how they recline their drowsy heads in the lap of Delilah, the great mother of harlots. The keen razor will work most deceitfully. Before they dream of their danger, their seven locks are gone.
> Our strength—our liberties—our republic—religion—God save us from such perdition. (334)

Emerson effectively coupled the biblical and patriotic references so important to early nineteenth-century Americans.

Such fear of convents moved west as Catholic women religious opened convents and schools in frontier areas. For example, Lyman and Catharine Beecher confronted the threat in Cincinnati. In *A Plea for the West*, Lyman continued his anti–convent school diatribe, claiming that the sole purpose of Catholic academies and seminaries was "to subvert the religion of protestant children" (1835, 93) and to extend papist control over the Republic. He asked, "Do they not studiously withhold Catholic children from the action of such causes in protestant schools, and tax their own people, and supplicate the royal munificence of Catholic Europe to rear schools and colleges for the cheap and even gratuitous education of protestant children high and low,— while thousands of Catholic children are utterly neglected, and uncared for, and abandoned to ignorance and vice? And is all this without design?" (94).

In reports that were published by other newspapers nationally, the *Cincinnati Journal* supported Beecher with tirades about dangers from Catholics, especially with regard to convent schools. Enumerating and describing the "SIXTY SEMINARIES FOR FEMALES, WITH HUNDREDS OF TEACHERS, all pledged to the church of Rome," the *Journal* warned, "The priests know the power of maternal influence—they know the strength and energy of female piety; and if they can mold to their purposes the daughters of America, they have made sure of coming generations" ("Statistics of Popery" 1835).

Similarly, in St. Louis, Elijah P. Lovejoy led the crusade against convents and convent academies with scathing pieces in his *St. Louis Observer*. Lovejoy, remembered primarily for his death during an attack by pro-slavery groups in Alton, Illinois, had earlier claimed that the real opposition to him was not slavery but popery "blown up by Jesuit breath" (qtd. in Lovejoy, Lovejoy, and Adams 1838, 149). As did other opponents, he posed Catholicism as a danger to U.S. freedoms—"Popery in its very essential principles is incompatible with regulated civil or religious liberty" (176)—and railed against those Protestants who would send daughters to Catholic academies, exposing them to licentious dangers. In one editorial, he asked, "What is a Nunnery? [but] a dwelling whose inmates consist of unmarried females.... They have been induced to take these vows and exclude themselves from the world, from various motives. Some whose affections were young and ardent, from disappointment of the heart; some from love of retirement; some from morbid sensitiveness to the world of society; and some others, from the blandishments of Priests and Lady Superiors" (105). After describing the isolated and beautiful grounds where convents were located, he scoffed at the notion of chastity among the sisters: "Talk of vows of chastity, in chambers of impenetrable seclusion, and amid bowers of voluptuousness and beauty! 'Tis a shameful mockery.... The Nunnery has generally been neither more nor less, than a seraglio for the friars of the monastery" (109).

Such rants against convents and their academies had become commonplace, especially by Congregationalists. The convents and their schools thus set the stage for the promotion of Protestant schools to educate girls and the women who would teach them with the proper religious and moral sentiments.

Saving the Nation

Anti-Catholic rhetoric and sentiment in general, and toward the Catholic convent schools in particular, had become pronounced at least as early as 1829 with Joseph Emerson's diatribe about popery and the Ursuline convent in Charlestown, Massachusetts. The angry mob that destroyed the Ursuline institution seems to have been embittered that the nuns provided education to mostly Protestant young women in their academy. Jealousy over the nuns occupying a stately and comfortable residence appears to have increased resentment. The Ursuline nuns had founded the convent in 1820, gradually improving the material circumstances of their academy until, by 1834, they had established a handsome brick building located on a twenty-seven-acre, well-groomed estate outside Boston.

Typical anti-Catholic rhetoric surfaced in connection with the convent, including rumors of dungeon imprisonment of young women; licentiousness, usually on the part of priests and nuns; murder of helpless infants; and brutality to boarders, providing an excuse for the attack by mobs fearful of "papist control." The incident also increased rhetoric regarding Catholic convents and schools in general. The occasion provided the stimulus for Sarah Josepha Hale, influential editor of the *Ladies Repository* and proponent of better education for women, to call for publicly funded seminaries for women to counter the proliferation of Catholic academies.

In a series of articles following the attack, Hale condemned "the awful crime of the rioters" because "evil is not to be commended though good may be the result" (1834b, 518). Although Hale acknowledged that the claims against the nuns were unfounded and denounced the injustice of the attack by relating a more accurate narrative than rumor had established, she nonetheless fanned the fear of a Catholic takeover to support her own call for Protestant academies and seminaries for women. Hale expressed concern regarding the "twenty convents, or Catholic seminaries in our land" (519) and warned, "The only effectual way to prevent the increase of conventual seminaries, is to found Protestant Schools" (520).[5] She insisted that "female education must be provided for—otherwise convents will increase, and Catholicism become permanently rooted in our country" (1834a, 564). As would other proponents of education, Hale raised the specter of a nation under the control of the Catholic Church. Echoing Lyman Beecher's call for a thousand young men to be sent to the West to establish moral leadership, Hale asked, "Where are the *thousand young women*, who are destined as wives for these Protestant clergymen, to be educated? . . . The convents are now considered the best and most fashionable places of education . . . and there, in all human probability, many of the future wives, of the pious students of Lane Seminary, are now receiving their impressions" (561). Hale's point was clear: unless good Protestant academies were established to compete with the convent schools, the future leading women of the Protestant churches, and the country, would be Catholic-educated and Catholic-influenced.

Other seemingly moderate critics warned against the schools. Mrs. A. G. Whittelsey, editor of *Mother's Magazine*, claimed, "We do not intend to excite or cherish a vindictive spirit toward the Catholics in our country," but nonetheless continued, "We must, however, be totally blind not to perceive, and very criminal not to use our best endeavors to counteract and prevent the evils which threaten our country from the silent, secret, systematic, and persevering attempt of Catholics to convert our children to the Romish faith by educating them" (1835, 77). Citing the need to *"go to work*, and do our duty" in the *"subverting of Satan's empire,"* Whittelsey followed with a letter from "A Young Lady" who appealed to mothers to stop the Catholics who have taken "vows to the sole object of converting our youth, particularly *young ladies*, to the Catholic faith" (77). And the *American Quarterly Register*, even while warning of an increasing population of Catholics whose "degraded, stupid ignorance, lead[s] to all intents and purposes an animal life, a life of sensation," attempted to appear moderate by being "willing to believe that some papists are finding their way to heaven under all the superincumbent mass of error and absurdity which belongs to the system." Nonetheless, this editor, citing "numerous Catholic convents and nunneries," then warned that "Catholics depend for success very much on the instruction of the young." The great danger for this editor was that Protestant children attended convent schools and "after having finished their education return to their homes, full of esteem and veneration for their instructresses. They are ever ready to refute the calumnies, which the jealousy of heretics loves to spread against the religious communities, and often where they have no longer the opposition of their relations to fear, they embrace the Catholic religion" ("Papacy in the United States" 1834).

Such rhetoric became pronounced, as well, among early Protestant educators of women, who often used fear of a Catholic takeover to support their schools' financial and missionary goals. For example, Mary Lyon's and Zilpah Grant's support for women's education was firmly embedded within the context of their zeal for Protestant ideals and hostility toward Catholics. Sarah Locke Stow, Lyon's student and later a teacher at Mount Holyoke, records Lyon's and Grant's concerns:

> They saw the hope of the nation in the training of the young, and this training passing more and more into the hands of woman. To the ever constant moral modeling by the mother was being added the mental training by both mother and teacher. And the Pope of Rome was looking on, not idly; Europe was sending millions of money across the sea to support schools for girls who were Catholics, or to become Catholics. (1887, 10)

If Lyon feared for the souls of her own students, she anguished for those under the influence of Catholic nuns. Porterfield claims that "Lyon was clearly alarmed by the organizational scope of the Catholic Church, especially with regard to its interest in female education," and that anti-Catholicism "was central to Lyon's vision of Mount Holyoke and its role in outstripping the efforts of Catholic sisters to educate American children" (1997, 40). Lyon incorporated these concerns into literature for potential donors. In her 1837 circular, she described the dangers posed by Catholic academies, claiming that "more than a hundred female schools" had already been established in the United States by the Catholic Church and warning that the church was spending large amounts of money to educate nuns "to lend their aid in converting this nation to the Church of Rome" (qtd. in Porterfield 1997, 40). Lyon had expressed fear of Catholic education explicitly in a letter to Grant: "How shall the mothers of future generations be so trained, that, with the common blessing of Heaven, they will refuse to give up their children to

THE RELIGIOUS NATURE OF EARLY WOMEN'S LITERACY

Catholic influences?" (Lyon n.d., 124); and Stow observed, "Rome knew that 'the hand which rocks the cradle rules the world,' and sought the control of that hand in America. A few Protestant observers, equally wise, sought to place that hand under the control of Christian intelligence" (1887, 11).

In an 1834 appeal to Thomas White, seeking funds for what would become Mount Holyoke, Lyon offered fame and salvation for those contributing to the struggle to save the nation and the world:

> My Dear Sir:—In your old age, would you not be glad, with a few other kindred souls, to be the means of commencing a great work, which, in importance to the welfare of our country, of the church, and of the world, shall not fall behind the home missionary, or any other of our leading benevolent societies? . . . He who, first putting his hand to the work, shall say to others, "Come and do likewise," will deserve a place with Mills, with Robert Raikes [founder of the Sunday school movement], and others of like eminence. (Lyon n.d., 13)

Lyon placed the evangelical value of Protestant schools for women and the subsequent reward for benefactors in heady company indeed.

Lyon continued to garner support for her school with anti-Catholic rhetoric. In her 1837 *General View of the Principles and Design of the Mount Holyoke Female Seminary*, intended to raise funds for Mount Holyoke, she told prospective donors that the church was fifty years behind in its support for women's education, allowing the Catholic Church a head start in encouraging parents to ignore dangers to their children: "We find them cheerfully giving them up to Roman Catholic schools, fearing not their secret and sure influence, though they would tremble at the thought, that the Pope of Rome may yet set his foot on the neck of this great nation, and on the necks of their children and children's children" (11). She continued to explain the dangers:

> In all the movements of the Catholic church in the Old World, what can be found more artful than her operations in the new? She cannot capture this nation by the sword. She cannot at once convert our enlightened and educated men. Her hope is through female schools, and to them she is devoting her principal efforts. For this object thousands and thousands of dollars are annually poured in upon us by Catholic Europe. For the same object, it is said, that $100,000 were brought into

the city of New York during the last summer. More than a hundred female schools have been founded, and the work is rapidly going forward. Every effort is thus making to prepare the females of our land, and through them the children and youth of the coming generations, to lend their aid in converting this nation to the church of Rome. (12)

Catharine Beecher, too, raised the specter of papal control. In fundraising efforts for her Western Female Institute, she drew upon the ongoing controversy regarding the use of Bibles in public schools to argue for the Bible as "the standard of rectitude in all moral and relative duties." She called for children "to be educated to understand its precepts, and urged by all the motives it presents to obey them" (1835, 12–13). Beecher correctly argued that "not one of the eight largest Protestant denominations... would refuse assent to any one of these positions" (13). However, Catholics and Protestants had long since bestowed allegiance to their own translations of the Bible, believing others inaccurate and, therefore, inauthentic. Catholics had consistently shunned public schools because of those schools' uniform enforcement of Protestant precepts and use of the King James Bible. Beecher's proposal was an obvious affront to Catholics.[6]

Beecher further played on nativist fears of unruly immigrants, implying Catholic Germans and Irish, in insisting that "we must educate the nation, or be dashed in pieces, among all the terrors of the wild fanaticism, infidel recklessness and political strife, of an ungoverned, ignorant, and unprincipled populace. What patriot, what philanthropist, what Christian, does not see that all that is sacred and dear in home, and country, and liberty, and religion, call upon him to waken every energy, and put forth every effort?" (1835, 18). At a time when Protestants rarely considered Catholics to be Christians, and when many "natives" feared that Catholics' allegiance to Rome precluded their support of republican government, the intent behind the words would have been clear.

Beecher's most explicit and methodical attacks come together in her "address to the Protestant Clergy of the United States" titled *The Evils Suffered by American Women and American Children: The Causes and the Remedies*. In this address, Beecher claims two purposes: to portray the "melancholy indifference" and "neglect of education interests... among Protestants, in contrast with the vigor and wisdom which the Catholic church exhibits on this subject" (1846, 17), and to "inquire into" the "disproportionate interest in plans of *curative* benevolence, compared with what is felt for efforts of *preventative* benevolence" (23). Beecher first demonstrates the strength of the Catholic Church in education; she quotes Leopold von Ranke's *History of the Popes* in an effort to show how the Jesuits, under Ignatius Loyola, had led the Catholic Church in Europe to "renovated strength" after the Protestant Reformation. "The greatest changes took place *without notice, without even finding mention in the works of historians,* as if such were the inevitable course of events," she noted (18). Beecher then demonstrates the similar pattern taking place in the new Republic, listing specifics about various states, especially those in the West. For example, she explains, "Last winter I visited the state of Kentucky, and on inquiry I found that there were only *two* Protestant high schools for young ladies, which received patronage from the more wealthy classes, and these were very limited in numbers. On the contrary, I learned from the residents of the state, that the education of the young ladies of the first families in that state was very extensively in the hands of the Catholics" (18). Beecher goes on to enumerate the many Catholic schools for women in Kentucky:

> In the diocese of Louisville, Kentucky, are enumerated the following Catholic female institutions. The female Academy of Nazareth, at Bardstown, conducted by Sisters of Charity, and a very large establishment; the Female School of St. Vincent of Paul, conducted by seven Sisters of Charity; the St. Catharine's Female Academy at Lexington, and another at Louisville, conducted by Sisters of Charity; the Female Academy of St. Magdalen's, near Springfield; the Calvary Female Academy, Marion Co.; the Preparatory School of Gethsemane; and the Loretto Female Academy, Marion Co. Beside these schools, there is the St. Magdalen's Convent, with thirteen sisters and a number of novices, and the *Mother House* of the Lorettines, where are forty-five sisters, and one hundred and fifty-six in the community. This *mother house* is a point from which their teachers are sent out to establish other schools. These are the Catholic female institutions in *only one* of our western states, while there are only two Protestant institutions that can at all compare with them in patronage. (18–19)

She continues with a description of Catholic convents and academies in such states as Indiana, Illinois, Ohio, and Maryland, warning that "future wives and mothers are being educated exactly after the plan devised by the general of the Jesuits in Rome" (19).

Beecher then turns to the second part of her argument. Her purpose here is to appeal to Protestant clergy for support of women's education, reinforcing the concerns she presents in the first part of the essay. Beecher decries Protestants' too-heavy reliance on legislative action in creating "popular education," a path she believes too passive in promoting "education in the great West, where the seat of empire is to be, and where population is increasing fastest, is constantly retrograding, while there really is no systemized, efficient organization for this object except that of *the Jesuits!*" (25). Beecher specifically states her aim "to secure to Protestant women that support of *public sentiment* which women find in the Catholic Church" (28). She outlines how the Catholic Church has "mournfully perverted" such benevolent impulses as self-denial and self-sacrifice in creating its massive educational system because "few will maintain that the great body of that corporation, which consists of pope, cardinals, bishops, and priests, have been engaged in any other work than that of extending the bounds of their own church and thus of their own domination over the human mind" (29); she charges, however, that "the Protestant world have swung to the other extreme" (29).

Here Beecher compares the encouragement toward benevolence and self-sacrifice that Protestant young women receive with that of Catholic women. She first presents attitudes toward Protestant young women: "But when a woman of education, wealth, or high standing, devises some plan of benevolent action, that would take her out of her present sphere, and involve the sacrifice of comfort and ease, a great array of influence and argument is turned against her, especially by family friends, and often too by those who profess to be Christians" (29). And when young women of more humble background wish to pursue benevolent goals, Beecher claims, "there has been no response of public sentiment, no organization or aid to encourage them to the attempt" (30). Beecher then contrasts this situation with that of Catholics:

> Now this is not so in the Catholic church. . . . The whole influence of the clergy, and the whole power of public sentiment, which they can control, are lent to encourage and sustain every woman who is disposed to sacrifice either time, position, or wealth, for the extension of the Catholic church. If she is of high rank, or possesses wealth, she is immediately lauded as a saint, and the post of lady abbess or lady superior is found for her, where she retains her high position, and gains still higher estimation and power. If she is of humble rank, then the establishments of sisters of Charity, or other religious houses,

open their doors and give all their benevolent energies full employ in educating the young, or nursing the sick. Meantime she is cheered by the hope that by this course she saves her own soul, rescues the souls of all she can persuade to enter the corporation of her church, and by her additional penances and self-sacrifices is perhaps laying up a stock of good works to supply the deficiencies of others. (30)

Beecher continues to explain that the efforts of Protestant women are more difficult than those of Catholic women as they must "seek confidence and support without the help of Jesuits" (30). She even quotes one authority as reporting that "many of our best and most educated Protestant women are constantly going over to the Roman Catholic Church, for no other reason . . . than 'for the power it gives them to throw their energies into a sphere of definite utility under the control of a high religious responsibility'" (18). Beecher continued to use fear of Catholic schools in fund-raising efforts.

Emma Willard has generally been portrayed as a neutral figure whose devotion focused solely on women's education, and her writings do display less hostility to Catholics than that of some other women proprietors. She was, however, a product of her time and culture. Frederick Rudolph notes that, "unlike Mary Lyon, Mrs. Willard did not . . . share the overwhelming sense of Christian mission that characterized the founder of Mount Holyoke" (1962, 310); however, Willard's writings, too, while they are less bigoted in some instances, in others display her acceptance of the common repugnance of all things Roman Catholic. Willard's part in her very popular geographies, coauthored with William Channing Woodbridge, focused on ancient geography. In *A System of Universal Geography*, Willard's account is taken entirely from the Protestant interpretation of the Bible, of course; her innovation is in the method of teaching (focusing on concrete and local first) and in the use of maps and other graphics. Because she writes about ancient geography, little occasion arises for her to address the inferiority of Catholics. However, Willard assents to Woodbridge's account of modern history, which she claims to be remarkably like her own (Woodbridge and Willard 1827, xii); in this account the Catholic religion is treated with disdain under many of the categories the pair consider to be important informers of geography. For example, in studying "National Character," Woodbridge looks at the "Influence of Moral Causes." Woodbridge claims that *"general ignorance* is almost invariably attended with general corruption, it is fully exhibited in Russia and the Catholic countries of Europe" (218). Similarly, when addressing "Learning," Woodbridge notes that "in Catholic countries, the progress of philosophy and natural science has been checked by the prevalence of superstition" (198) and that "the joint influence of an absolute government and the Catholic religion has prevented the advance of knowledge in *Austria, Poland, Italy, Spain, and Portugal,* and the *Spanish and Portuguese colonies* of South America" (199). In addition, under "Education" he notes that *"the Protestant States of Germany* are distinguished from the Catholic, by the superior education of the people" (203), and that "in *Ireland,* the mass of the people are involved in the grossest ignorance. . . . One of the strongest motives to the acquisition of knowledge is destroyed by the Catholic priests in Ireland, who prohibit the people from reading the scriptures" (204). In his writing, then, Woodbridge is rather typical of other Protestant educators of his time.

In her single-authored histories, Willard's own sentiments are more evident. Nina Baym notes that in her history textbooks, "Willard accepts Manifest Destiny as the territorial expression of a millennial role for the United States. She interprets the Mexican War as a conflict between a Christian (i.e. Protestant) and a non-Christian (i.e. Catholic) nation" (1991, 23n24). In *Last Leaves of American History: Embracing a Separate History of California,* Willard writes:

> At the time when Mexico was colonized, Spain stood at the head of Roman Catholic countries,—regarding all heretics in exterminating abhorrence, and cutting them off by the inquisition and the sword. As the Reformation proceeded, England, the land of our forefathers, took the lead of Protestant nations. But while we, mingling with the world, changed,—Mexico, shut up, retained her native aversions; and these, coupled with the national pride and jealousy of the Spanish character, may be marked *as the first and predisposing cause of the late Mexican war.* (1853, 21–22)

Willard's *Universal History in Perspective* also demonstrates her bias. In her preface, Willard insists, "No wise man presumes to form conclusions concerning the future destiny of nations, without first acquiring a knowledge of the past" ([1835] 1850, 7). Her goal is clearly to assure that "correct" version of the past. In her narrative of the seventeenth century, Willard tells her reader of "Christina, the daughter of Gustavus Adolphus, who was seated on the throne of Sweden at the conclusion of the thirty years' war."

THE RELIGIOUS NATURE OF EARLY WOMEN'S LITERACY

Acknowledging Christina's renown for "attention to literature," Willard tells her reader,

> Her literary labors, instead of qualifying her to fill with usefulness and honor the station in which Providence had placed her, wrought in her a distaste to the cares of royalty, and the mere selfish wish of following, undisturbed, her own propensities. Resigning her crown to CHARLES GUSTAVUS, she repaired to Rome; and, that she might enjoy the charms of Italia society there, she renounced the protestant faith, in which she had been bred. Thus the imputation of being a heretic did not interfere with her pleasures. In her visits to Paris, her dissolute life shocked even the French court, and her cruelties to her attendants excited their abhorrence. (47)

Willard names moral goodness as the "best of all things to be taught" and defines it as follows: "That respects God and man: God first, and man second. To infuse into the mind of a child, therefore love and fear towards God—the perfect—in wisdom, goodness, justice and power—the Creator, Benefactor, and Savior, the Secret Witness and the Judge—this is of all teaching the very best" (qtd. in Hale 1856, 819). Both the Catholic sisters and the New England leaders of women's schools would have agreed with Willard; however, the emphasis on religion in the proprietor schools clearly came from a Protestant, anti-Catholic focus. In many of the schools, anti-Catholic messages were part of the curriculum.

In her circular to teachers, Willard suggests that teachers follow the example she set at her esteemed academy at Troy and impresses upon them the need to infuse the Almighty into every subject. She provides examples for geography, chemistry, and other subjects. For history, Willard suggests, "bid your pupils remark the proof that God exercises that continual sway over human affairs which is denominated his Providence." To demonstrate that God "orders the affairs of man," she tells teachers to show how "the Papal tyranny, that most unjust and soul-subduing of all usurpations, became in the hand of God, the instrument of bringing forward the most important event of profane history—the discovery of America; for without the supposed power of the Pope to give to the sovereigns of Spain the discovered countries, Columbus had never been furnished by them with the means of discovery" (1838, 24). Willard's circular was intended for all those teachers who had attended Troy but who were now conducting schools or classes of their own.

Most evidence about the anti-Catholic sentiment in curricula surfaces in information about Lyon's schools, partly because we have more extant records concerning her schools. Fidelia Fiske, one of Lyon's students, gathered letters in which students related memories of their time with Lyon. The memories overwhelmingly reference the religious emphasis at the schools rather than academic subjects. Students remembered the division of students into groups according to their being Christian (or saved) and recalled the religious conferences with Lyon and her religious lectures. Lucy Lyon (Mary's niece and a student at Mount Holyoke) wrote Fiske, "The senior class have all been writing on Popery the last two months. . . . Miss Lyon was chiefly induced to give them this subject from a suggestion of Mr. Perkins last year" (qtd. in Porterfield 1997, 158n29). According to Porterfield, Lyon had made the assignment after Justin Perkins wrote her about the "resurgence of Roman Catholic missions to the Nestorians": "'Had we not come to their rescue,' wrote Justin Perkins, 'the incessant working of the artful machinations of the Jesuit emissaries . . . would, in time, have gradually obliterated the Nestorians and transferred the last man of them to the Romish standard'" (qtd. in Porterfield 1997, 158n29).

Lyon often invited missionaries to the Mount Holyoke campus to feed what Porterfield calls the "seminary's appetite for compelling scenes of heathen life" (1997, 65). In July 1845, for example, Lyon brought a missionary to campus to speak about his work in southern Europe: He contrasted the "unimaginable splendor of the Vatican" with the "wretched, filthy, degraded" people held in its thrall. Lucy Lyon reported, "He says it is not strange for a Catholic mother to break the arms and legs of her infant, so as to make it a successful beggar" (qtd. in Porterfield 1997, 66). Lyon had been mentored by both Joseph Emerson and Zilpah Grant. According to Fiske, both Grant and Lyon used methods learned from Emerson, especially the grouping of students in order to more readily attend to their conversion (1866, 77). The strong anti-Catholic sentiment of all three infused curricular content, and probably that of their students who later became teachers.

Mutual Interests and Influences

Early nineteenth-century "good" academies for women were remarkably similar in the subjects they taught. Although he included few Catholic academies in his study, the courses Thomas Woody outlines for the better academies for girls in the nineteenth century (1929), and those that Margaret

A. Nash (2001) and Mary Kelley (2006) found in later studies, are very much like those in Catholic academies for girls, as shown in the following two chapters. Kelley suggests that "local, regional, and national networks" allowed for an institutionalized general curricula throughout the country as early as the 1820s (2006, 75). As demonstrated above, Protestants promoting women's education were well aware of the convent academies; those in the convent academies likely benefited from the advances in the proprietor schools as well, as educational issues became a mainstay of popular newspapers and periodicals, and the two groups were in competition with one another. The intelligent, dedicated, and savvy leaders in both groups would have assured their currency to other prominent academies.

The early New England schools and the Catholic academies probably influenced the curricula and school management of one another. Certainly, some aspects of the Catholic schools, such as normal schools and boarding accommodations, influenced the proprietor academies, as we hear from the proprietors themselves, especially Catharine Beecher. Beecher and others took notice because the Catholic academies became, in many instances, the most respected and successful schools in the country, often with the most cutting-edge facilities.

The Catholic schools had been able to set the pace for and stay current on the expectations for academies. Inadvertent though it may have been, Protestants often called attention to the superiority of Catholic academies. Sarah Josepha Hale, one of the most influential women of the century, repeatedly testified to the excellence of the sisters' institutions. Not only did she sound the alarm about the spread and quality of Catholic convents in 1834, but she continued to support Protestant women's education, often by measuring Protestant academies against Catholic academies. As late as 1860, in extolling the merits of her friend Emma Willard's Troy Female Seminary, Hale ended her article by citing the comments of New York bishop John Hughes regarding the courses offered at the sisters' St. Vincent Academy. Hughes had praised the school's academic curriculum but asked the sisters to spend some of their time helping students to become knowledgeable in homemaking. Hale replied,

> Nearly all large seminaries for girls are deficient in this particular; there is no department of household science; but this is soon to be remedied in one denomination, Roman Catholic schools for young ladies.... These Catholic schools are popular with many who do not

belong to the faith, because of the careful attention paid to the pupils; if this neglected branch of the "science of the *cuisine*" is also taught in those schools the advantage will be increased. (1860)

Even the vehemently anti-Catholic American Tract Society inadvertently praised the schools. For example, a tract that it distributed continuously, titled *Roman Catholic Female Schools: A Letter of an American Mother to an American Mother*, warns of the dangers for Protestant girls sent to Catholic academies. The tract responds to reasons "assigned as grounds of preference for these schools" in order to discount them (n.d., 1) and lists three of the most common reasons Protestant parents preferred Catholic academies:

1. You thought it a duty to be *liberal*;
2. The Catholic school was *the best in your vicinity*; and
3. You had received a pledge from the teachers that they would *not interfere with the religious instruction of your children*, and therefore your children would not be affected by the tenets of their instructors. (1)

While the tract continues for eight pages in its efforts to dissuade parents from sending their daughters to Catholic academies, in arguing against the second point, the tract makes no attempt to refute the point but insists that Protestant parents "are greatly to be blamed" for not making more effort to procure fitted Protestant teachers: "You have waited until foreigners have done for you what you should have done for yourself: until Rome in her kindness has sent you teachers for your children" (2). The tract continues with the usual warnings about dangers to daughters in Catholic academies, but those who were familiar with the schools and their reputation might be further convinced that the best education for their daughters was in the sisters' schools. Indeed, all the warnings about Catholic academies seemed to attest to their reputation for superior education rather than to argue that the Protestant schools were better—or even equal.

Indeed, many of the wealthiest and most high profile citizens were schooling their daughters at the Catholic academies. In the nation's political capital, the children of ambassadors to the United States and of many elected officials attended the Visitation Academy in Georgetown. The well-to-do in other areas sent their children to Catholic academies as well. Clearly, many Protestants recognized the superior education of the Catholic academies and did not fear the Catholic influence on their children. The Ursulines' Mount Benedict Academy near Boston had been home to many of Boston's Unitarian elite.[7] Unitarians might have been particularly uncomfortable with the emphasis on religious conversion in some proprietor schools. Even Congregationalists often expressed concern about the intense emphasis on religion, as had the trustees at Adams Academy in Derry.

The pressure for conversion does seem to have been relentless. For example, Lyon wrote to Grant, "The first week, I made a separation in the school after the plan that you have generally practiced" (qtd. in Fiske 1866, 72). According to Fiske, this "devotional exercise" at the beginning of each term, and which Lyon had learned from the practice of Joseph Emerson and Zilpah Grant, consisted of students being "asked to class themselves among the friends of God, or otherwise, according to their own conviction of their state" (77). The grouping according to the state of students' souls, as detailed by Fiske, reminds one of Jonathan Edwards, a major influence on these New Divinity adherents, with his dire warnings for those who have not been saved. Fiske remembered Lyon:

> We can even now, after the lapse of years, see her loving eye resting upon us after the names had been taken of those who had professed Christ publicly; of those who had not done this, but still had some hope in him; then of those who had no hope. We hear her say: "This should remind us of the last great day of separation. If death should come to us to-night, would the separation be the same as this now made? Is it not almost certain that some whose names are written as Christians, if called away, would hear the fearful words, 'I never knew you.'" (77–78)

The proprietors met separately with the groups created according to the states of their souls. As conversion was a process,[8] the efforts at converting and advancing conversion were constant. Porterfield calls the pressure for conversion "almost a prerequisite of graduation" (1997, 50), and Sizer and his colleagues note the "ever-present threat of an early death" in Grant's academy (1993, 58). One student wrote to Fiske that "the lukewarm professor and the openly irreligious alike trembled for their personal safety" as "the burdened souls came together to plead once more for their companions who were still out of Christ" (qtd. in Fiske 1866, 115–16). Another former student, Emily Dickinson, who spent one unhappy year at Mount Holyoke, called herself "one of the lingering *bad* ones" (qtd. in Porterfield 1997, 50). Few girls classified as having "no hope" could have been comfortable in such a system; the atmosphere seems only somewhat better for those who had "some hope." While many parents would have appreciated the heavy conversion emphasis, others, such as the Unitarians who patronized the Ursuline convent outside Boston, and many other New Englanders as well as most outside New England, would not have been comfortable with such pressure on their daughters.

Emma Willard set a tone that some may have found disquieting as well. In addition to inclusion of "Christian truths" throughout her curriculum, Willard also held personal conversations with students and gave religious Saturday lectures. She collected daily summaries of students' faults and credit marks and read them to the school before her Saturday lecture. In instructions to teachers, Willard suggested, "Take advantage of passing occurrences, as the death of friends, to impress your pupils with the shortness of the time allotted them for preparing their last account" (1838, 22).

Even some who professed to disdain all things Catholic willingly entrusted their daughters to the sisters. Editor of the *Louisville Journal* and Know-Nothing supporter George D. Prentice, whose anti-Catholic rhetoric infused the rage that brought on Bloody Monday in Louisville, a deadly attack that killed many Catholics and demolished Catholic neighborhoods, sent his daughter to Nazareth Academy. Another Know-Nothing supporter, John J. Crittenden, who served in the U.S. House and Senate and was appointed U.S. attorney general, enrolled his daughter Anne Mary at the New Orleans Ursuline Academy. She may have imbibed some of her father's disdain for Catholics. In 1821 she wrote her father, "The Sisters are becoming vaine, they are too sure of patronage and if they do not change they will ruin their school" (qtd. in McCluskey 1964, 46). One might surmise either that these anti-Catholic men were disingenuous in their rhetoric denigrating Catholics or that they found the sisters' academies so superior that they were willing to entrust their daughters to the hated sisters. At any rate, the fact that so many prominent figures sent their daughters to Catholic academies would have increased their prestige and made others feel comfortable in sending daughters there.

The Catholic academies probably also enticed Protestant parents because of their boarding schools. At a time when those attending Protestant academies most often boarded with nearby families, parents entrusting their daughters to others might have preferred the Catholic boarding academies, where life was rigidly regulated and girls lived among other girls, usually of their own standing, protected in country settings. In entrusting two daughters to St. Joseph Academy at Emmitsburg, in Maryland, a South Carolina father explained that in "a more open and unrestricted school, so far removed from home, the same security would not be felt" (qtd. in Oates 1994, 127).

Fidelia Fiske had described boarding situations near Mary Lyon's academy when she referenced a "gentleman [who] gave up a large room in the attic of his house, which was divided into four apartments, by suspending bedquilts and blankets, and was occupied by eight persons" (1866, 82). She also detailed the wife's reservations. Fiske admired the efforts made to accommodate students for Lyon's academy, but some parents may have balked at the makeshift apartments even as they feared repercussions from unhappy wives forced to take on extra work. And sometimes circumstances necessitated changed plans. For example, when Roxanne Foote Beecher became ill, those boarding at the Beecher home found it necessary to find a new boarding home. In contrast, the Catholic boarding academies were proven dependable and almost always announced the healthy country air, loving care, tradition, and charming environments of their institutions. For example, the Ursuline Mount Benedict Academy proclaimed:

> The garden adjoining the establishment, to which the Young Ladies always have access, during the hours of relaxation, is beautifully laid out, and consists of two acres of land. Besides this, they are allowed, on days of recreation, to extend their walks over the whole farm, which embraces twenty-seven acres, always, however, under the immediate superintendence of one, or more of the Ladies. During the Summer season, they are allowed two acres of land, which are divided into flower-gardens and are cultivated by themselves. (*United States Catholic Almanac* 1833, 92)

And the Georgetown Visitation described its facility thus: "The Academy is situated on the heights of Georgetown, in the District of Columbia, commanding a view of the Potomac, and a distant perspective of Washington city. The ladies, under whose superintendence the studies are conducted, are members of the Religious Order founded in 1610, by St. Francis of Sales, and first governed by St. Jane Frances Frémoit De Chantal" (84). Even their most vocal critics unintentionally described the beautiful grounds and magnificent structures the Catholic academies offered, as had Lovejoy to his St. Louis readers.

In addition, the all-female staffs of Catholic academies supervised and cared for students in an atmosphere that quickly gained a reputation for meticulous attention. The environment was often rather posh; however, girls were encouraged not to take on airs, not to dress frivolously, and to adhere to nineteenth-century standards of humility, self-control, and benevolence. The academic curriculum offered a serious, well-rounded education that prepared students to participate in intelligent conversation. The schools fulfilled the educational and social expectations many hopeful parents had for their socially prominent or aspiring girls.

Interestingly, religion was taught far less in most Catholic academies than in Protestant ones: because they relied to a large extent on tuition from Protestant families, the sisters promised not to proselytize, while teachers in Protestant proprietor academies were expected to do so. Clearly, the New England "pioneers" of women's education, to varying degrees, believed themselves a part of a great religious and national enterprise. They also felt themselves in competition with the Catholic sisters, an opposition that spurred their efforts on behalf of women's education. Both Beecher and Lyon tried to establish an effective "system" for countering the Catholic threat. Beecher spoke openly of Protestant women's "competitors the Catholic nuns or Sisters of Charity" (1846, 32) and warned of the dangers of having "no systematized, efficient organization for this object except that of *the Jesuits*!" (25). Lyon continually railed against the "systematized organization" of Catholics and believed her mission to be not only religious but also patriotic. She feared the "money for the education of girls in convent schools... pouring in from Catholics in Europe, constituting... a threat to 'the safety of the country'" (qtd. in Green 1979, 118). Both Beecher's Western Female Institute and Lyon's Mount Holyoke were attempts to create a system similar to the Catholic ones.[9]

Ironically, Beecher's explicit proposals for Protestant female seminaries, as well as the quieter efforts of other proprietors, modeled the very academies they opposed, those established by the Catholic congregations. In her *Evils Suffered by American Women and American Children*, Beecher clearly calls for "the establishment of *permanent institutions*, which should embrace all the *good features* of the *mother houses* established by Catholics. Such should include a high school and a primary school, in which every branch of education, from the first to the last, should be taught in the best possible manner, so as to serve as *model schools*" (1846, 31). Throughout her career, Beecher argued for institutions very much like the Catholic ones: for teachers to be educated for their profession in institutions that could also place them in teaching positions and serve as home "when seeking for a location, or when thrown out of employ from sickness or other causes" (31); for the proliferation of seminaries for teachers as initial graduates were dispersed; and for enough teachers in each academy to specialize, as one or two teachers could not adequately teach the many necessary subjects—all characteristics of the Catholic convent system. Throughout her career, Beecher also deliberately distanced herself from some aspects of the Catholic system, condemning celibacy, although she and many of the other proprietors never married, as well as women's communal living, for example. Beecher's educators, instead, would "consecrate at least a certain number of years" to teaching, "until they assume the responsibilities of domestic life" (1835, 19). She insisted that "vows of matrimony often involve far more self-denying benevolence than vows of celibacy" (1846, 32).

In speaking of Beecher's schools, Kathryn Kish Sklar claims that "no contemporary female seminary provided room and board for its students since the alternative of boarding in nearby private homes was believed more efficient and less costly" (1973, 91). She sees George Bancroft and Joseph Cogswell's Round Hill, Massachusetts, boarding school as the model for Beecher's proposals for women's education, as well as Emma Willard's early unsuccessful efforts. However, the convent academies had embodied the tradition of boarding schools for centuries in European countries and had created boarding schools in the United States since their inception in the late eighteenth century. Beecher was familiar with the workings of the successful convent boarding schools and clearly called for this model based on her knowledge of the convent schools.[10]

Lyon's Mount Holyoke also evoked the Catholic institutions. Lyon established Mount Holyoke in 1837 as a boarding school "so that her control could be complete" (Scott 1978, 691) and insisted on keeping tuition as low as possible so that poor women might become teachers. Her institution in many ways resembled the Catholic convents, where women might enter with little or no money and receive education to prepare them for teaching. Similar to Catholic convents, Lyon set the tuition and board at Mount Holyoke at sixty-four dollars per year by having students contribute to upkeep and chores, with any profit used to keep future costs for students low. Whereas Beecher called for better pay and support for women teachers, Lyon argued for minimal compensation for women teachers, expecting their religious fervor and commitment to promoting their religion to adequately compensate them, much like expectations for women joining Catholic convents.[11] Sisters, who took a vow of poverty, were not salaried but received material necessities and board. Both Lyon's and the Catholic sisters' institutions operated under a missionary mandate, Lyon promoting missionary work both abroad and at home in the name of the New Divinity Congregational Church, and the convents branching out across the United States in service to the Catholic Church. As did members of convents, Lyon encouraged her students to call one another "sister," often referring to them as her daughters. Beecher's efforts at creating training schools for teachers were far less successful than those of Lyon and the Catholic sisters. Her Western Female Institute lasted only a few years.

Emma Willard's school was dissimilar from the Catholic convents but similar to their academies, both in the offerings to students and in those they served. Unlike Beecher, Lyon, and the convents, Willard's mission was not to train teachers. As Nina Baym explains, Willard's plan "solicited government funding to educate wealthy young women" (1992, 125). Just as Catholic academies sometimes included orphans or other less wealthy students while instructing primarily well-to-do students who paid usually expensive tuition, Willard's school was for elite young women but included a small minority of those less affluent. She sought government support not to lower costs to students but because she believed with government support their education would be superior, as it was less susceptible to pressure from parents (1992, 126). Willard expected less wealthy young women who wanted an education to attend normal schools or less prestigious academies.

Although Beecher repeatedly referred to the Catholic convents and academies as "endowed by foreign funds, conducted by foreign women, and sustained by Jesuit skill and power, and for the well-known purpose for which the Jesuit order is established" (1846, 33), most who began the early convent academies lived very frugal, often ascetic lives, until their academies became profitable. Even then, their vows of poverty permitted only necessities, their money going instead to expand and strengthen their existing schools and to fund new ones. This mode of living and cooperation facilitated the rapid expansion of their schools and academies. Little foreign money found its way into these schools. And although some European women religious established academies in the United States, most of the teaching congregations in the early decades of the nineteenth century were founded by and made up of American women—all of those Beecher identified in her speech were founded by native women. Only two European communities had schools in the United States at the time of Beecher's claim. The Jesuit order did assist some communities in developing curricula, but some of the sisters worked with other male religious orders, such as the Sulpicians and Dominicans; others developed curricula without assistance from the men's orders.

The anti-Catholic sentiment and Protestant evangelical purpose that figured so prominently in the early proprietor academies for women is representative of the circles within which the leaders lived and moved. Emma Willard's primary influences at Middlebury, Vermont, where she began forming her educational philosophy, were the Reverend Horatio Merrill, pastor of the Congregational Church in Middlebury and "a recognized leader throughout the State in matters of education and religion" (Brainard 1893, 4), and Dr. Henry Davis, president of Middlebury College and later president of Yale, acceptable in those posts because of his orthodox Congregationalist stance. Catharine Beecher's influential father, Lyman, had helped to stoke the fury of the Charlestown mob by delivering vehemently anti-Catholic invectives; he convinced many that "the Catholic Church holds now in darkness and bondage nearly half the civilized world. . . . It is the most skillful, powerful, dreadful system of corruption to those who wield it, and of slavery and debasement to those who live under it" (qtd. in Hennesey 1983, 119). In a July 1830 letter that suggests he is replying to Catharine's query (he says, "I believe I have now touched on all your topics" [1961, 168]), Lyman Beecher writes, "The moral destiny of our nation, and all our institutions and hopes, and the world's hopes, turns on the character of the West, and the competition now is for that of preoccupancy in the education of the rising generation, in which Catholics and infidels have got the start of us." He further suggests his need to go west to "the great battle" and expresses his intention that Catharine accompany him (167). Catharine's brothers, especially Edward and Henry Ward Beecher, also preached copiously about the dangers of popery.[12]

Zilpah Grant and Mary Lyon, too, were enculturated into the Calvinist tradition that encouraged their missionary zeal as well as their fear of Catholics. The conservative western Massachusetts region of their childhood was staunchly Congregational, greatly influenced by Jonathan Edwards in religious matters and the Whig Party politically. In addition, their mentors and friends held equally conservative views. Grant's and Lyon's experiences as students and their early involvements as teachers represent the area in which they lived; both claimed the Reverend Joseph Emerson as one of their greatest and most admired teachers. Lyon studied and later taught with Emerson at his Female Seminary in Byfield, Massachusetts, where she met Zilpah Grant, already a teacher there. Lyman Beecher, a friend of Emerson, visited often. Beecher also influenced the early proprietor school run by Sarah Pierce in Litchfield, Connecticut. Although Pierce's school for girls was rather rudimentary in its early years, she is hailed as one of the pioneers of women's education in the United States.[13] Reminiscences of Pierce's students are filled with comments about Lyman Beecher, pastor of the Congregational Church in Litchfield from 1810 to 1828. Catharine Beecher writes that while they were in Litchfield,

> among those associated most intimately with my father, (Rev. Lyman Beecher) and his family during his whole Litchfield life was Miss Sarah Pierce, a woman of more than ordinary talent, sprightly in conversation, social and full of benevolent activity. She was an earnest Christian, and, being at the head of a large school of young ladies, found frequent occasions for seeking counsel and aid from her pastor. In return she gave gratuitous schooling to as many of our children as father chose to send, for occasionally young boys found admission. (qtd. in Vanderpoel and Buel 1903, 179)

These Calvinist leaders were the most powerful and authoritative men in early nineteenth-century New England. Adhering to the beliefs of such leaders, the New England "pioneers" of women's education led an admirable, committed effort on behalf of eternal salvation for young women and children and protection from Catholic dangers.

Despite the strong anti-Catholic sentiment they faced, however, Catholic sisters gradually gained the confidence and support of many non-Catholics as well as Catholics. Their schools attracted students regardless of religious affiliation, and the academies provided education for the children of distinguished Protestant national figures. For example, Nazareth Academy near Bardstown, Kentucky, enrolled daughters of such dignitaries as Zachary Taylor, Jefferson Davis, and Henry Clay (whose daughters, granddaughters, and great-granddaughters attended and who, as secretary of state, distributed premiums at the first commencement ceremony), as well as those of regional notables, such as governors and newspaper editors. The

Georgetown Visitation Academy drew children of famous national and international representatives in the Washington, D.C., political community; sitting presidents often delivered premiums at academy commencements. The academies included students from great distances, and traveling dignitaries made a point to visit the schools when in the vicinity. When the sisters decided upon the need for incorporation, which some members of the public opposed for fear of papist control, Protestant state legislators whose children attended the academies championed their cause.

Beecher and others took notice of Catholic academies because they became, in many instances, the most respected and successful schools in the country, often with the most cutting-edge facilities. The rapid proliferation of convent academies and their patronage by the well-to-do alarmed many Protestants, and fear of Catholic power and indoctrination began to drive efforts to build quality Protestant schools for girls and young women. Strong anti-Catholic sentiment was evident in nearly all Protestant literacy efforts for women in the early nineteenth-century United States, and Catholic women religious responded by increasing their own efforts at women's education.

3.
U.S.-Based Convents and the Literacy Experience

Prior to U.S. independence, few Catholics resided in the English-controlled American colonies, and even fewer gained a good education or attained prominent positions, largely because of prejudices and laws relegating Catholics to second-class citizenship. "Because Catholics had been forbidden throughout the colonial period to maintain their own schools," says John Tracy Ellis, "the national period opened without a single Catholic educational institution" (1969, 53). Wealthy Maryland Catholics, such as the Carrolls, Neales, and Brents, were exceptional and sent children abroad to be educated, but the less well-to-do had few literacy opportunities. Because of state-sponsored religions, Catholics were free to practice their religion and teach only in Pennsylvania. Although Maryland had been founded as a refuge for Catholics by Lord Baltimore and the 1649 Maryland Toleration Act had established religious freedom there, Catholics had always been a minority in the colony. As the Protestant population increased, laws of religious toleration were overturned and the Anglican religion established.[1] Restrictions had increased in many of the other colonies after the British 1688 revolution, as the British reenacted penal laws throughout Great Britain, influencing the colonies to put an end to the few schools run by Catholics prior to that time. The Congregationalist Church in the New England colonies, for example, branded as dissidents any who failed to join that church, making nonchurch members ineligible to participate as citizens and subject to other penalties; teaching outside church-approved schools was prohibited. The Anglican Church in Virginia and other southern colonies imposed similar restrictions on those outside their church.

However, by mid-eighteenth century, enforcement of laws restricting religious freedom had become problematic, as demographic and philosophical changes began to undermine the established churches. "Individuals emboldened by the Great Awakening and the Enlightenment were no longer willing to defer to ministers in religious matters," Frank Lambert notes. "Moreover, growing pluralism meant that no one church could possibly speak for all Protestants" (2003, 194). Unlikely alliances between evangelical dissenters, such as Baptists, who chafed at established religions set by Congregationalists and Anglicans, and leaders influenced by the Enlightenment and Deist movements, such as Thomas Jefferson and James Madison, created a strong momentum for religious freedom as the new nation's Constitution was written.

Following the Revolutionary War, Jefferson and Madison had led Virginia delegates to include religious freedom in their state constitution. Subsequently, Madison effectively used the Virginia model in shaping the First Amendment assurance of religious freedom, making the practice of religion a matter of individual conscience. Many states continued some form of state-supported or state-established religion in their constitutions; however, all included some form of toleration clause. Gradually all states moved to disestablish a state religion.[2] The changes were not intended to support Catholics (or other persecuted religious groups, such as Quakers and Jews) and did little to diminish hostility where it existed. However, Protestants became pitted against Protestants as sects vied for their own rights. As anger toward and fear of powerful clerics and churches grew, ensuing laws eased legal hardships for Catholics.

After the U.S. Constitution assured religious freedom, much prejudice remained, but Catholics were no longer legally disenfranchised or forbidden to openly practice their religion and teach. Immigration of Catholics increased, and their religious leaders became concerned for Catholics' spiritual and educational needs. Male religious orders began establishing schools, especially colleges and seminaries for men, and in 1797 women began establishing their own religious communities in the young United States with missions largely or entirely devoted to the education of girls and young women where none or little had existed; they hoped, too, to reduce prejudice toward their religion, as demonstrated in their rules and constitutions. For example, the *Rules of the Society and School of Loretto, Kentucky* proclaimed,

> The glory of God and the attainment of one's personal sanctification is the primary and essential purpose of the Society: but the special object must never be lost sight of by those belonging to this Society which is to devote one's self completely to the education of females and implanting in them the principles of our holy religion instilling in

the minds and hearts of the Catholics entrusted to our care its teachings and leading their conduct to virtue but, in the case of Protestants committed to us, removing the prejudices that may have been instilled in them against our religion. (1820, 2)

Similarly, the Oblate Sisters of Providence's constitution read, "A religious society of Coloured women . . . renounce the world to consecrate themselves to God and to the Christian education of young girls of color" ("Original Rule" 1829, n.p.).

Because their constitutional mission was education, women who began and joined these early religious communities were afforded unusual avenues for education otherwise unavailable to them, the convents becoming major centers of literacy for women. In the first years of the convents, many members were prepared for teaching by local priests and professors at nearby men's colleges and seminaries and by highly educated women recruited for their advanced literacy and proficiency in teaching. The women lived in community, mostly without children or other family obligations, and focused as a group on improving their own literacy and on learning how to effectively impart their knowledge to other young women and girls.

Most convent communities coming as missionaries from Europe observed long-standing religious rules and pedagogical guidelines, with curricula established during a long tradition in education; however, women forming new convents in the United States had no such tradition from which to draw. While many of the new foundations modeled their religious rules on European communities, they lacked access to established European curricula and found it necessary to create their own. This chapter examines the literacy influences and experiences of religious foundations whose missions were the education of girls and young women but who had no prior community tradition for providing education and, therefore, no established communal curriculum from which to draw in the early years of their U.S. formation.[3] It points to the importance of the convents themselves as literacy sites for women and details the sisters' curricular efforts and concerns in providing education for the young women and girls in the schools they created.

Initial Literacy Levels

In her extensive study of the eight earliest permanent U.S. communities of Catholic women religious, Barbara Misner attempted to determine the literacy levels of community members at the time of entry. Misner found hard data difficult to come by but located "some information" for 17.4 percent of the women she studied. Based on available evidence, she determined that seventeen members of the eight communities were illiterate at entry, as they marked rather than signed registers. She concluded that "many young women, especially in the first years of any religious community's existence came with very little, if any, formal education" (1988, 136) and inferred that literacy levels were lower in rural areas. This was undoubtedly true. The availability of and expectations for literacy would have been greater in urban areas, as more densely populated locations were better able to support schools and the need for literacy was more pronounced. In addition, because of early laws and prejudices, women in Catholic communities often had fewer opportunities for education than other women.

Correspondence among members of the Catholic clergy often demonstrates the concern for the low levels of education in their communities. For example, in an 1815 report to Pope Pius VII regarding his fledgling seminary for men in Bardstown, Kentucky, Bishop Benedict Joseph Flaget discussed the slow progress he witnessed in his seminary students: "At first very many of the pupils had to be instructed not only in Latin and grammar, but also in the very elements of reading and writing, such is the great and almost barbaric ignorance of this district" ([1815] 1978, 315). The concern was not for men alone. Bishop Jean Baptiste David wrote of the difficulty in "form[ing] good teachers especially in these parts [Nazareth]; postulants come to us with little knowledge, hardly able to read" (David 1824). Similarly, in an 1823 response to the request of Bishop Louis DuBourg of the Louisiana and Florida territory for teaching sisters from the Sisters of Loretto, the Reverend Charles Nerinckx wrote, "You will observe, my Dear Sir, how unaccomplished they must be, being all brought together in such a hurry" (161).

In his demographic study of early professed sisters in Maryland communities, Gerald Mannard found that, "in their early days of organization, the Sisters of Charity [Emmitsburg, Maryland] primarily attracted women like Mother [Elizabeth] Seton, native-born and middle to upper class." He found, too, that "the profile of the Sisters of Charity began to shift during the 1830s, however, with increasing numbers of women of Irish birth or descent, and of working-class background" (1989, 174). Misner also determined (based on small numbers) that most women who joined early communities tended to be middle class. However, we should not assume that the status of middle class assured high levels of education. For example, according to Mannard, the Emmitsburg sisters were among the more affluent members of early communities. Still, on 30 May 1810, Elizabeth Seton, whose duties at St. Joseph Academy, which she opened in 1809, had been primarily administrative, wrote her friend Julia Scott that "so many are daily applying that I suppose I must be school dame again—our good Sisters can teach the country children very well, but when the class is higher it is not so easy" (2002, 2:134). Other members of her community were clearly not so well educated as she and found it difficult to offer the challenging and sophisticated curriculum necessary for more advanced students.

In rural and frontier areas, members may have been even less educated. In Kentucky, for example, where three early convents were formed between 1812 and 1822, educational opportunities were scarce. At the turn of the nineteenth century, Kentucky was still largely a frontier area where inadequate resources and the perceived greater need to build roads and establish other essential material necessities limited support for education. In addition, the largely agricultural economy did not necessitate a high level of literacy. Although Kentucky became a state in 1792, a system of common schools was not inaugurated until 1830, and effective implementation of the schools came much later (Barksdale 1914, 34).[4] According to Paschala Noonan, early members of the St. Rose Dominican sisters were poor (1997, 31). Overall, many new members were poor; and middle-class women, especially outside metropolitan areas, often had a rudimentary education at best. When Mary Rhodes, one of the founders of the Sisters of Loretto, moved to Kentucky from Maryland, she began a small school because her brother's children, who would have been considered middle class, were illiterate and had no other opportunities for education. The sisters in Kentucky seem to have experienced less hostility than those in some English-speaking parts of the country, probably partly because most sisters were from the immediate area but also because the literacy needs were so great. Protestants often supported the building of Catholic institutions.[5]

The few opportunities for education, especially for women and girls, created a void the sisters would help to fill; however, the limited literacy of many early members required a concerted effort to prepare them for schooling duties, and the convents became the primary opportunity for women to gain literacy in many areas. In the earliest years, the sisters' schools, especially the rural schools, only hinted at the esteemed reputation the convent academies would hold in a short period of time. Although some of these schools initially offered a basic education, by the late 1820s and 1830s the sisters had gained the educational expertise to provide some of the most prestigious academies for girls in the country.

Unique Literacy Opportunities

The early sisters enjoyed learning opportunities rare for women of their time, as they were often taught by some of the best-educated teachers the country could provide. Many of Europe's most highly accomplished Catholic clergy had fled to America to escape the Reign of Terror. These clergy, with a high cultural value for education, promoted literacy for Catholic citizens in their adopted country, opening schools and seminaries for men and boys in the new nation. They also saw a need for schools for girls and encouraged the founding of women's religious communities for that purpose. Concerned for the limited expertise of the sister-teachers (and the larger Catholic population) and sometimes aware of the possibilities for prestigious academies, leaders contributed to the sisters' knowledge and preparedness for teaching at every opportunity. Although they had historically educated men, the professors at newly established U.S. Catholic colleges and seminaries—professors trained in such scholarly traditions as those instituted by the Sulpicians and Jesuits—instructed the new sisters.

In Kentucky, for example, the numerous Catholic colleges and seminaries afforded women at newly formed convents a wealth of support. The professors at nearby St. Joseph College in Bardstown[6] provided instruction in rhetoric, philosophy, and science for both the Sisters of Charity of Nazareth and the Sisters of Loretto. For the Sisters of Loretto, the president of neighboring St. Mary's College gave instruction in advanced composition and English literature, and the sisters traveled to nearby St. Thomas Seminary to attend chemistry and physics classes. The sisters also learned French, bookkeeping, and higher mathematics from the Reverend Simon Fouché, a learned French Jesuit (T. Kelly n.d., n.p.; Bede 1926, 47; Carroll 1937, 58, 65). In addition, they studied piano, harp, guitar, and vocal music with a variety of music teachers (Bede 1926, 48). Even the local bishop, Benedict Joseph Flaget, who had taught at seminaries in Nantes and Angers, France, as well as at Georgetown College and St. Mary's College and Seminary, Baltimore, "provided instruction in grammar" (Ewens 1978, 54).

In addition, their ecclesiastical superiors, also members of learned societies, often provided instruction for the sisters. Jean Baptiste David, the

French ecclesiastical superior for the Sisters of Charity of Nazareth, had acted as private tutor to a wealthy family in Nantes and served on the faculty of the French College of Angers and later at St. Mary's College and Seminary in Baltimore, as well as at Georgetown College in Washington, D.C. He gave "each of [the teaching sisters] two lessons in grammar and arithmetic a week. I am training them also in reading and writing" (David 1813; see also Howlett 1915, 51–52; Doyle 2006, 32; and *Mother Frances Gardiner* 1972, 4).[7] Similarly, Dominican Samuel Thomas Wilson, "an avid scholar and well-versed in languages" (Noonan 1997, 25) who had studied at several colleges and the University of Louvain and later served as professor and rector at the Dominican College of the Holy Cross in Belgium and in England, gave daily instruction to the sisters who began the Academy of St. Mary Magdalen in Springfield, Kentucky (O'Daniel 1932, 8–20; M. Spalding 1844, 64). He also appointed another Dominican, Pius Miles, as their chaplain and instructor. "Wilson and Miles conducted classes in English, history and mathematics. Wilson, being a linguist, probably also taught French to the sisters," Noonan notes, as the archives hold an extant letter from one of the earliest sisters "in eloquent French" and the sisters included French in their early curriculum (1997, 38). Similar situations prevailed at Loretto, as the Reverend Charles Nerinckx, who had studied at the College of Geel, the University of Louvain, and the Seminary of Malines, worked to advance the literacy skills of the Sisters of Loretto. Such assistance happened in other locations as well. For example, Father Joseph Cloriviere "helped the [Baltimore Oblate Sisters of Providence] become accomplished teachers" (Morrow 2002, 184). The priests and professors in many locations also assisted the sisters by teaching some courses in the academies. In many locations, the sisters reciprocated by helping the Belgian and French priests to improve their English.

The priests helped to provide the sisters with books and their schools with an incredible array of state-of-the-art materials known only to the most elite institutions in this country. Nerinckx made his extensive personal library available to the Sisters of Loretto, and when he visited Europe in 1816, he returned with maps, charts, globes, and "philosophical apparatus" for the Lorettines' academy (Boas 1935, 6; Carroll 1937, 60–64). The president of nearby St. Mary's College, Reverend William Byrne, instructed the sisters in the classroom use of these materials. Similarly, Father Cloriviere helped to begin and Father Michael Wheeler helped to complete an odeum for Georgetown Visitation Academy, a magnificent music hall that also functioned as a science lab. The "Philosophical and Chemical Apparatus" Wheeler ordered cost the sisters $2,448.32 in 1828 and allowed the sisters "to demonstrate the theories of many useful branches of natural philosophy—such as astronomy, pneumatics, electricity, Galvanism, chemistry, Chladni's Acoustic figures, etc." In addition, the sisters acquired "an increasing collection of minerals and Hauy's Primitive Forms to assist in the study of crystallography" (Sullivan 1975, 74). As Kim Tolley (1996) has demonstrated, nineteenth-century academies for girls emphasized science, and the Catholic academies were clearly leaders in this regard. By the late 1820s, most flagship Catholic academies either had the best equipment and laboratories available, or their students visited nearby men's colleges to participate in scientific demonstrations.

Highly educated women were also recruited for the communities to further the learning of less literate members; most early communities boasted one or more well-educated member in their original or earliest numbers, many of whom had taught and administered schools previously. Early members of at least four communities had attended girls' academies. As mentioned previously, Mary Rhodes, of the Sisters of Loretto, had received a convent education before moving to Kentucky and initiated a school in an area devoid of formal educational opportunities. Similarly, Sister Stanislaus Jones joined the Visitation nuns in 1825, having received her education in a New York academy ("Sister Stanislaus Jones" n.d.). Seton, of the Sisters of Charity at Emmitsburg, and Elizabeth Lange and Marie Balas, of the Oblate Sisters of Providence, seem to have been academy-educated.

Archival records demonstrate the great value placed on good teachers, with letters praising their work and obituaries acknowledging a major loss at their deaths. In fact, Visitation Academy suffered greatly at the death of Sister Ignatia Sharpe in 1802. The nuns struggled to maintain the quality and reputation of their academy after her death and began to recover only after Father Cloriviere and Jerusha Barber (who would later become Sister Mary Augustine, a member of the community) devoted themselves to educating the younger members whom Sister Ignatia would have taught. When Augustine Decount joined the order in 1817, her presence brought both knowledge and prestige because she had taught music at a celebrated Philadelphia academy (Misner 1988, 180).

Such women served as examples for other sisters, taught less-prepared members, and oversaw development of the curriculum, both in content and in pedagogy; they also assumed administrative duties. For example,

Elizabeth Seton, who founded the Sisters of Charity of St. Joseph in Emmitsburg, Maryland, in 1809, had previously conducted a school for girls in Baltimore and was clearly quite literate, as exemplified by her prolific and sophisticated extant writing. According to Mary Bernard McEntee, Seton "had read the classics, studied philosophy, and was fluent in French" (1972, 23). The breadth and depth of Seton's knowledge are demonstrated in the four large volumes of her collected writings. Her texts are primarily religious and spiritual, along with correspondence. However, in volume 3a, editors Regina Bechtle and Judith Metz provide a schema of the contents of three of Seton's early extant copybooks, which included a wide variety of excerpts from histories, philosophies, literature, and theology, a very impressive accounting, with Seton's reflections on some (2006).

The Sisters of Charity of Nazareth's Ellen O'Connell joined the community in 1813, the year after its founding. O'Connell was the daughter of "an eminent professor of language and rhetoric. Ellen, his child, left motherless at a tender age, was the object of his greatest solicitude. He cultivated her gifted mind with care and delighted in her progress" (Webb 1884, 247). O'Connell had become experienced in both teaching and school management before arriving at Nazareth. Father David had recruited her specifically for her ability to lead educational efforts in the community. A prolific writer of poetry and essays, O'Connell became directress of studies at Nazareth from 1814 to 1831. Her students often commented on her strengths, asserting repeatedly that Sister Ellen had educated every sister in the early schools ("Early Annals" n.d., 75). The "Early Annals" describe her as follows:

> In addition to the possession of a mind of rare intelligence, she had received an excellent education and was gifted with a facility for imparting her own knowledge to others. With so much spirit did she enter into the views of Father David that within a few years she had succeeded, with the valuable assistance which he himself was enabled to render, in forming a body of teachers at that day unequalled in the State. (n.d., 76)

By 1821 Ann O'Connor had joined the Nazareth convent, bringing a piano and initiating a music department. Ben J. Webb describes her as "a most important valuable acquisition" because of her liberal education and strength in teaching music and drawing (qtd. in *Mother Frances Gardiner* 1972, 5).

O'Connell and O'Connor added to and gradually took over the education of the upper classes in the academy as well as the teaching and training of novice sisters.

Elizabeth Lange and Marie Balas, initial members of the Oblate Sisters of Providence, the earliest U.S. African American teaching congregation, had received a formal education before immigrating to the United States. Early accounts identify Lange and Balas as refugees from the St. Domingue Revolution, and numerous sources, including Carter Woodson, cite the 1871 U.S. government's special report on education, which praised the Oblates' school, stating that "the colored women who formed the original society which founded the convent and seminary are from Domingo, though they had some of them, certainly, been educated in France" (U.S. Department of Education 1871, 205). Diane Batts Morrow, who recently published a well-researched study of the Oblate sisters, convincingly claims that more likely they attended the academy of the Sisters of Notre Dame du Cap-Francais in Le Cap, St. Domingue (2002, 18), noting that "had either Lange or [Marie Therese] Duchemin studied abroad . . . they would have undoubtedly acknowledged it given their Francophile tendencies" (32). According to Sharon Knecht, current archivist for the Oblates, Lange "received an excellent education" in a "culturally rich" and "primarily French speaking community of Cuba."[8] Regardless, all agree to the sophisticated education of the original members. Marie Therese Duchemin, an early recruit, had been adopted by and educated in the school Lange and Balas had operated prior to establishing the community's academy; some evidence exists, as well, that Duchemin attended St. Joseph Academy in Emmitsburg for some period to study English in order to take charge of English instruction at the Oblates' St. Francis Academy, as the initial members were primarily French speakers (Morrow 2002, 32).[9]

The St. Domingue Revolution brought another invaluable contribution to Catholic literacy in the United States. Julia Datty had also escaped the revolution, settling in Charleston, South Carolina, and establishing a well-respected academy. Catherine Clinton cites a parent's payment of $772.52 for his daughter's year at Datty's boarding school, demonstrating the school's high esteem (1982b, 55). When the Charleston Sisters of Charity of Our Lady of Mercy (known as the Sisters of Mercy) were struggling to enhance the pedagogy and reputation of their schools, having lost their best teachers and seemingly rudderless, Datty joined the community and directed the sisters in both content and pedagogical techniques.

Leading Literacy Centers for Women

By the 1830s, the convents boasted the best academies for girls in the country, as well as scores of day schools and orphanages. To achieve this position, they had made other substantial investments in members' literacy. The Emmitsburg Sisters of Charity had assured time for sisters' continuing study by 1818 when their council "resolved to hire women for ironing or washing, &c. &c." to allow sisters to further their education and to prepare for teaching: "Mother, the Assistant & Treasurer were requested to form a plan of who should be taught, who to teach & what" ("Council Minutes" 1818). Similarly, "teacher training became a very thoroughly conducted department of Loretto by 1820" (Bede 1926, 47), and the original rule of the Oblate Sisters of Providence emphasized that "those sisters who will be appointed to teach must possess a sufficient knowledge of the different branches of education over which they preside: for how could they possibly instruct the children entrusted to their care, in the things of which they themselves would be ignorant?" ("Original Rule" 1829, n.p.).

The sisters would continue to make every effort to protect the effectiveness of teachers. When demands for teachers and burgeoning enrollment threatened to harm pedagogical effectiveness, the sisters at Emmitsburg ruled, "No Sister shall keep a larger number of children in her class than she thinks she can do justice to. The number assigned by those who have long experience in public schools (Free schools) is 40" ("Council Minutes" 1818; see also McNeil 1996, 196–97).

The best-educated sisters in the orders not only taught in the schools and academies but also provided educational training for novices and other sister-teachers in the evenings and on weekends. As the convents grew and the sisters opened schools too distant to allow for regular instruction during the school year, they returned to the motherhouse during the summers to further their education and to prepare for the coming school year. Such systematic preparation of sisters became typical of all communities. Sister Margaret George, first directress of studies at Emmitsburg, "began with great zeal, to fit the young Sisters for efficient teachers. She made them review their studies, go through a course of history, etc.," and organized systematic courses and review for the young teachers (Metz and Wiltse 1989, 25). One celebrated early directress of studies at Nazareth, Sister Columba Carroll, had come to Nazareth when she was orphaned and was a member of the first commencement class. Praised widely by sisters, students, priests, and historians for her intelligence, she directed teachers from 1832 to 1862, when she became superior (see McGill 1917, 136–47; and Webb 1884, 259). Carroll wrote both a manual for boarding school teachers (*On Education Book 1st: Boarding Schools for Young Ladies*) and a manual for teaching literature ("Course of Literary Studies") for use by novice teachers. The teachers also improved pedagogy through practice. Ellen O'Connell helped the sisters in her charge "to learn by experience. Little classes or some superintendence was given them and Sister Ellen watched at a distance, never interfering, seldom appearing where the young Sister was at work" (qtd. in *Mother Frances Gardiner* 1972, 4).

The directress of studies often encouraged and counseled distant teachers through mail. For example, Sister Frances Gardiner said in a letter to one sister, "I wrote to Sister G. and told her she must take her leisure time to improve herself and that I would ask you to let her have the time—although I know you have tried to get her to study. I hope you will insist upon her doing so in future, by my request." To another she penned, "You must not neglect to improve yourself all you can. Write every day, but with care. Your letter was well done. Review and study and never think you have reached the point beyond which you need not aim" (qtd. in *Mother Frances Gardiner* 1972, 5). The sisters wrote of Sister Frances Gardiner with respect and admiration: "You never saw anyone more anxious than Sr. Frances to improve that she may go to your aid. She would study day and night, if she were permitted" (Harriet 1822).

The mother superiors encouraged apprentice teachers as well. Mother Catherine Spalding wrote to one of her teachers,

> My very dear Sister, I have only time to write you a few lines—to tell you how much I was delighted to get your long letter & to see you have improved so much in your writing & spelling—You see now I was right when I told you practice was all you needed. You need never be afraid to write. I can read your letter with great ease & always with much pleasure. (1844)

At remote locations, a local directress of studies or superior supervised and observed teachers during the school year, encouraging their progress. For the Sisters of Charity at Emmitsburg, for example, regulations provided for supervision by the "Head School Sister" who would be "free from class—possess all talents—be impartial—have authority over discipline": "Once a month, Mother will endeavour to attend every class herself, choosing for it the time which will suit her best and the least for[e]seen either by the girls or even by the Sisters, in order to witness herself . . . the talents, application, teaching, attention, and success of the different teachers" (qtd. in Crumlish 1945, 3). The "Head Sister" taught by modeling and one-to-one mentoring.

The sisters often noted with admiration the ability of their soft-spoken mentors to command the respect of students. One wrote of Mother Catherine Spalding, "I could never have forgotten the tones of her voice, so soft, so gentle, but so deep and earnest, or the expression of her dark blue eyes, which seemed to me to read your inmost heart" ("Early Annals" n.d., 53). Another remembered her mentor's personal impact:

> Like all young Sisters, I had a hard time keeping them [students] in their seats. Sister Mary Martha would come to the door, every once in a while and just look in, and those children would get so quiet you could hardly hear a pin fall, but she would not be gone ten minutes when they were noisy again. One day I said to her, "Why can't I do that?" and she smiled at me and said, "Well, you will in time. Don't expect it right now. You'll learn how." (qtd. in Eiting n.d., 3)

Literacy levels of convent members grew quickly, not only because of the concerted effort to increase members' knowledge but also because many new members came from among the educated academy students. Mannard determined the number of sisters who had been educated by the Maryland communities they joined to be 22.4 percent for the Visitandines and 32.7 percent for the Oblate Sisters of Providence (1989, 158). In 1825, Nerinckx wrote of membership at Loretto: "At present we [Sisters of Loretto] have about eighty, not one-third over twenty-one, and most of them have been students of our schools" (qtd. in Barrett n.d., 32). In 1959, *Loretto Magazine* claimed that one of its schools, Bethlehem Academy (formerly Mount Carmel Academy) in Breckinridge County, Kentucky, founded in 1823, had provided 123 former pupils to the Sisters of Loretto community and 35 who had joined other religious communities ("Bethlehem Academy" 1959).

Curriculum, Pedagogy, and School Schedules

While most very early convent schools provided elementary schooling initially, the curriculum became more advanced as more sisters became better educated. By the 1820s, for example, Emmitsburg had expanded offerings to include rhetoric, philosophy, chemistry, botany, algebra, and astronomy (McEntee 1972, 12–14). The sisters were making use of Father Simon Bruté's basement for a chemistry and physics laboratory (15) and a cupola and belvedere for the study of astronomy (Crumlish 1945, 23). At the same time, Visitation Academy's "Prospectus" of 1828 announced a cutting-edge curriculum, promoting its enticing new scientific equipment and odeum:

> The ladies of the Visitation, with proper counsel, have sent for *apparatus*, by which they will be assisted in imparting an elementary insight, in at least fourteen branches of modern science. They have completed an edifice, named from an extension of the classic term, ODEUM, adapted for its reception, and for the annual public Examination and Exhibition. Within its limits are also comprised an extensive hall for recreation, bath apartments, laboratory, and mantua-room. To the basic subjects previously taught will be gradually added Algebra, Versification and Poetic and Composition, Female Elocution, Popular Astronomy with the assistance of the newly invented Geocyclic of Delamarche, Logic, Ethics, Metaphysics, Natural Philosophy in its various branches, Anthology, the Spanish, Italian, and Latin languages if required, Vocal Music, the Guitar, and Painting on Velvet. (qtd. in Sullivan 1975, 75)

Although many of the founders and their ecclesiastic superiors wished the sisters to devote themselves completely to education for the poor, the sisters created tuition academies (sometimes called select schools), usually attended by the well-to-do. Women who joined U.S. convents were not wealthy; therefore, the convents did not have the advantage of endowments and dowries that supported most European convents.[10] Most U.S. communities of Catholic women lived in dire poverty in the early years and were able to provide for themselves, the poor, and orphans only through the profits from their academies.

The sisters' day schools generally provided a basic curriculum, while the academies focused on more advanced learning; however, a clear distinction did not always delineate the schools. The Sisters of Loretto, for example, created an "academy" at Gethsemani, Kentucky, on more "moderate terms" than those established for their prestigious Loretto Academy:

Although there now exists in our State several flourishing and highly useful schools and Academies for the education of young ladies, it may nevertheless be apparent to all that many parents and guardians are prevented by their circumstances from availing themselves of those Institutions. Many indeed would prefer sending to an institution whose only object would be to afford means of acquiring a plain and competent education, on the most moderate terms. Considering this, the conductors of the Loretto Female Academy have resolved to establish a preparatory school of this sort, wherein young pupils may be instructed in the elementary and most indispensable branches.... The only branches taught will be Reading, Writing, Arithmetic, English Grammar, Geography and Plain Sewing. ("Preparatory School" 1838; see also Barrett n.d., 52)

Such schools mixed features of day schools and academies. Gethsemani was a boarding school, like the academies, important for students who did not live close enough to attend by making the daily trips to school; however, subjects focused on were far more limited and "practical" than those of the academies while providing a more complete education than that found in the day schools. In addition, the cost was somewhat less than that of the academies, although not as much less as one might expect, with means of payment similar to the day schools:

Terms—(Including Boarding and tuition)
per session $33.00
Extra, for bedding...2.00

One half may be paid in produce, at the market price. Teachers will be appointed who will devote themselves with maternal care to the improvement and welfare of the children entrusted to their charge. ("Preparatory School" 1838; see also Barrett n.d., 52)

Although produce was accepted as partial payment in most early academies, by 1838 tuition payment at the academies was generally in dollars rather than in produce. In 1838 the tuition charged at Loretto Academy, the sisters' main academy, was thirty-five dollars board per session, with tuition at six dollars for the lower classes (reading, writing, English grammar, plain sewing, and marking), four dollars extra for higher classes (geography with the use of maps and globes, fancy needlework, embroidery, beading, drawing and painting, rhetoric and history, botany, and philosophy), and extra charges for music and use of piano (fifteen dollars per session), music on guitar (twelve dollars), French language (five dollars), and dancing (ten dollars per quarter) ("Loretto Literary" 1838). Costs for the two schools remained the same two years later ("Preparatory School" 1840; "Loretto Female Academy" 1840). Tuition for Loretto's Deaf and Dumb Asylum was one hundred dollars per year ("Loretto Deaf Academy" 1840). At nearby Nazareth Academy, the motherhouse academy charged fifty dollars per session with charges for extras similar to those at Loretto ("Nazareth Female Academy" 1840). Nazareth's Bardstown academy charged rates similar to the Loretto motherhouse academy ("Female Academy of Bethlehem" 1837). By comparison, after moving to its handsome new building outside Boston, the Ursuline Mount Benedict Academy cost "$125 a year, plus some extras" (Buetow 1970, 84). A later ad for day schools (1853) gives a sense of the different expectations for students who did not board: "Those who can afford . . . pay full price. The poor pay 25¢ each first Monday of the month. Those who cannot pay shall have tuition of their daughters gratis, but all must be decently clad" (qtd. in Greenwell 1933, 26).

Sometimes "convent schools" took boarders and published prospectuses, or descriptions and advertisements for their schools, similar to those of academies, though not equal in breadth and quality. The Sisters of Loretto's school in La Fourche, Louisiana, struggled, partly because of insufficient financial support but also, importantly, because the diocesan bishop, Joseph Rosati, had published a prospectus for the school promising an academic schedule akin to larger academies but impossible to meet for the three sisters assigned to the school (Campbell 1987, 18). This must have been especially disturbing to the sisters, who advertised the excellence of their main academy by pointing out that their "community, being numerous, are enabled to give the fullest and most prompt attention to every department" ("Loretto Literary" 1838). At the main academy, and often at other large schools, the many sisters who specialized in one or two areas provided a large variety of subjects taught by teachers well versed in the area. Three women could not begin to provide the excellence the sisters (and parents) had come to expect. Still, the "academies" generally were boarding schools for the wealthy or relatively wealthy who could afford the tuition, providing a high level of formal education for girls at the time.[11] Day schools and orphanages offered a more elementary curriculum with an emphasis on basic literacy, religion, morality, and vocational skills.

DAY SCHOOLS AND ORPHANAGES

We know much more about the convent academies than about the day schools and orphanage schools the sisters operated. McEntee claims that boarders and those attending the day school at St. Joseph Academy at Emmitsburg "received the same lessons" (1972); however, if this was true initially, demands placed on the teachers changed that policy quickly for nearly all schools run by the sisters.[12] According to Misner, "All the original communities except the Carmelites taught the elementary subjects in day schools referred to by such terms as pay schools, free schools, poor schools, or benevolent schools.... Since these schools served the local community there was no need to publish a prospectus and there is, therefore, little documentation to consider" (1988, 191–92). We generally learn about schools other than academies through the sisters' letters, and because the sisters' purpose in correspondence was not to define the curriculum for prospective students, the letters are less clear and detailed about specifics in the schools.

Increasingly, the demand for teaching sisters to provide additional schools often required them to begin teaching before they were completely prepared, and some teachers were intellectually, temperamentally, and educationally better fitted for teaching than others. The best teachers generally taught in the academies, as patrons who paid the academy tuitions that subsidized the free schools demanded the most advanced curriculum and expected well-prepared teachers. In addition, the sisters themselves were products of their culture and not above pervasive nineteenth-century classist notions about benevolence; they seem to have approached their free schools in a manner similar to that of their orphanage schools. Still, the sincere concern that all students' education be protected is pervasive in their records, as demonstrated in this passage from the Emmitsburg sisters' 1812 rule:

> The Sisters of St. Joseph's shall endeavor to educate gratis as many poor orphan children as it will be in their power.... The time of those children shall be divided between manual labor and their education. The morning will be devoted to the first and the afternoon to the last, or vice versa, if the Mother thinks necessary to change it. But whatever rule is adopted in this respect, it shall be constantly observed. The Sisters will, in this respect, be scrupulous of taking any of the time allowed to them for their education by requiring of them services which would take away their attention from their studies. (*Rule* 1812)

However, like others in the nineteenth century, the sisters' perceptions about literacy needs differed according to station in life, a fact based partly on the reality of students' future lives. Students in day schools had a more limited curriculum than did those in the academies, intended to prepare them for a different, less "refined" world than those in the academies were expected to inhabit:

> During the part of the day appointed for their education, they shall be placed by the Mother under the care of a School Sister and be taught, as much as possible, separately from the other boarders with whom they shall not be permitted to have much intercourse in order to prevent them from contracting habits of idleness, pride, and forming notions above the sphere of life in which they may have to live if one day they return [to] the world. Accordingly the education shall be confined to reading, writing, the principal rules of arithmetic; and the greatest care shall be taken to teach them how to sew, spin, knit, and all the details of housekeeping as the best means to get their living if they had to live in the world. As for embroidery, grammar, foreign or dead languages, geography, history, those branches of education shall be left aside for them as useless for them and calculated only to take up their attention from the useful branches. (Seton 2006, 3b:534–35; Kelly 1981, 263–64)

Similarly, in an 1818 letter from the Georgetown Visitation Academy to Shepton Mallet, he was told that orphans were educated "sufficient for honest industry" and "clothed by our own manufactory, maintained and educated sufficient for their station" (Sullivan 1975, 63); in an 1819 letter to the Visitation nuns in Paris, the academy representative also explained that the "poor school" educated orphans "sufficient for their station" (63).

Sisters were aware, too, of their religious, moral, and social responsibilities. Although constitutions rarely dwelled on religious training and the schools' circumstances in a Protestant country curtailed the sisters' religious focus, they, nonetheless, expected to shape students to an acceptable moral and socially acceptable character, as expressed in the Emmitsburg rule:

> Above all things the Sisters will endeavor to form their hearts to a solid piety which [is] the chief motive of educating them. But should any of them announce extraordinary talents for some branches of education not mentioned above, the Mother may have them taught

to her, but so that it should not interfere either with their usual labor or their necessary branches of education. Whilst employed in manual labor or in recreation, they shall be under the care of a Sister who shall take care to check them whenever acting or speaking improperly. They shall be subject, as for silence, to the same rules as the Sisters while at work with them. In sickness they shall be treated as the Sisters themselves. (Kelly 1981, 264)

According to John Mary Crumlish, the "extra" education prepared students to work as governesses if ability demonstrated (1945, 16–17). However, girls with great promise and those who the sisters thought interested in becoming members of the religious community also received further education. They would have been prepared above their "sphere of life" to better fit them as sister-teachers; if they did not join the community, they might be governesses.

ACADEMIES

The day schools drew local children who could make the daily trip to school, but the boarding academies drew from larger regions. The Nazareth Academy, for example, enrolled girls from throughout the Southeast, while St. Joseph Academy at Emmitsburg was "made up mostly of the elite of New York, Philadelphia, and Baltimore. Those delicate young ladies had to wash on the porch, the water sometimes freezing, then they drank their rye and carrot coffees out of tin cups, had only dry bread for breakfast" ("Annals . . . at St. Joseph's" n.d., 249). The curriculum was rigorous; the academies advertised their comparability to men's colleges. For example, an ad for Nazareth Academy in the 1833 *United States Catholic Almanac* boasted that "a course of lectures on Rhetoric and Philosophy (Natural and Moral) shall be annually given by the Professor of St. Joseph College" (96). Loretto Academy alternately claimed affiliation with St. Joseph College and St. Mary's College. In fact, the prospectuses of both Nazareth Academy and Loretto Academy explicitly state their being "conducted on the principles similar to those of St. Joseph's College" and St. Mary's College, nearby men's colleges. (See, for example, "Nazareth Female Academy" 1840; "Loretto Literary" 1838; and "Loretto Female Academy" 1840).

In order to promote their academies, the sisters placed the prospectus for their academy in newspapers and, after 1833, in the annual *United States Catholic Almanac*. These sources can tell us much about the schools. Because the sisters depended on paying Protestant students to supplement paying Catholic students, the promotions for nearly every early academy include a disclaimer similar to the following outlined in the promotion for Loretto Academy in the 1833 *Catholic Almanac*: "They make no attempt at proselytism, and the only religious influence they exert is that of their individual piety and exemplary conduct" (109). Similarly, the prospectus for St. Joseph Academy at Emmitsburg reads, "Pupils of all denominations are admitted without distinction. Uniformity requires that they should attend Divine worship, but no encroachment is made upon the liberty of conscience" (*Prospectus* 1831).

As in the day schools and orphanages, the days in the academies were strictly scheduled, every minute closely supervised. In 1820, the Sisters of Loretto published general "Rules for the School," providing twenty-two guidelines. The rules addressed who was accepted to the academy (including Protestants), time for rising and retiring, a general schedule for the entire day, and expectations for students and parents (see appendix B). The rules demonstrate, too, the academic effectiveness of the academies. Days were rigorously structured, with short breaks for meals and recreation, but with time devoted primarily to academics. Even during meals, students kept silence and listened to readings; after a lengthy and fully scheduled day, students devoted an hour to writing, reading, or ciphering before preparing for sleep. The advantage over other schools is demonstrated, too, in the length of terms. Parents paid up front for tuition and board, and students were not admitted for fewer than three months; the regular school year lasted eleven months. One of the greatest difficulties for free and common schools was students' infrequent attendance, but sisters had control of boarding students' time. The curriculum in the academy encouraged years-long attendance, as well. For example, as demonstrated in the 1828 prospectus for the Visitation Academy, outlined above, the "gradually added" cutting-edge courses became available to students on a graduated basis, after the mastery of basic subjects and prerequisite courses.

Academy students were set apart from day and orphan students in other ways. Most wore uniforms, or at least clothing according to a specified description, and rigid rules governed activities around the clock. Visits, even by relatives, were rare and closely supervised; students' letters were read before being posted, and received correspondence was screened before being given to students. The academies thus established a comprehensive culture of study, protection, discipline, and moral governance rare elsewhere in girls' education.

U.S.-BASED CONVENTS AND THE LITERACY EXPERIENCE

By the 1830s, most academies run by U.S.-based communities offered a curriculum similar to that of the Visitation Academy in Georgetown: "Orthography, reading, writing, arithmetic, grammar, English composition, Sacred and profane history, ancient and modern chronology, mythology, philosophy and chemistry, rhetoric, versification and poetic composition, geography, astronomy, the use of maps and globe, French and Spanish languages, music on the harp and Piano Forte, vocal music, painting in water color, painting on velvet, plain and ornamental needlework, tapestry, lace work or embroidery on Bobbinet, headwork, etc.—first class taught domestic economy" (*United States Catholic Almanac* 1833, 85). The exceptions to this extensive curriculum were found at the Oblates' St. Francis Academy and the Sisters of Mercy's Female Academy in Charleston. The course of study for the Oblates lists "English, French, Cyphering and writing, sewing in all its branches, embroidery, washing and ironing" (142). Perhaps acknowledging the reality for African American students in a racist society, the school taught basic literacy skills and emphasized vocational needs. However, the sisters may have taught more extensively, with that information excluded from public consumption in a society that rarely supported and often feared literacy among African Americans.[13] The Oblate sisters also included all students in one school, not differentiating among orphans, day scholars, and academy students. The Sisters of Mercy in Charleston were required by the local bishop to confine their academy to more basic subjects, as well; he was unable to see the Mercies as capable of offering the higher branches, never supported them in that effort, and finally demanded that they maintain a basic curriculum in order to allow the Ursulines to offer the city's elite an academy of extensive and advanced subjects.

The academies enrolled very young children through sixteen years of age, with the young and uneducated beginning in the first class. An example of what constituted the various classes can be seen in a list of studies from the Sisters of Loretto's academies:

First Class.—Tuition in the common branches. Viz.: Spelling. Reading. Writing. Arithmetic. English Grammar, Geography, Plain Sewing, and Marking.

Second Class.—Tuition in the common branches, with the use of Maps and Globes, Rhetoric, Composition, Botany, Fancy Needle-work, and Bead-Work.

Third Class.—Tuition in any of the above named branches, with Mythology, Music, vocal and instrumental, French, Drawing, and Painting required additional fees. ("Early Schools" n.d.)

The boarding schools offered unique opportunities for the sisters, but they presented many difficulties as well. Sister Columba Carroll's manual for boarding academy teachers, *On Education Book 1st*,[14] demonstrates the demanding responsibilities for sister-teachers in boarding academies. Handwritten in the elegant, calligraphic script typical of well-educated women in the nineteenth century, Carroll's instruction manual for novice teachers helps us to understand life in the academies; it also demonstrates her understanding of the difficulties encountered by boarding school teachers, whose twenty-four-hour supervision of adolescent girls they must have found challenging. Her book repeatedly encourages teachers, beginning with "My dear friends—The mission which you have accepted, however modest it may appear, is of great importance in the eyes of the church, of the family, and of society; it is highly meritorious before God." Carroll alternates descriptions intended to prepare sisters for the hardships they will face with bits of encouragement. Accompanying almost every set of instructions are warnings: "You will find amongst your scholars intellectual idleness, moral idleness, and sometimes also, but more rarely, physical idleness. All this you will have to correct." These forewarnings are accompanied by such encouragement as "Be not too greatly discouraged, however, and do not grieve like those who have no hope. See what we have beheld frequently."

Carroll makes every effort to address the tensions created by constant responsibility for children to whose parents the sisters were answerable, the pressures in the day-to-day efforts to discipline and inspire, and the need to discuss and address the very difficult issue of homoerotic relationships that might surface in close living arrangements among adolescent girls. She clearly held great affection for both teachers and students and understood the trials her sister-teachers would face, constantly exhorting them to "be kind, be also firm" and acknowledging the drudgery and difficulties of their role, while at the same time giving them comfort and hope that their efforts were worthwhile.

To ready them for resistant students, Carroll impresses on her teachers the need for method and preparation, always finding a positive frame:

Observe I beg of you, your lazy little pupil, and admire the tactics she knows how to put in play, to weary you, to triumph over you. She will sustain her role for some time, and you must also sustain yours calmly, with dignity; be firm, struggle, struggle__abandon not the field of battle. Your pupil, however little sensible and intelligent she may be, will finally understand that she should yield__you will break her little will; she will learn her lesson, she will perform her duty. This struggle may last one year—two years. Do not lose courage.

In another place she beseeches teachers: "Awaken then this sleeping beauty and this slothful nature by reasonable demands, by positive orders and by encouragement founded in the ardent charity of your heart. Think of the future of the indolent young girl, of that future already so badly compromised at the present. Pity this poor soul who will be subsequently tempted to sacrifice to this wayward inclination the most sacred duties. And she warns,

A taste for study comes spontaneously, but to a very limited number of girls. How ingenious and persevering then should be your affection in order to inspire the mass of your scholars with this taste. How necessary it is for you to have excellent methods in order to make study loved by those children, who naturally hold it in horror, and above all by those young persons who commence late, whose minds are little cultivated and whom it is necessary to lead with great discretion.

Always gentle, always encouraging, Carroll demonstrates respect and affection for both students and teachers. Throughout the 170 pages, she implores her teachers to become positive role models. At one point, she includes a portion of a letter one father had addressed to his daughter while she was a student at the academy: "You are then always dissatisfied and but little satisfied, not satisfied, discontented; it must be disagreeable to live with you. No, truly, it is not agreeable to live with a person who is habitually 'discontent.'" Carroll uses this as a humorous reminder to her teachers that they should strive to be agreeable to live with as well.

Carroll addresses directly the concern for homoerotic attractions among adolescent girls living in close quarters. I have found numerous warnings for both sisters and their students regarding "special friends." Usually, such addresses come in short, rather covert clauses simply warning that one should be equally affectionate toward all and take care not to have special friends. However, in six pages of her manual, Carroll clearly outlines warning signs for homoerotic relationships and the appropriate action sisters should take if they suspect them in their academy. In chapter 6, "Purity—The Affections," she addresses "excessive intimacies between pupils," acknowledging teachers' inclination to ignore such friendships as innocent affection among those who have much in common. But she asks teachers, if they have any concern, to "observe them carefully for a long time. . . . Study the variety of expressions . . . oversee private conversations" through "notes and extracts from classical and serious works"; watch for "little presents of various kinds" and "locks of hair exchanged between them." She lists other signs of concern: if "studies falter and all attention is on the object of their passion," if they become "dreamy, absent-minded in appearance" or write poor examinations. "You must hasten to throw water on the tome, to extinguish this little volcano," Carroll states.

Understanding that neither students nor teachers may realize what is happening without due vigilance, Carroll gives the many reasons teachers may dismiss dangers as seemingly normal affectionate ties but outlines the peril: "From confidence to confidence they will go still farther without being aware of it, they will pass the prescribed limits; at first, they had no wrong intentions but they were on the brink of a precipice, and they have slipped; and already they are not far from the sink of sensuality." Carroll explains that "these cases are rare, even exceptional, but they would become frequent if you had not the courage to oppose the evils from the beginning." Understanding the very delicate nature of the situation, she warns the sister-teacher to take action only with absolute proof: "after having seen with your own eyes, and being armed with incontrovertible evidence, with palpable facts in your hands that you must make serious observation to your poor dear culpable ones, who have given themselves up to an exercise so dangerous, who have truly played with the fire."

After 169 pages, Carroll ends her manual by addressing the rewards for the sisters in their old age: "Oh how somber must not the Autumn of life be for the lay-teacher!__When you, my sisters shall have reached the evening of existence, you will not have to withdraw entirely from the animated scene of the schoolroom nor to dwell in sad isolation far from the children of your love; for it is precisely when the leaves become [unclear] and fall to the ground, that you will gather the sweetest fruits of your labor." Indeed, retired sisters could visit and invite visits from the children in the academies. Living on the premises, they could participate in the activities of the academy, witness plays and commencement ceremonies, and remain a part of the students' lives to the extent they wished. They also had economic security and a community of friends. It was these rewards Catharine Beecher had longed for—for herself and for other single women.

TEXTBOOKS AND CLASSROOM MATERIALS

As demonstrated in chapter 1, most textbooks for use in U.S. classrooms were blatantly anti-Catholic, a fact not lost on Catholic educators. By the time David had written in search of more satisfactory texts for use in the schools, there were, indeed, some more acceptable ones, as demonstrated by those found in some convent archives or listed for use by academies in the *Catholic Almanac*. We have evidence that *Tooke's Pantheon of the Heathen Gods and Illustrious Heroes* was used at the Loretto and Visitation Academies, as well as at the Ursuline academy in Charlestown before its burning (*United States Catholic Almanac* 1833, 94). Andrew Tooke, an English schoolmaster, had translated the standard Latin work of the Jesuit François Pomey into English in 1698, without acknowledging Pomey, but European clergy educated in the classical tradition of the Jesuits and Sulpicians would surely have known the original authorship. *Tooke's Pantheon* became a popular school text for English-speaking students through the middle of the nineteenth century. Classical mythologies were relatively free from bigotry anyway, chronicling information uncontested by religious factions. However, geographies and histories were among the most egregious partisan texts, and convents apparently found texts less disparaging of Catholicism.

The archives of the Sisters of Loretto contain a complete series of Charles Rollin's *Ancient History* (eight volumes). Published in Boston in 1807–9 in English, the Loretto texts had clearly not been a part of Nerinckx's library and would have been obtained for the convent. The priests and professors at nearby schools would have used Rollin in the classroom, as catalogs for all the Jesuit men's colleges list Rollin as a text, and both Georgetown University and St. Louis University archives contain complete early editions. The Rollin texts were probably used by the sisters to prepare for teaching, and perhaps as textbooks for the upper classes, as the 1833 *Catholic Almanac* promotion for Mount Benedict Academy in Charlestown, Massachusetts, lists Rollin's *Ancient History* as a text for the senior class (94). Likely used in many of the academies' lower division classrooms, if texts were used, were history texts by William Grimshaw; Grimshaw's histories of Greece, Rome, England, and France were also archived at the Sisters of Loretto convent.[15] As described in chapter 1, Grimshaw's texts narrated historical events in terms much more acceptable to Catholics.

No extant texts of the earliest days remain at the archives of the Sisters of Charity of Nazareth, but David was clearly looking for more Catholic-friendly texts, and he worked closely with the ecclesiastical superiors at Loretto. He also was in communication about the issue with Bruté at Emmitsburg; therefore, those at Emmitsburg likely knew about the more acceptable history texts.[16] As noted in chapter 1, in 1793 John Carroll wrote Mathew Carey that he would suggest Carey's edition of William Guthrie's geography book for use in the Georgetown academy, and Joseph Mobberley had ordered seventy-five copies of either Reeve's *History of the Old and New Testament* or the *Catholic Christian Instructed* for use in New York free schools, which would have been taught by the Emmitsburg Sisters of Charity.

As noted earlier, Columba Carroll wrote manuals for the sister-teachers she trained. These manuals were apparently used more than at the motherhouse academy, as extant copies in the Nazareth archive indicate that the manuals were duplicated for use in the communities' academies outside the original Nazareth Academy. Carroll's manual on teaching literature offers a curriculum that includes both classic and contemporary authors and reads much like today's anthologies—she provides a lengthy background history for British literature, followed by authors, their dates, and information about their lives and work. She follows with a somewhat shorter background history for American literature, with American authors and suggested works. The indexed manual would have been a very useful support material for teachers but does not include the authors' works, suggesting that she expected teachers and pupils to have access to those works.

Carroll includes Lucian, Horace, and Virgil and more contemporary authors such as Lord Byron, Alexander Pope, and Nicolas Boileau-Despréaux. As was typical in the nineteenth century, the "literature" course included a broad reading in humanities, including such categories as historians, philosophers, and orators and statesmen. While she provides dates and background for most authors, she simply lists others under the appropriate categories, organized for teachers' immediate needs. For example, one category, titled "Modern Infidelity, Reflections on War, and the Sentiments proper to the present Crisis," includes Thomas Chalmers, who "possesses great intellectual vigor" ("Course" n.d., 99) and John Foster: "Though his manner was rough, his earnestness and thorough abandon enabled him to thrill his audience with his own emotions" (99). A teacher wishing to assign reading meaningful for a specific discussion or purpose might readily find the appropriate authors or texts. Carroll's curriculum also included fiction and poetry by popular women writers. She defines "domestic reading" as "a species of books intended for the family, and designed to teach science, religion, the love of nature, &c." (105). Under this category she mentions such contemporaneous American women as Catharine Maria Sedgwick, Lydia Sigourney, Lydia Maria Child, Eliza Leslie, and others, as well as Europeans Jane Austen, Felicia Hemans, Ann Radcliffe, and Frances Trollope. For Carroll, these were writers who had "devoted themselves, equally, to the youngest and to the most advanced of the family circle" (105).

She includes women outside this category as well. For "Mary Shelley 1798–1851" Carroll writes,

> The wife of the poet, and the daughter of W. Godwin, wrote in Italy in 1816 the powerful tale of Frankenstein, in which a young student of physiology succeeds in constructing out of the horrid remnants of the churchyard and dissecting-room, a kind of monster to which he gives by the agency of galvanism a kind of spectral life. This existence rendered insupportable to the monster by his vain cravings after human sympathy, is employed in inflicting the most dreadful retribution on the [unclear] philosopher. ("Course" n.d., 91)

In her manual *On Education*, Carroll had insisted that her teachers "speak to the kind of reading which is suitable for young girls," and Maria Edgeworth was clearly a favorite with her. About Edgeworth she writes,

> The most valuable pieces of her educational stories are the tales entitled "Frank," "Harry," "Lucy," "Rosamond" and others, combined under the general heading of "Early Lessons." These are written in a simple style, and the sound practical principles they inculcate make them pleasing even to the adult reader. In the "Parents' Assistant" the same qualities are applied to the improvement of a more advanced age. . . . Many of Miss E's works show a delicate appreciation of the merits and weaknesses of the human character, and she has in some sense done for her countrymen what Scott did for the Scottish people. Her writings display much common-sense, and to the young she has proved herself a valuable friend. ("Course" n.d., 95–96)

Because of her stress that writing be suitable for young girls, Carroll's attention to some authors informs but fails to recommend. For example, she devotes several pages to Byron, detailing the problematic nature of his parents' lives and of his own, and follows with his better-known works. His dramatic works, she explains, are more typical of Vittorio Alfieri than of Shakespeare. She gives him modest praise for appeals to emotion and sympathy; however, she also outlines problems, including the "highly immoral" nature of some works, especially *Don Juan* ("Course" n.d., 74–76).

Carroll's manual would prepare students to discuss classical works while gaining familiarity with more recent writers, and she was concerned that what her students read would enhance their moral character.[17] Although her curriculum cannot be said to represent that of all Catholic academies at the time, it was almost surely used in various academies of the Sisters of Charity of Nazareth.

Evidence suggests similar appreciation of women's writing elsewhere. For example, extant copies of the premiums, or prizes, distributed by the Sisters of Charity at Emmitsburg for the categories of Latin, translation, history, logic, and geography include primarily popular women's works, such as that of French author Angeline de Mazili, *Poems by Lydia Sigourney*, and Felicia Hemans's early poems and *Life and Work of Mrs. Hemans*.[18] Thus, students were encouraged to appreciate popular writings by women as a reward for good work. At a time when many warned about the dangers of secular readings, especially novels, such prizes made a statement about appropriate recreational reading.[19]

CREATIVE EXERCISES AND STRICT CONDUCT

The sisters and priests who taught in the academies appear also to have constructed their own exercises for students. Reverend Simon Bruté taught geography to the students at Emmitsburg "by traveling on the maps to different countries." In an 1822 letter to Josephine Seton, Sister Jan Frances Gautland explains her students' journey "to a few of the New England states, and after sailing up the Connecticut to Hartford, we sailed through the Sound to your New York and there we remain. We examined some of its islands, buildings &c., but as our guide had to make a voyage on business of the utmost consequences, we still remain in the city" ("Annals . . . at St. Joseph's" n.d., 238; Crumlish 1945, 5). Father Bruté clearly modeled such instruction for the sisters, providing exercises the sisters might use while giving lessons to academy students as well.

The first directress of studies at Nazareth (1816–32), Sister Ellen O'Connell, drew up rhymes for students to define and demonstrate rhetorical devices, as in the following example:

TROPES AND OTHER FIGURES OF RHETORIC ILLUSTRATED

A Trope, a sovereign power o'er language shows
    And upon words a foreign sense bestows—
God is a rock and guards His Saints from ill
    Herod's a fox and will be cruel still
A Metaphor compares without the sign
    Virtue's a sun and shall forever shine
An Irony in smooth mellifluent phrase
    Its poison shoots and wounds with deep disgrace
"Ye are the men of all mankind most wise."
    "And when ye die no doubt all wisdom dies"
Sarcasm is irony in excess
    King of the Jews thee humbly we address
Low at Thy feet we bend submissive down
    Receive Thy reed and hail Thy thorny crown.
Hyperbole the truth will oft neglect
By bold excess and by as bold defect—
Mark how it rises "Yon tall mountain shrouds.
Its height in heaven and towers above the clouds."
Again it sinks, "Shall man his grandeur boast,
An atom of an atom world at most?"   (n.d.)

O'Connell followed with similar definitions and examples, providing help with classical rhetorical terms that might assist in one's own writing and in appreciating the writing of others in the belletristic tradition so important in early nineteenth-century American colleges:

A Figure

Though figures no new sense impose
Yet language with their radiant beauties glow,
So clothes on men, nor shape nor size bestow,
Yet 'tis to them we half our graces owe.

Apostrophe

Apostrophe diverts the speaker's strain to other objects.
Witness earth and main;
"Witness thou love and all ye rolling spheres,
How good how great the Lord of all appears."

Epanorthesis

Epanorthesis our too languid words,
Repeats and thus more emphasis bestows
Witness thou, Sun and all ye rolling spheres
How good, how great the Lord of all appears.

Asyndeton

Asyndeton cashiers to speed its pace
The cop'lative from its accustomed place,
"I came, saw, conquered" mighty Cesar cried,
Victory and fame attendant at his side.

Polysyndeton

A polysyndeton each thought to show
Distinct with cop'latives will overflow
And bagnios and slowth and swimming bowls,
Dissolved their virtue and unmanned their souls.

Apophasis

Apophasis while feigning to impose,
Strict silence will fullest sense disclose
"I might have mentioned, but I choose to spare,
"How like a tiger or a raging bear,
"You rushed upon me and shed my blood,
Had not this arm your curs'd attempt with stood.["]

Prosopopaeia

Prosopopaeia into persons turns,
The qualities of mind - See valor burns
"From virtues threaten'd head t'avert the blow,
And crush oppression her insulting foe."   (n.d.)

The compilation demonstrates not only the classical emphasis typical of Catholic schools but also O'Connell's efforts to make terms accessible and concrete for students.

Writing, a major focus at academies, gets specific attention in the attenuated rules. In Elizabeth Seton's instructions for "School Department at St. Joseph," three of the eighteen directions pertain to writing, instructing those in charge of writing to "have their pens, copybooks, ink and ink horns ready before their respective classes begin" and to keep the "ink, paper, pens and wafers" when students are not using them. The importance of writing is demonstrated, as well, in her instruction that "during the time of classes and particularly during the writing class, the greatest silence must be observed even by the School Sisters except when the duties of their office require they should speak. No children can be allowed to speak, even on pretext of wanting books, paper, ink, or pens, but must address themselves to the School Sister in a whisper so as not to disturb others" (Seton 2006, 3b:538). Writing's importance was evident, too, at Loretto Academy, where students initiated a literary paper in the 1820s or 1830s (Barrett n.d., 83).

Even outside writing class, students (and teachers) were dissuaded from talking, except during brief periods set for recreation. The rules and constitutions also emphasize the necessity of sisters' deportment providing a good model for students. And in her school rules, Seton wrote,

> The greatest attention shall be paid to the behavior of the children in class. They shall not be permitted to loll, sit where they please, stoop too low, sit cross legged [or] leaning upon one another, talking or whispering to one another, pushing or making faces to one another. Impudent behavior or answer to the School Sisters shall be punished instantly. They shall not be permitted to come in class too late or to walk in a rude noisy manner. (2006, 3b:539)

Christie Anne Farnham notes the emphasis on extravagant dress at southern girls' academies and suggests that the effort at "self-discipline, self-denial, and personal achievement was slow to make headway" (1994, 139); however, this was untrue of the sisters' academies, the majority of which were located in the South in the early nineteenth century. Girls wore simple dress or uniforms, and any forms of vanity and frivolous behavior were discouraged. In her guide for young teachers, *On Education Book 1st*, Columba Carroll had written, "There is a passion for the toilet, there is a necessity for the toilet," and she urged her young sister-teachers to assure that students treat the toilet as a necessity, not as a passion. In another passage she wrote, "Those of your scholars who belong to the aristocracy should disdain neither sewing, nor household chores. Let them learn to put their white hands to useful labor" (n.d., n.p.).

Sisters' ways of conducting themselves served as an example for students. Some sisters gave "polite" classes,[20] but their effectiveness rested primarily upon the day-to-day behavior exhibited by the sisters themselves, reinforced by the rules and expectations for students. And the sisters could also use their space to address concerns that arose from student interaction outside the classroom. An example is this note Carroll posted to students:

> Mother Columba, as a special favor, requests the pupils of the Nazareth Academy to discontinue using certain inappropriate and slang words and phrases. Among them, for example, are <u>awful</u>, <u>real</u>, instead of the adverb, <u>really</u>; <u>'taint</u> for <u>it is not</u>, <u>was you</u> for <u>were you</u>.
>
> Please apply to the teachers who will point out further instances. (qtd. in Corcoran 1966, 23)

Difficulties for Subordinates

Although their primary mission was teaching, all sisters clearly were not blessed with such a vocation. Initially, many sisters not only taught but also spun, wove, and sewed, for themselves and neighbors, in addition to performing farm labor, in order to sustain themselves. As the number of members grew and academies became profitable, sisters less adept at teaching could be assigned to the kitchen and laundry. However, the demand for teachers and their small number at some mission locations sometimes necessitated placing sisters in teaching positions when they were not so well prepared or adept.

While the sisters got extraordinary support from many quarters as they began their communities, they also often encountered antagonistic or unfavorable actions on the part of superiors who perceived the sisters' roles as subordinate and menial. Most communities lived in grave poverty during their early years, and the bishops and priests sometimes found that fitting. Louis DuBourg, bishop of Louisiana (which included all of the Louisiana Purchase at the time), sought and won a branch of the Sisters of Loretto to establish schools for girls. He wrote enthusiastically to his brother:

> The great advantage of these Sisters is: to establish them it is enough to give them a piece of land, a hut, some farming implements, kitchen utensils and looms; with these they provide for all their wants and find means of giving a solid education to the children in return for a few provisions furnished by the parents. They even take upon themselves the care of destitute orphans. This is the admirable foundation of Mr. Nerinckx of Kentucky. (qtd. in Ware 1999, 2)

Bishop Rosati expressed similar sentiments after three sisters had made a difficult trip to La Fourche, Louisiana, and learned that their assignment took them to a place far more rustic than promised. When a church member beseeched him to have the filthy building cleaned for the sisters, he told the sisters, "That is the way Providence procures for you opportunities of practicing well the virtues of the beginnings of your foundation—poverty, mortification, in a word, the cross without which we cannot sanctify ourselves. Therefore, you ought with gratitude and with a great desire to profit by them for your sanctification" (qtd. in Campbell 1987, 5). Such attitudes often played out in demeaning and harmful ways for the sisters, even among usually supportive superiors. The sisters lived under a vow of poverty, but sometimes they found themselves suffering under conditions more dismal than necessitated by their vow, with insufficient food and deplorable living conditions. Despite their difficult conditions in the early years, the sisters strove to improve their schools, but their property was often taken from them. In 1821, the Sisters of Charity of Nazareth learned of problems related to the handsome new brick structure they had built on the property offered by their bishop: "The ground on which they had built was not their own, and never could be theirs. On it they had expended all their savings during those ten years of indescribable hardships laboring in-doors and out and enduring privations which are met only in a life in the wilderness. Childlike in their confidence, they had never doubted their right to the ground" (Fox 1925, 100). The sisters bought property a few miles away from this location and began to build anew.[21]

The annals of the Sisters of Charity at Emmitsburg that date from 1821 to 1832 explain what happened in the early 1820s to their property in Frederick, Maryland, a substantial mission location: "By a great mistake, the Sisters' title to the property [Frederick—schoolhouse—frame and then brick—orphan asylum, boarding school and free school with added brick wing][22] was given up to the Jesuits, who in the year 1846, replaced us by the nuns of the Visitation" (243).

Similarly, the Sisters of Loretto were required to move from the convent grounds they had initially established—the property owned and improved by the sisters—to a location some five or six miles away when their bishop deemed the property ideal for the expansion of a men's seminary. The sisters were given another farm in exchange for their property, but the move was not of their choosing, and the money and effort they had invested to improve the property was lost to them.[23] In Cincinnati, the bishop simply claimed the property of the Sisters of Mercy as his own, providing no compensation.

While the sisters were technically under the authority of the bishop and of their ecclesiastical superior, they were generally allowed freedom to manage their internal affairs and to make assignments. The various communities' constitutions and religious rules were not uniform, however, and could be interpreted differently by diverse parties; some bishops and ecclesiastic superiors repeatedly worked to assert greater control over the sisters. As late as 1841, Bardstown's Bishop Flaget considered at length exactly where authority over the Sisters of Charity lay—with the bishops in whose dioceses they were located or with their ecclesiastical superior. Tellingly, he mentions that the superior general of the Sisters of Charity in France clearly did not have authority over these American institutions, but he fails to consider the American mother superior as the ultimate authority (Flaget 1841). After the death of the initial ecclesiastical superior and cofounder of the Sisters of Loretto, the sisters' constitutions and religious rule were revised by the bishop and new ecclesiastical superior, partly because so many young sisters were dying due to their rule's austerity, but also because the bishop and new superior felt the mother superior was given too much power in the original rule.

In 1829, the supportive ecclesiastical superior of the Dominican Sisters of St. Rose was replaced by an unsympathetic superior who tried to disband the group: "He advised them to ask for dispensation from their vows and to return to their homes and wait a more favorable time to make an establishment, if they persisted in their object." When he later learned that the sisters were in debt (as many communities were as they built their schools), "he decided there was no alternative for the sisters but to sell their farm, pay their obligations and disband" (Minogue 1921, 64). Despite his pressure, the sisters refused and became a successful community.

Bishops sometimes tried to manage sisters without consent of the mother superior and often encouraged the splintering of communities. Many Sulpician priests had long wished the Emmitsburg Sisters of Charity to join the French Daughters of Charity, with whom they were familiar, and the Reverend Louis Deloul eventually took steps in that direction, first ordering that the sisters no longer care for boys in their orphanages in order to comply with the French rule, and finally making the decision that the union would take place, without seeking the sisters' opinions or approval—"in his wisdom [he] thought it well to keep them from such information till initiatives had been taken in obtaining the opinion and approval of the bishops most interested" (anonymous letter qtd. in Metz 1996, 233). Some members subsequently broke from the motherhouse and continued in their own tradition.

Bishops often spent years imploring sisters from distant motherhouses to come to their dioceses, but once there, the sisters sometimes found themselves involved in contentious battles when the bishops tried to exert control in opposition to the rules and directions of the motherhouse. Concerned for their own interests, the bishops of New York and Cincinnati directed large numbers of members from religious communities assigned to their dioceses, primarily from Emmitsburg, to break from their motherhouse and begin separate communities that would be more directly under the control of the bishops (Metz 1996, 231–40). When three Sisters of Loretto had difficulties at La Fourche, Louisiana, brought on primarily by the impossible promises made by Bishop Rosati (mentioned above), he arranged for the sisters to join the Sisters of the Sacred Heart, without the approval of the mother superiors of either community. This desire to maintain control over the sisters is clearly stated in an 1830 letter from Bishop John England to Judge William Joseph Gaston: "The sisters I am endeavoring to establish will not be a band of those at Emmitsburg, nor dependent on them, as I do not wish to make my institutions depend upon superiors over whom I have neither control or influence. Hence I shall try what can, within the diocese, be done upon the same principle. I have four who cost me very little and do much service" (qtd. in Guilday 1969, 2:135).

Sisters also often got caught in conflicts between male superiors or found themselves at odds with their ecclesiastical superiors. Elizabeth Seton became engaged in a struggle with Father Louis DuBourg, who "forbade us to write our dear former confessor Father Pierre Babade." DuBourg resigned after Seton's protest to Bishop John Carroll. She also struggled with Father Jean Baptiste David, who contested her rules for the school and tried to replace her as superior with a postulant of his choosing (McNeil 1996, 191). David was moved from Emmitsburg to Kentucky, where he helped to found and became ecclesiastical superior to the Sisters of Charity of Nazareth. Seton and Catherine Spalding, whose manners were nonconfrontational but who usually persuaded superiors to agree with their wishes, were two of the more successful at resisting interference, but many sisters lacked the authority or ability to effectively defy male superiors.

Some superiors became involved even with dress, especially as it signified affiliation with European orders. Surmising the pleasure of French tourists to America "when in our great cities, they would see the cornette so known and so venerated in Europe," Flaget assured Deloul, "I am quite sure that our Sisters of Charity in Kentucky will be ten times more content to adopt the white cornette than the black bonnet of your Saintly daughters" (Flaget 1841). While the Emmitsburg sisters adopted the dress of the European order, the Kentucky sisters, in fact, did not agree and refused to accept either the affiliation with or the dress of the French sisters. The sisters won some battles, as shown above. However, the stress and consumption of time in already too-busy schedules were clearly burdensome, even when events ended favorably.

The sisters clearly experienced personal advantages, however. Some early members of the Emmitsburg community were widows, often with young children. Elizabeth Seton, widowed with five children and concerned with how to properly educate them, brought her daughters to St. Joseph Academy; her sons were provided for gratis at the nearby Sulpician College. Seton would have been unable to educate her sons in this manner on her own. Her improved circumstances can be seen in her 4 July 1808 letter to Julia Scott:

> You would scarcely believe the change I experience in my manner of life since I am in my New Home—after so long a period of trouble and confusion to lead a life of regularity and comparative repose—accustomed to find recreation and amusement only in my books, and considering every visitor a thief upon my few precious moments and almost an intruder, my poor heart was wrapped up in its own solicitudes, or indifferent to every temporal object—but such is the contrast of my present situation I scarcely dare think of it—we were received by each of the Reverend gentlemen of the Seminary as their adopted charge.... My boys are finally received in the college by the voluntary offering of these kind beings who are the Professors without the least expense. (2002, 2:14)

Rose White and Margaret George, two other early members of the community, were also widows, White with a young son. Some of the first members of the Oblates and Visitandines were widows as well. In the early years, religious communities served as a way for women to provide for themselves and sometimes for their children. The convents also offered a means of salvation, a way of serving God and avoiding temptation. In addition, they permitted mothering without the dangers of childbirth and a life lived within a community of women with limited interference from men. Furthermore, for those interested in learning, the convents provided unique lifelong, often advanced, educational opportunities and professional careers in such fields as teaching and school administration, nursing, and hospital administration, roles rare for early nineteenth-century women.

While twenty-first-century readers might see major sacrifice in the life these women chose, Sarah A. Curtis suggests that for lower-class women who were unlikely to marry, vows of poverty, chastity, and obedience did not differ markedly from the dependent or submissive lives they might lead outside a religious order (2000, 79). With regard to literacy for themselves and other women and girls, these sisters' lives demonstrate a heretofore barely acknowledged opportunity. The convents brought literacy, both basic and advanced, to numerous young women and girls who otherwise had little or no access to such learning.

"Massacre of the Protestants." From "Narrative of the Irish Rebellions; and Massacre of the Protestants, 1641–2," in Charles K. Moore, *A Book of Tracts*. Courtesy University of Louisville Rare Books Archives.

"Popery Undermining Free Schools, and Other American Institutions." From E. Beecher (1835).

POPERY EXPOSED;

OR,

THE SECRETS AND PRIVACY

OF

THE CONFESSIONAL UNMASKED.

THE HUSBAND'S REMORSE AT HIS WIFE.

WILLIAM R. TAYLOR: NEW YORK.
PRICE ONE DOLLAR.

Title page, *Popery Exposed*, no author, n.d. Courtesy Notre Dame University Archives.

Cover, *The Priest, the Woman, and the Confessional,* by Charles Chiniquy, n.d. Courtesy Notre Dame University Archives.

BARBARA UBRICK, In the Dungeon

CONVENT HORROR

Story of Barbara Ubrick, who for twenty-one years was locked in a stone dungeon eight feet long and six feet wide in the basement of the convent because she refused to surrender her virtue to a Romish priest. Never saw the face of a human being; never saw daylight; never had water to wash with—clothes rotted off her back; slept on a pallet of damp straw; hair grew out all over her body; lived in her filth for twenty-one long years; fed on mouldy bread, and potato peelings and water once a day; became a raving maniac; weighed 40 pounds when the authorities got her out. This portrayal is one of Rome's blackest crimes on record.

Buy this book and scatter broadcast. Help to wake up the American Protestants, save the government from the hands of Rome and forever abolish the nunnery system from American soil. Nunneries are un-American.

Price 25 Cents

Tract No. 40

NUNNERIES

Must be Abolished from American Soil

Help Free one hundred thousand girl slaves from these un-American Popish-prison Sweat Houses.

Buy these books and Scatter them out.

Address
Protestant Book House,
1415 Palmetto Ave., - Toledo, Ohio

Title page, *Nunneries Must Be Abolished from American Soil*, n.d. Courtesy Notre Dame University Archives.

MARGARET L. SHEPHERD, (Ex-Nun)

"My Life In The Convent"
Or Nunnery Life Unveiled.

SIX YEARS BEHIND POPISH NUNNERY BARS

This is the greatest book on the nunnery system in print today, giving the most complete information relative to the objects, rules, treatment—the lives of the priests with the nuns, etc.—in the various orders of convent sisterhood, and the most complete exposure of the Black Nunnery life in print today.

She was the daughter of a priest of Rome—seduced by a priest—married to a priest—abandoned in the convent by a priest—her baby destroyed in the convent!

It is one of the saddest narratives on the subject ever written. Buy this book above all others. It will hold you in its grip until through tears and heart throbs you have read the last line. 258 pages. Price 50 cents.

No Stamps Taken

Send Check or Money Order

HELEN JACKSON, (Ex-Nun)
CONVENT CRUELTIES

But This is a People Robbed and Spoiled. They Are All of Them Snared in Holes, and They Are Hid in Prison Houses. They Are For a Prey and None Delivereth for a Spoil and None Saith Restore. (Isaiah 42:22).

Known in religion as "Sister Rose Virginia."

Helen Barnoski-Jackson born of Polish Catholic parents in the state of Pennsylvania, placed in the Good Shepherd Nunnery, Detroit, Mich., when 13 years of age, five long years were spent in this prison house at hard labor. Later was smuggled to the pope's penitentiary at Newport, Ky. Six more years there at the ironing board without any remuneration whatever. Broken in health and starved, she begged the Mother Superior to let her return to her home, refused—she and another convict planned to escape—dug a hole under the convent wall, and fled. Now married and lives in Toledo, Ohio. Giving her life for the salvation of the girls of America.

Her book abounds with horrible cruel incidents of brutal treatment at the hands of inhuman task masters—(Mother Superiors, and bachelor fathers). Fully illustrated.

Price 50 Cents

Book advertisements for *Nunneries Must Be Abolished from American Soil*, n.d. Courtesy Notre Dame University Archives.

First Ursuline convent, Quebec, built 1642. From *Glimpses of the Monastery* (1897).

Ursuline convent, Quebec, 1759—after fire destroyed earlier buildings. From *Glimpses of the Monastery* (1897).

New Orleans Ursuline Convent, completed 1753—the oldest extant building in the Mississippi valley, now Old Ursuline Convent Museum. Photo by Frank J. Methe.

View of Visitation Convent and Academy, Georgetown, Washington, D.C., 1829. Courtesy Georgetown Visitation Preparatory School.

St. Joseph Academy, Emmitsburg, Maryland, circa 1846. Daughters of Charity Province of St. Louise Archives, Emmitsburg, Maryland.

St. Michael School, Convent, Louisiana, built 1825. Courtesy Society of the Sacred Heart Provincial Archives, United States–Canada Province.

Nazareth Convent and Academy, Kentucky, 1848. Courtesy Sisters of Charity of Nazareth Archival Center.

Motherhouse, Sisters of St. Joseph of Carondelet. Sisters of St. Joseph of Carondelet, St. Louis Province Archives.

First convent and school for the deaf, Sisters of St. Joseph of Carondelet. Sisters of St. Joseph of Carondelet, St. Louis Province Archives.

Arrival of the Ursulines in New Orleans. Charcoal by Madeleine Hachard, circa 1727. Old Ursuline Convent Museum, Archdiocese of New Orleans.

Elizabeth Ann Seton, DC. Courtesy Daughters of Charity Province of St. Louise Archives, Emmitsburg, Maryland.

Mother Catherine Spalding, SCN. Courtesy Sisters of Charity of Nazareth Archival Center.

Mother Mary Lange, OSP. Courtesy Oblate Sisters of Providence Archives, Baltimore, Maryland.

Mother Theresa Duchemin, OSP. Courtesy Oblate Sisters of Providence Archives, Baltimore, Maryland.

Sister Rose Boegue, OSP. Courtesy Oblate Sisters of Providence Archives, Baltimore, Maryland.

Madeleine Sophie Barat, RSCJ, artist unknown, circa 1879. Courtesy General Archives of the Society of the Sacred Heart, Rome.

Rose Philippine Duchesne, RSCJ. Courtesy Society of the Sacred Heart Provincial Archives, United States–Canada Province.

"Consolation." Sisters of Mercy of the Americas, Mercy Heritage Center, Belmont, North Carolina.

The Daughters of Charity at Satterlee Military Hospital, Philadelphia. Daughters of Charity Province of St. Louise Archives, Emmitsburg, Maryland.

4.
Literacy in Convent Schools of European-Based Congregations

The need for educators in Catholic communities was so great that religious leaders regularly sought missionaries from established convent teaching communities in Europe to create mission settlements in the United States. The teaching in these European communities was similar to the teaching in U.S.-based congregations. After all, Catholic religious communities constructing teaching philosophies and pedagogies in the young United States often drew from a European tradition, as many of their ecclesiastic mentors were European. For example, nearly all communities named one sister head of each school and placed a sister in charge of each classroom to be responsible for instruction and order. Continuing professional advancement was also emphasized in both European and American congregations. The constitutions of the Sisters of St. Joseph required that the sister-teachers "devote all the time possible under obedience, to their own improvement," and that they prepare carefully before lessons (*Constitutions of the Sisters of St. Joseph* [1693] 1860, pt. 3, ch. 4, p. 136). However, the communities also differed. Most of those who formed their curricula and pedagogies in the United States were guided by women, and sometimes men, who had been born in and imbibed the American culture; in contrast, those emigrating from Europe brought a very different background and a curriculum created for a French, historically Catholic, society, and they held to that curriculum as much as possible during the early decades of the nineteenth century.

These European-based communities of teaching nuns brought established curricula and methods for teaching girls and young women. Because they had written constitutions and extensive manuals for teaching, we can get some understanding of the sisters' missions, their expectations, and the teaching methods they used in their schools. However, because there are fewer letters and journals describing their teaching than what is found in the archives of the U.S.-based communities, we get fewer personal accounts describing teachers' perspectives and experiences.[1] Although these women religious had been well prepared for their teaching mission, the Catholic culture in which they had learned to teach was very different from the culture many would experience in the United States; their schools differed from those of native sisters, therefore, especially in a greater emphasis on religion but also with more attention to needlework and other traditional feminine arts and a later move to include the sciences in the curriculum. Their European background also presented challenges with language, class, and other social and cultural expectations, especially for those who settled outside French American communities. However, they brought innovations, too, most notably, perhaps, curriculum for teaching the hearing impaired. The three communities who provide the primary focus for this chapter gradually adapted and became a permanent and influential part of the American culture.

The greatly different culture into which they immigrated made survival difficult for many European communities. From 1790 to 1829, twelve communities of women religious were founded in the United States. All six of those founded by or with a majority of Americans became successful permanent communities, while of those founded from European motherhouses during this period, "only one [Sisters of the Sacred Heart] achieved permanent stability" (Ewens 1978, 32). Mary Ewens found that the "ability or inability to adapt European customs and role definitions for nuns" (33) was instrumental in determining their success. For those who settled in areas where Catholics did not make up the majority of citizens, the adaptation was much more difficult. This chapter examines the three European-originated communities that became permanent parts of the United States prior to 1840: French Ursulines, who became part of the United States in 1803 with the Louisiana Purchase; the Sisters of the Sacred Heart, another French community that arrived in 1818; and the French Sisters of St. Joseph, whose first members arrived in 1836. Irish Ursulines also established a successful convent and academy in Boston in 1820, although it was destroyed by a mob in 1834, and a later group of Irish Ursulines settled permanently in South Carolina in 1834. These communities also contribute to this chapter.[2]

As Sarah A. Curtis has discussed, French convents had long provided women rare acceptable opportunities for training and careers, as well as a sense of community (2000, 61). Unlike in the United States, European convent life had an extensive tradition and, for some communities, a teaching profession that had enjoyed centuries of acceptance and development. European groups also possessed economic security. Most had been established with endowments, and members were expected to bring dowries to the organization upon entry. These congregations were, thus, also based on a class structure largely absent in U.S. communities. Choir nuns focused primarily on prayer (as well as teaching if their mission included education); lay nuns, from less wealthy families, took responsibility for most of the domestic and manual labor.

Before coming to the United States, European communities had already created detailed plans for operating schools and for the systematic education of students in their charge. Women from these communities arrived prepared both academically and pedagogically to offer an education they deemed appropriate for girls and young women. However, there was no systematic preparation for the material and cultural differences they would find in the New World, which were often immense. For example, rather than providing new opportunities for literacy, at least literacy as traditionally defined, as U.S. convents were doing for entering women, life in the New World often diminished European nuns' opportunities for furthering their education. The more difficult material life in the United States necessitated increased time and effort for providing day-to-day necessities and less time for educational advancement. Access to books and other materials, both for their own benefit and for use with students, was hampered as well.

On the other hand, once established, these European-based convents would provide access to literacy for Americans in a way similar to U.S.-based convents, as American recruits often had not had the education of European novices. For example, by 15 August 1821, three years after her arrival in Missouri, Philippine Duchesne, the U.S. superior of the Sisters of the Sacred Heart, wrote Madeleine Sophie Barat, founder of the European community, "The four novices we have are very good, especially the Americans." Duchesne does not explain how many of the novices are American, but she does describe the uniqueness of their situation, as the books they were expected to study were unavailable, and they clearly did not have the level of education required of European recruits: "As the novices have not had much formal schooling and not one of them had a copy of *L'Hommand's Grammar*, I also made an outline of that which each one copies and studies from" (qtd. in Callan 1957, 348).

The earliest successful European nuns migrating to the New World chose destinations where immigrants from their home country had already established settlements. For example, French congregations had settled first in the French-speaking territories of Canada and Louisiana in the seventeenth and early eighteenth centuries. The early Canadian Ursulines received much support from the French aristocracy, allowing them to feed themselves and also the Indians they catechized and educated. The New Orleans Ursulines seem to have lived in conditions inferior to those of the Canadians. As late as 1822, when three Ursulines from Quebec arrived in New Orleans to assist the nuns there, "one of them wept hot tears on seeing the poverty of our house that she likened to the stable of Bethlehem, although we had spent several weeks preparing for their reception" (qtd. in Heaney 1992, 270).

Still, while the New Orleans nuns' living conditions were somewhat rustic initially, the group's contract with the Company of the Indies, along with support from the French crown and local community, provided necessities, and the nuns, having settled in a French-speaking culture, became a comfortable and successful segment of the population. By the early nineteenth century, when Louisiana became part of the United States, the Ursulines had been an important component of the local culture for nearly a century. However, the Sacred Heart nuns, who were just entering the New World, found conditions in the United States trying. Although the European motherhouse wished to support the missions in the United States, the challenging circumstances made such assistance difficult. After the French Revolution, the nuns could not count on financial help from the French aristocracy, as had earlier groups, and their new communities often did not offer the support seen by the earlier Ursuline congregations, as the French Catholic population in their Missouri communities was mostly poor and shared space with English-speaking, often hostile, Protestants.

Mother Philippine Duchesne repeatedly expressed her dismay and discomfort at hostility from Protestants. As she prepared to leave New Orleans for Missouri on 9 July 1818, she wrote Barat about her frustration with the simple black dress she and her companions would don to deflect unwanted attention: "We wore our religious costumes on the ocean vessel, and no one thought it out of place. On the contrary, they commented that it was a well-chosen habit, having nothing singular about it. The Ursulines, even those who have come out during the last thirty years, have traveled in secular dress, and we shall have to do so on the steamboat" (qtd. in Callan 1957, 249). The Sisters of St. Joseph, too, wore secular clothing for travel in the United States and expressed dismay at the necessity. The nuns, having come from a Catholic culture, seemed unprepared for the indifference and even open hostility of Protestants toward Catholic women religious. Other signs of dissonance appear in Duchesne's journal and letters. A gentle woman, loved and admired by nuns and students, she nonetheless struggled with a culture so alien to her own.

In addition, the nuns' work increased far more rapidly than their ability to handle it. In France, numerous new members helped to supply teaching and domestic needs; however, French recruits to the American community did not arrive in numbers sufficient to relieve their overburdened colleagues. Barat often wrote her nuns in the United States with regrets and apologies, similar to this 29 June 1829 letter to Lucille Mathevon, head of one of the Sacred Heart schools:

> What grieves me more than anything is that I just cannot get as much help as I should like to send you. Sister Duchesne will help you all she can, and we shall send others in a year or eighteen months. The three we are sending now will have to be replaced in the houses from which they come, and it will be hard to find religious, for every superior has only what she really needs. The young nuns whom we send fresh from the noviceship have so much to learn. (1850, 2:154)

The nuns would feel the need for additional help for decades.

Whereas the Sisters of the Sacred Heart struggled to provide for themselves and their schools, the Sisters of St. Joseph, who came to the United States in 1836 and settled in mostly Catholic regions of the St. Louis diocese, appear to have had a somewhat less difficult beginning. Some of these nuns' first years were very challenging materially, as they moved to the impoverished area of Carondelet, Missouri, providing most of their services gratis to people with little money; others settled in Cahokia, Illinois, a somewhat more favorable location because it was occupied by more affluent French Canadian Catholics who were able to offer more material assistance. However, Josephites' work among mostly Catholic populations made them an appreciated part of the communities in which they toiled, and by the end of 1839, Carondelet village officials agreed to salary the teachers there "to educate in the ordinary branches of the English and French languages the female children of the town of Carondelet, from six to eighteen years old" (Missouri state laws qtd. in Keenan 1934, 48). In the same year, because of the nuns' special mission for teaching the deaf, the Missouri legislature began appropriating annual tuition for the students in the school for the deaf. The Sisters of St. Joseph's later date of arrival clearly made a difference, as numerous other women religious communities already in the St. Louis area provided support when necessary. For example, when they first arrived in St. Louis, the Josephites received English lessons at the Sacred Heart convent and were housed with the Sisters of Charity until their own convent could be readied. These sisters no doubt also assisted with their new friends' acculturation in other ways. Still, material circumstances for all these communities were far more difficult than what they had known in Europe, and language barriers often created problems as well.

The Jesuit Influence

By the seventeenth century, inspired by the wildly popular Jesuit missionary reports from New France, the *Jesuit Relations (The Relations de Jesuites de la Nuevelle-France)*, many French girls dreamed of traveling to the New World, especially to teach the Indians. The *Relations* became "popular in the court circles of France . . . and assisted greatly in creating and fostering the enthusiasm of pious philanthropists, who for many years substantially maintained the mission of New France" (Thwaites [1896] 1925, li). The *Relations* became popular reading in the nuns' monasteries as well, where they inspired the earliest missionary nuns to New France, including Marie Guyart (Mother Mary of the Incarnation), founder of the first American school for girls in Quebec (Greer 2000, 23).

Although public dissemination of the *Relations* was suspended in 1673, Jesuits continued to be the luminaries of the time; returning Jesuit missionaries spoke in the churches and circulated through communities in an effort to raise money for their missions. Such activity assured the continuing interest of young French women in becoming missionaries to the New World, bringing women religious to the United States in the early nineteenth century. For example, the Sacred Heart's Philippine Duchesne had been thrilled by accounts of heroism and martyrdom in Jesuit mission life, especially those of Father Jean-Baptiste Aubert, who had been in Louisiana and the Illinois country as a missionary to the French and Indians (Callan 1957, 22). Duchesne wrote her French superior in 1818:

> My first enthusiasm for missionary life was roused by the tales of a good Jesuit Father who had been on the missions in Louisiana and

who told us stories about the Indians. I was just eight or ten years old, but already I considered it a great privilege to be a missionary. I envied their labors without being frightened by the dangers to which they were exposed, for I was at this time reading stories of the martyrs, in which I was keenly interested. The same good Jesuit was extraordinary confessor at the convent in which I became a pupil. I went to confession to him several times, and I loved his simple, informal manner of speaking, a manner he had used with the savages. From that time the words *Propagation of the Faith* and *Foreign Missions* and the names of priests destined for them and of religious in far-away lands made my heart thrill. (qtd. in Callan 1957, 23)[3]

Jesuits were also instrumental in the formation of some societies of women religious, supporting them and helping to form their teaching plans; later they participated as the nuns refined their educational curricula and methodology. Both the Sacred Heart plans of studies and the *Règlements* of the Ursulines of Paris were modeled on the Jesuit *Ratio Studiorum*. According to Marie de Saint Jean Martin, "It has often been said that the Ursulines of the first house of the Order at Paris received their method of education from the Jesuits. This is very probable since three Jesuits, John Gontery, Charles de la Tour, and Pierre Coton helped to prepare their Constitutions" (1946, 285). Martin has outlined the comparable histories of the Ursulines and Jesuits and the parallel between the Jesuit *Ratio Studiorum* and the Ursuline *Règlements* to convincingly demonstrate the close affiliation (1946, appendix A).

Support for the nuns' teaching mission was ongoing, with experienced members of the nuns' communities and Jesuit spiritual and educational experts conducting workshops and conferences for the nuns; American missions received information from conferences held in France. For example, Jesuit Bartholomew Jacquenot gave a thirty-day retreat for the early Ursulines, as did Jesuit Nicolas Loriquet for the Sacred Heart nuns.[4] The ongoing education continued as nuns sought to assure their currency in curricular matters. In 1827, for instance, Father Julien Druilhet, who had served as rector of the College de Saint Acheul at Amiens, conducted a series of educational conferences for the Sisters of the Sacred Heart at their motherhouse in Amiens. He also adapted some Jesuit works to the nuns' needs; among these was the *Instruction for Young Professors Who Teach the Humanities*, written by Father Judde, a learned eighteenth-century Jesuit

(Callan 1937, 732). These materials became part of the educational curriculum for the nuns in both France and the United States.

While members of these religious communities often referred to the Ignatian spirit that saturated their curricula and pedagogical methods, they clearly adapted the *Ratio* to what the Jesuits and the nuns saw as appropriate for girls and young women. Classical languages, the bedrock of Jesuit schools, were not included in the curricula for girls, at least not as rigorous studies. As Louise Callan notes, while the Sacred Heart schools included Latin from the earliest periods, the "pupils learned to pronounce it carefully and fluently in order to take part in the offices of the Church . . . to follow intelligently the liturgical services" (1937, 726), not as part of a classical studies agenda. In New Orleans, French and English shared equal time in the curriculum.

While the educational collaboration with Jesuits was very important to the Sacred Heart nuns, the cooperation in mission and moral support proved important for them as well. Duchesne often wrote of her relief when Jesuits moved into her Louisiana area, and Barat counseled her to "follow the advice of our friends," even choosing to keep or close missions according to the proximity of Jesuit friends (qtd. in Callan 1957, 425). The Sacred Heart nuns were a cloistered community, and they often relied on the counsel of the Jesuits in matters outside their walls. Many women religious also had brothers or other family members in the Society of Jesus; these ties, along with the traditional relationship created in France, provided a comfort that helped to sustain members of these communities.

Curricula and Schedules

While the Jesuits influenced the teaching plans of a number of women's congregations, the earliest Sisters of St. Joseph had been most closely associated with the Oratorians in their educational mission; the activist community, in addition to teaching, worked in hospitals and other social services. When they re-formed after the Revolution, they became diocesan communities, their normal schools aligned with and approved by the state. The Josephites' *Méthode d'enseignement pour les classes des soeurs de St-Joseph*, published in 1832, provides an extensive, step-by-step manual typical of other French teaching congregations (Frances 1936, 104). Although the Ursuline and Sacred Heart plans were influenced heavily by Jesuits, the three plans are similar in emphasis and in detailed instructions for teachers.

While teachers' personalities, location of schools, and numerous other factors necessarily influence curriculum, we might gain some understanding of the curriculum in the early schools of European-based communities by examining academy promotions, the congregations' constitutions, and their guides for teaching. These communities arrived with clearly outlined procedures for schools and those who administered them, carefully crafted plans of study with criteria for courses to be taught, daily schedules to be followed, and pedagogical practices to adhere to. The guidelines are helpful for understanding what was taught in the schools to a certain extent, as the communities intentionally established as much conformity as possible in order to accomplish the society's goals and to assure an effective, sequenced education.

In the United States, the Sacred Heart "plan of studies was inaugurated as far as possible from the very beginning. Modifications were made as required, but dispensed with whenever conditions warranted a closer adaptation of the plan" (Callan 1937, 747). The 1705 Ursuline *Règlements* continued to be the primary guide for Ursulines until 1860, when the nuns revised their manual. The Josephites, too, mandated conformity. Their constitutions required that they carefully follow the method adopted by the congregation for teaching (*Constitutions of the Sisters of St. Joseph* [1693] 1860, pt. 3, ch. 4, p. 65). In addition, "constant communication with the Mother House, the frequent arrival of recruits trained in France and, above all, the unswerving determination to preserve uniformity among the convents of the Society were factors which facilitated the transplantation of the system from Old to New World soil" (Callan 1937, 746).

In the early years of their settlement, the nuns in charge of education in the United States were also repeatedly instructed by their European superiors to make every effort to conform to community educational practices. For example, responding to the hardships the nuns in Missouri were facing, Madeleine Sophie Barat wrote Philippine Duchesne on 19 February 1820, "I understand perfectly, from the account you have given of your circumstances, that you cannot follow the Plan of Studies; you must do the best you can, and try to come in line with it as soon as you can" (1850, 1:204). Later, on 13 November 1821, Barat warned Eugenie Audé, head of a Louisiana school, "Sister Anna Murphy can work with you for the boarders, as she is well educated and has a good knowledge of English, but she might not follow the Society's plan of studies in her teaching, so you must guide her" (1:236–37). Therefore, we can assume that examination of extant sources such as constitutions and plans of studies, accompanied by promotions for schools, can help us to understand literacy practices in the schools of early European-based nuns.

Whereas American sisters slowly constructed their own guidelines with lived experience of their own culture, receptive to needs in their English-speaking country, the women religious who emigrated from Europe relied on curricula established for French girls, a very different population. These nuns faced the classroom armed with meticulously detailed and remarkably sequenced plans of studies. For example, the Ursulines' *Règlements* was nearly two hundred pages long. In addition to rules for the nuns and students and guidelines for conducting and managing the schools, the *Règlements* provide specific pedagogies for the teachers. Similarly, "The Method of Instruction" used by the early Sisters of St. Joseph in Missouri and Illinois "is a book of three hundred pages, a model course of study, with minute instructions regarding the matter to be taught and the manner of presenting each subject" (Savage 1923, 95–96). By contrast, the U.S.-founded Sisters of Loretto's *Rules of the Society and School of Loretto, Kentucky* contains thirty pages, the "Rules for the School" making up only six pages of the document. These rules applied generally to the operation of the school and who might attend rather than offered pedagogical guidelines.

The Ursuline *Règlements*, typical of guidelines for schools of the European-based communities, spells out, step-by-step, the teaching of writing, spelling, reading, arithmetic, manual training, and religion for young students. The detailed pedagogical treatment of these subjects may be seen in the method of teaching writing, covered in chapter 6 of part 1: Children should begin learning to write *o* and *i*, with the teacher watching carefully to assure proper formation of them. When they have mastered these letters, students continue with *a, w, u, m*, and *n*, followed by *b, d, l, f, g, h*, and *c*. Students proceed to new letters only after mastering the previous ones. They then learn to write two-letter combinations, short words without consonants, followed by longer words with consonants and, finally, lines or sentences. The teacher forms the model for students to duplicate, sometimes before class, sometimes during the allowed instruction period, and watches closely. The *Règlements* provides guidelines about where children should learn and practice writing (in the dining room at long tables, with small pieces of fabric to absorb ink when necessary), about their posture during writing (erect), and how they should hold pens (with three fingers only) (1705, 75–81).

Similarly, for spelling, which covers three sections of chapter 8 in part 1, children are taught in groups of eight or ten, each given a printed book and a sheet of white paper. Each works in her own book, correcting any misspellings by writing the corrected form above the misspelled word. The pupils write as the teacher dictates word for word, very clearly, two or three lines from the book. All students are asked to write the same passage again without seeing what they had written previously. The following day, they are asked to write the passage on a clean sheet of paper. When they can write that lesson correctly, they may advance to the next. Teachers are offered a second method for teaching spelling as well. In this way, they can adjust the method according to their own personalities or those of the children or vary the presentation as children improve:

> The pupils are furnished with an exercise book. The teacher reads from her book three or four lines which they write in their blank books. She then calls upon some one in the class to spell the words aloud, and each one corrects her own work. Then the teacher examines to see if they have done the work properly. The following day, she has them write on fresh paper the same passage in order to fix it in memory. (qtd. in Monica 1927, 381)

Other subjects are treated with similar detail. The specific instructions address those in the early stages of learning such areas as reading, writing, math, spelling, and grammar. This would have included those in the junior division of the academy as well as those in the day schools.

For academy students literate beyond the two-year basic program, the 1820 curriculum outlined by the Society of the Sacred Heart included "Christian Doctrine, chronology, mythology (abridged), grammar, spelling, elements of literature, sacred and profane history, geography and cosmography, arithmetic, needlework and accomplishments (drawing, painting, music and deportment), domestic economy and habits of order" (Callan 1937, 735). The efforts at thoroughness may be seen in instructions in the teaching of history: "The method of *resumé* is considered most advantageous, not only for the actual mastery of history, but for the several features included in the method itself: it teaches the pupils to express their ideas clearly, it gives purity, facility and fluency to their style, and it infallibly removes from them that awkward embarrassment which people never fail to experience who have not acquired the habit of writing" (qtd. in Callan 1937, 738). This pedagogical philosophy includes specific guidelines for implementation. Students keep a notebook exclusively for history. The teacher reads the day's lesson, asking questions, repeating the material, summarizing, and responding to questions. Later, during study time, each student writes a summary of the day's material in her own words. During the next history class, the teacher asks various students to read their summaries, assuring that the entire lesson has been covered. The teacher then points to any important information that has not been included, but she also addresses style, discussing any matters of incoherence or awkwardness. Each week, or at least monthly, the teacher collects the exercise books, examining and correcting for mistakes, with attention also to penmanship, spelling, and style (Callan 1937, 738–39).

Students at the upper levels did a great deal of writing, as was typical of nineteenth-century academies for women. Penmanship and grammar were practiced extensively at this level, as clarity was necessary for effective communication at a distance. In addition, both were important identity and class markers; middle- and upper-class women were partly identified by their penmanship, with expectations that they write clearly, correctly, and beautifully. Writing was thus also incorporated into subjects such as history, as outlined above. In addition, students wrote numerous compositions and letters. Such thoroughness is seen throughout the guidelines. In all subjects, teachers were reminded to assure students' understanding of the material before proceeding. At the end of each unit, the teacher was to determine students' command of the unit by review (both her review with them and their review of their exercise books) and an oral or written exam.

Proper etiquette, too, was stressed. Etiquette, sometimes referred to as politeness or courtesy, was a regular subject in academies of U.S.-based communities as well, and the general assumption of all seems to have been that definitions were concrete and universally accepted, needing little elaboration. The rules of etiquette clearly outline specific social expectations for women. For example, the Ursuline *Règlements* instructs teachers to

> give special attention in etiquette at table, helping the children to form habits acceptable in good society. They will give lessons in politeness and courtesy. They will watch over their pupils so that they may develop poise, good manners without affectation, a serene and pleasing face, a soft and moderate voice. They will correct children who are guilty of improper speech. At recreation they will train them

to delicacy and deference which make relations easy and agreeable. In a word, they will strive in all circumstances to form them in the delicate art of "savoir-faire" which religion makes perfect. (qtd. in Monica 1927, 78)

These guidelines for academy students clearly imposed societal expectations for white middle- to upper-class girls.

Religion in the Schools and Academies

European nuns migrating to the United States came well equipped for their mission educationally. They had received impressive schooling and training prior to their arrival in the New World, evident in the letters written by early members and in their constitutions, which explicitly outline expectations that entering members "must have a good education" (*Constitutions and Rules* [1800] 1890, 18).

Attention in their early years in the congregation, then, focused primarily on formation to a religious life, not on literacy acquisition, as was necessary for many of the native foundations. For example, on 15 August 1821, Duchesne wrote Barat in Amiens, "The novices are studying Rodriguez, the Catechism of Perseverance, and Sacred History" (qtd. in Callan 1957, 347). Whereas the novices in early U.S.-based convents focused much of their time on gaining literacy, knowledge about academic subjects, and pedagogic techniques, the European-based communities could devote their time almost completely to religious study and contemplation. As Mary O'Leary explains of the Sacred Heart nuns, "Intellectual work of an absorbing or of a purely secular character is not given to the novice until the second year of her training, and then for not more than three hours a day. The point of this restriction is to give freer scope for spiritual growth and to avoid distracting, by some passing interest, the mind intent upon the serious question of vocation" (1936, 152). Such study also helped to prepare future teachers for their schooling mission, as much of their teaching focused on religion. The *Catechism of Preservation* by Reverend Francis B. Jamison, subtitled *An Historical, Doctrinal, Moral, and Liturgical Exposition of the Catholic Religion*, provided extensive knowledge about the church's history and its position on every aspect nuns would need for teaching and answering questions about the Catholic religion. Their focus on sacred history would serve a similar purpose. Such study not only prepared the nuns with deep theological understanding of their faith but also confirmed the importance of their mission of Christian formation for girls and young women.

Greater emphasis seems to have been placed on religious instruction in academies operated by those immigrating with prepared and uniform curricula than in U.S.-based schools, at least initially and especially in primarily French-speaking communities. While constitutions of U.S. groups include Christian formation in their mandate, this goal was not the major focus of constitutions. Created under difficult material conditions and without the academic Jesuit communities who helped to shape teaching plans in Europe, the U.S. versions seem spare. Additionally, surrounded by Protestants and aware of some hostility to the Catholic religion, U.S. sisters may have consciously avoided extensive emphasis on extending their religion, but their focus was largely on providing education for girls, especially in areas where none existed. The intentions of seeking legal incorporation from a largely Protestant legislature may also have contributed to the focus of their constitutions. In addition, because they relied on tuition from Protestant students in their academies and promised not to proselytize, U.S. communities necessarily concentrated on other academic subjects, especially in academies.

Teaching communities in European countries, especially those whose cultures were overwhelmingly Catholic, such as the three permanent French communities established in the United States prior to 1840, were founded with the teaching focus largely on a Christian (Catholic) formation. For example, the Sacred Heart nuns were founded specifically to "rechristianize" French families after the French Revolution and to support the faith in opposition to the Protestant heresy, while the schools and teaching communities arising in the United States formed largely out of need to provide education for girls, especially in areas where none was available, and to dispel prejudice. This is not to suggest that U.S.-based groups had no purposes of proselytizing and conversion; however, the emphasis as curricula and pedagogies developed within a largely Protestant country necessarily differed from that in a primarily Catholic culture.

The constitutions of the European teaching groups in the early nineteenth century demonstrate the approach with which these women had prepared for teaching before coming to the United States. The Ursuline constitutions state explicitly, "The principal end and aim of Ursulines [is] the instruction of young girls in Christian piety, and becoming manners, in order to draw down the blessing of heaven" (*Constitutions of*

Ursuline Religious [1705] 1812, ch. 1, p. 3). This mandate surfaces throughout the constitutions:

> Although much time must be employed in teaching the children to read, write and work in a manner suitable to their sex and age, Ursulines must nevertheless remember that the Christian Doctrine and correct manners are the chief points to be alluded to. Let them keep simply to the text of the Catechism, without introducing any studied discourse or questions, repressing the curiosity of their pupils, in order to accustom them to treat divine things with respect, and to be humbly submissive to the simple truths of faith. (ch. 5, p. 6)

The constitutions of the Sisters of the Sacred Heart place similar emphasis:

> Religion should therefore be at once the foundation and the crowning point of the education they intend to give, and consequently the chief subject taught; the rest is only accessory, but yet necessary in its degree, since their object is to form those who, for the most part, are called to live in the world, which they should edify without offence, and whose customs they should know and follow in all that is not contrary to the rules of the Gospel. (*Constitutions and Rules* [1800] 1890, pt. 3, ch. 3, p. 85)

The same emphasis prevails in the rules of operation and curriculum. The Ursuline *Règlements*, the community rules for operating the schools, devotes the most extensive instructional guidelines to the teaching of religion. Approximately fifty of the nearly two hundred pages of instruction are dedicated to teaching catechism and preparing for communion, confession, and confirmation. And in addition to these, numerous pages relate to the celebration of feast days and other holy days. Guidelines for teaching catechism and religion receive more space than any other subject in the Sacred Heart plans of studies as well. And teachers are prodded to make the religious curriculum enticing. The Ursuline Règlements directs: "The teachers shall endeavor to make the catechism classes interesting and attractive so that the students will be pleased with them and will love religious instruction more than other subjects" (1705, pt. 1, ch. 5).

A considerable portion of the schedule in both the Ursuline and Sacred Heart guidebooks is given to religion, as well. The Sacred Heart inclusion of religion in its four more advanced classes proceeds as follows: the fourth class studies "the Gospel (a portion memorized daily), Diocesan Catechism explained (daily lesson memorized) and Bible History"; the second and third classes are taught "the Gospel, Catechism, Church History"; and the first class learns catechism. Callan explains, "Catechism, Bible History, the Gospel of the Sunday learned during the preceding week and, for the older children, *La Doctrine Chrétienne*, by [Charles François] Lhomond, were studied after explanations had been given at class." In addition, the syllabus prescribes "'every morning reading interspersed with comments, and in the afternoon two half hours devoted to religious instruction, the one entirely informal, mingled with questions, for the younger girls, the other more *advanced* in tone and matter, for the better instructed pupils'" (qtd. in Callan 1937, 736–37).

The daily schedule included religious activities aside from the academic classes that focused on religious subjects. The day began with a regimen of prayer followed by attendance at mass. Students recited litanies prior to dinner at 10:30 and listened to inspirational readings as they ate. Just after noon, they attended classes until 2:00, when they again prayed before a short period of recreation. From 3:00 to 5:00, classes focused primarily on catechism and prayers. Before retiring to sleep, students joined in prayer once more, prepared for bed, prayed, and examined their consciences. The emphasis on religion is demonstrated in letters and journals as well. Philippine Duchesne's journals also outline the many religious feast day celebrations in which the schools participated.

The *Méthode* of the Sisters of St. Joseph similarly addresses school details in this order:

1. The Entrance into School
2. The Beginning of Class
3. Prayers for Beginner and More Advanced
4. Manner of Learning and Reciting the Rosary, and on Confession
5. Recitation of Lessons
6. Teaching of the Special Subjects
    - a. Writing
    - b. Reading
    - c. Arithmetic
    - d. Orthography
    - e. Geography
    - f. Chant
    - g. Prayers
    - h. Catechism (Frances 1936, 104)

As in the Sacred Heart schools, much of the emphasis was on religious instruction.

The emphasis on religion surfaces in students' memoirs as well. Sacred Heart student Mary Ann Rourke wrote,

> The strongest point of the education was religious instruction. Those nuns spoke like priests. I can still remember an instruction in which the Mistress was trying to make us understand the pain of loss felt by the reprobate soul. She told us the story of the Babylonian Captivity—how the Jews hung up their harps by the rivers of Babylon and wept in thinking of their homes lost forever. The picture of homesickness was brought out in all its details as "worse than death," then applied to the homesickness of the soul for God when it is freed from the body. (qtd. in Callan 1957, 547)

The purpose of women religious in France had been to educate girls primarily in their religious and Christian piety. Although they offered a thorough general literacy as well, the primary focus was on religion.

Traditional Curriculum for Women

Academies overseen by European congregations appear to have been more traditional than those of their U.S. counterparts, especially in the early years and in those places where populations and students were primarily French. All academies focused on a strong basic literacy and academic subjects deemed important for the well-educated nineteenth-century woman, such as geography and history; however, emphasis elsewhere seems to reflect a culture different from that developing in the United States. Both the Ursulines and the Society of the Sacred Heart stressed their adaptation from the Ignatian *Ratio Studiorum* to that appropriate for females; while the male congregations emphasized the classics, the nuns adapted their curriculum to traditional expectations for girls.

In culturally French areas, the imported curriculum caused few problems; however "the imposition of a rigid French curriculum on American school children caused much dissatisfaction," and the curriculum gradually altered after "considerable discussion on both sides of the Atlantic" (Ewens 1981, 24). Cheryl A. Bodine-Reed claims that "the curriculum of the Sacred Heart nuns changed as conditions in France seemed to necessitate a fuller education for women, as public education positions became available to well-educated women from bourgeois and elite families"; according to Bodine-Reed, some changes came in the 1850s, but the most significant broadening of curricula came in the 1860s, as demonstrated in the Society's 1867 plan of study. That revision includes "no mention . . . of the Society's original aim involving the ReChristianization of French society" (2013, 36–37).

Before 1840, most U.S. schools of European-originated congregations held to a predominantly French traditional curriculum. As late as 1840, little evidence of a focus on science appears in the ads for academies of these congregations, especially those located in areas with relatively large French populations. As noted in the previous chapter, scholars have demonstrated the prevalence of science in women's academies in the nineteenth-century United States, especially in the more prestigious academies (Tolley 1996; Woody 1929, 2). In 1833 with the first national *Catholic Almanac*, the flagship schools of U.S.-based convents already demonstrated a focus on science. As noted in chapter 3, priests at nearby colleges had instructed many sisters in teaching such sciences as chemistry and permitted them to use their laboratories and science facilities. Visitation Academy in Georgetown had advertised a science focus at least as early as 1828. Such emphases remained and increased through the 1830s. By 1839, Nazareth Academy included "Botany, Natural Philosophy, Astronomy, Optics, [and] Chemistry" (*Metropolitan Catholic Almanac* 1839, 158) as curricular inclusions, and Loretto Academy advertised "Botany, Optics, and the Elements of Mechanics, Hydrostatics and Astronomy, Chemistry, and Natural Philosophy" (161). Curricular reports for the European congregations' schools, however, show a far more restricted emphasis on science in the academies, even by the end of the 1830s. The exception is the Ursuline Academy in New Orleans, where the nuns made "the elements of Natural Philosophy, of Botany and Chemistry" available "to those young ladies whose parents desire it" (165). This adjustment came late, however, and was not offered as part of the core curriculum. Mount Benedict, the ill-fated Ursuline academy begun by Irish nuns and located outside Boston, catered to non-French students and appears to have been more typical of U.S.-based academies.[5] In 1833, the promotion for that academy lists Blair's chemistry and philosophy for use in the lower classes; the senior class included astronomy, natural and moral philosophy, chemistry, chronology, arithmetic, geometry, and botany.

LITERACY IN CONVENT SCHOOLS

By 1834, the Sacred Heart's Philippine Duchesne acknowledged the lack of science in her schools. On 26 January she wrote, "I am entirely behind the times. Here one must now talk of advanced sciences, astronomy, chemistry, philosophy. But I am drawn to know nothing but Jesus as the subject matter of the one science necessary, and to seek Him in solitude" (qtd. in Callan 1957, 559).

The academies seem to have differed in emphasis on "feminine" decorative arts as well. For example, the U.S.-based Emmitsburg Sisters of Charity prospectus for 1833 promoted "Music, Drawing, Painting on Velvet, Embroidery, Plain and Fancy Needle-Work," and the Loretto Academy likewise offered "Plain Sewing, Marking and Ornamental Needle-work, Drawing, Painting in water colors, Fancy work and Embroidery" (*United States Catholic Almanac* 1833, 100). Evidence of students' impressive needlepoint and other needle projects survives in the archives of many of these U.S.-founded convents. However, the promotions for European-based academies placed much more emphasis on "accomplishments," decorative sewing, and crafts. Throughout the 1830s, the St. Louis Sacred Heart Academy listed "Sewing, Marking, Lace, Muslin, Tapestry and Bead work; Painting on Velvet and Satin, drawing, Painting in water colors and crayons; shell and chenille work. Artificial Flower making; Filagree, Hairwork and chrystallized Parlor Ornaments; Music, vocal and instrumental" (*United States Catholic Almanac* 1833, 103); this ad remained unchanged through 1839 (see also, for example, *Metropolitan Catholic Almanac* 1839, 145). The Ursulines' Mount Benedict Academy in Charlestown, Massachusetts, offered "every kind of useful and ornamental Needlework; Japaning; Drawing in all its varieties; Painting in Oil Colours; also, Painting on Velvet, Satin, and Wood; and the beautiful style of Mezzotinto and Poonah Painting" (*United States Catholic Almanac* 1833, 91). In the schools of the Sisters of St. Joseph, "handwork came next in importance after religion and reading" (Coburn and Smith 1999, 31). According to Carol K. Coburn and Martha Smith, handwork "was considered essential for all girls" in order to "'avoid the evils of idleness'" (31).[6] Aside from cultural expectations, the European nuns probably made use of arts in which they were greatly accomplished. For example, the Sisters of St. Joseph had long been identified with ribbon making and the making of fine lace in Europe and brought that tradition with them. The nuns understandably used their skills and felt comfortable with established teaching patterns. At the Sacred Heart academy, students "began by learning to knit and to stitch, and were taught gradually how to mend and make their own garments, as well as various articles of utility in the household. From work of this kind they passed on in the course of time to ornamental work, such as embroidery in muslin and silk, crocheting and the making of artificial flowers" (Keenan 1934, 13).

The European orders capitalized not only on their expertise in artistic needlework but also on their language and culture. Polished young American women were expected to read and speak French, and while all communities boasted the ability to teach French, often by a native speaker, those congregations whose numerous nuns' first language was French often offered a special enticement for students. At the Young Ladies' French and English Academy, established by Les Dames de la Retraite, a European group whose American community seems to have lasted just over a decade, "the course of instruction embraces the French and English Language, sacred and profane History, ancient and modern Geography, Mythology, and all the various kinds of Fancy and Ornamental Needle-work.... The French is exclusively the language of the house, except in the classes of English studies" (*Catholic Calendar* 1834, 76). Similarly, an early student at the Josephite Carondelet academy explained that she had come to the school because her mother "was anxious of my acquiring a French education in all the purity of the language" (Brouillet 1890–91; see also Byrne 1986, 250; and Coburn and Smith 1999, 50–52). And, according to Patricia Byrne, the "French character of St. Joseph's Academy attracted daughters of Southern planters until the Civil War" (1986, 250).

However, while language might have proven positive in some ways, it created problems for many. Les Dames de la Retraite's schools were short-lived, and language may have been a barrier for the women in charge of those schools, as they worked in English-speaking areas. The Sacred Heart sisters often acknowledged the problem created in English-speaking areas because their nuns were not fluent in English. On 28 August 1818, Duchesne explained to Barat that Americans' "national pride seems to make them scorn those who do not speak their language, so English is a real necessity" (qtd. in Callan 1957, 302). Later, on 2 January 1820, she would write Father Louis Barat,

> English is a very difficult language. I do not speak it, nor can I understand it yet. Mother Eugenie stammers out a little, and Mother Octavie speaks it badly and will never be able to teach it, so Monseigneur thinks, because of the extreme difficulty of the pronunciation and the

very delicate ear needed for speaking it. But all the parents require the study of this language, and we have no nun to teach it. Mother Octavie is aided by an American pupil. Pray that God may destine her for our Society. Her innocence of soul and natural disposition would make her an outstanding subject and just the kind we need for teaching English. (318)

Class in the Convents and Schools

European congregations had come initially into areas with settlers united by their European roots, accustomed to the traditions of the old country. The congregations had been formed within a culture delineated much more formally by class than the one they met with in the United States. Their convents were often founded with large endowments and with members of the well-to-do among the "choir," who provided a substantial dowry upon entering; "lay" nuns, from lower economic classes, were expected to assume the manual labor for those in the choir. Such structures differed from that of U.S. foundations, who more typically declared that new members "are to be received *gratis*, having with them the religious dresses and bedding. A free gift, as an alms, may be accepted, but no stipulation made" (*Rules of the Society* 1820, 5). U.S. communities had no formal delineation based on class among members; however, the practice among European congregations was deeply embedded. As Emily Clark has pointed out, the New Orleans Ursulines retained the distinction between choir and lay nuns even after acquiring slaves to do domestic work, demonstrating "a social conservatism that indicated an individual's role in the community according to family wealth, occupation, and perhaps race" (1998, 60). According to Margaret Susan Thompson, "Communities often found it difficult to attract native-born candidates to the lay ranks, and eventually found it necessary to recruit them from provinces outside the United States" (1987, 16). The nuns in these congregations often promoted their academies as devoted "particularly to the polite education of young ladies" (*Metropolitan* 1839, 144), something most often aspired to or available to the affluent.

U.S. bishops with a European background clearly thought of these communities in terms of class. For example, Irish-born John England, who helped to found the Charleston, South Carolina, Sisters of Mercy to educate and conduct works of mercy among those in his diocese, nonetheless continued to urge the Irish Ursulines to come to his parish. Having finally convinced the Ursulines to do so, he removed the Sisters of Mercy from academy work, relegating them to works of mercy and day schools, and installed the Ursulines as teachers of the girls' academy; he repeatedly praised the Ursuline academy as "one of the best schools for the education of young ladies in the useful and ornamental acquirements that befit those of their sex who are to decorate the most polished circles of society and in those virtues which win the esteem of man and secure the approbation of Heaven" (qtd. in Guilday 1969, 2:157; see also 1:527–28).

England's notions were not unfounded, as communities did prioritize according to class. For example, the constitutions of the religious of the Sacred Heart specify as the community's primary educational purpose the "foundation of boarding schools for the upper classes," with schools for the poor whenever feasible (Callan 1937, 733). The attitude toward class can often be seen in the differing curriculum and treatment of boarders and day scholars. For example, needlework would have been essential for women of all classes, but day scholars were taught sewing skills for their own use and for possible employment, while boarders were expected to demonstrate their skills in both basic sewing and a variety of decorative projects. The well-to-do daughters were often expected to create artistic sewing for display in their homes and to participate in "the making of clothes for the poor and of altar linen and vestments" (742).

This attitude played out in the different presumptions about the academies and day schools. While the Sacred Heart constitutions insisted that members should "consider as a favour and as an enviable mark of preference, the choice made of them to labour" among the poor (*Constitutions and Rules* [1800] 1890, 102), typical nineteenth-century attitudes toward class and the poor are unmistakable. The Sacred Heart constitutions stated explicitly the aim of the day schools in terms of expectations:

> As the eternal and spiritual good of their souls is the object aimed at, the utmost endeavor shall be made to teach them the Catechism well, and to give them on the truths and duties of religion all the instruction suited to their age, capacity and station. They shall be taught to know the excellence and merit of poverty, and learn how to sanctify it by an esteem and love of it, based upon the sentiments and example of Jesus Christ. (101)

LITERACY IN CONVENT SCHOOLS

This difference is also seen in the attitude toward manual labor. Whereas girls in the boarding schools were expected to help fold laundry, those in the day schools were required to do manual work "during part of the class hours, to protect them early from the dangers of idleness and later on to procure them means of subsistence and of gaining a suitable and respectable livelihood" (*Constitutions and Rules* [1800] 1890, 101). Other differences appear in the curriculum. In the free schools, "pupils, divided into three groups, or classes, were taught the elements of reading, writing, spelling, grammar, arithmetic and sewing, along with Christian Doctrine, which was considered the essential branch. They were prepared for the reception of the sacraments and trained to habits of Christian virtue. Hymns and prayers learned at school enabled them to take part in the services of the Church. In the early days the monitorial system was followed in Missouri" (Callan 1937, 746). Monitorial and similar systems allowed the nuns to assure instruction to large numbers of children in the day schools, but the academy students saw a much smaller teacher-student ratio and greater care to individual attention.

A similar system was used by the Ursulines, The *Règlements* outlines clearly the duties of the student monitor, called a *dixainiere*, as students were broken into groups of ten with a *dixainiere* at the head of each. As Mary Ellen Keenan has pointed out, the system was very much like the Lancastrian system introduced in the United States a century later (1934, 13). The *dixainiere*, chosen for her "excellence," distributed books and generally kept order among students in her group, reporting infractions to the teacher in charge. She also posed catechetical questions and monitored replies for accuracy. As with the Sacred Heart nuns, this system was used in the day schools. In the academies, where parents expected special treatment and more sophisticated learning for the children for whom they were paying handsome tuitions, the nuns acted as teachers for all, and the student-teacher ratio was much smaller.

The day schools were rigidly regulated. The supervisor in charge took responsibility for the general running of the school. She also monitored who entered and left the school and how they did so. During school hours students circulated promptly among classrooms and teachers, for catechism and religious instruction by the primary classroom teacher and for reading, arithmetic, writing, and needlework by others. In all schools, religion was assigned to the primary teacher because of its importance.

Books and Teaching Materials

The procurement of teaching materials may have been even more difficult in the European-based communities than in the U.S. groups. In the early U.S.-based communities, male religious mentors often assumed ownership of communities as founders and made every effort not only to help educate the early sisters but also to obtain teaching materials for them. For example, Reverend Charles Nerinckx donated his library to the Sisters of Loretto, and in trips to Europe he obtained maps, globes, and other up-to-date materials for their use. The Sisters of the Sacred Heart often received some assistance from their European motherhouse, but the European communities struggled to make even essentials available to their American missions. American clerics, who did not consider themselves founders, also believed the European nuns already prepared to teach and, therefore, less in need of their help; they, then, appear to have focused more on other projects.

The schoolbook problem was a serious one for European religious communities in America, for they could find few substitutes for the books listed in the French syllabus. Efforts by the European motherhouses helped to a certain extent, but distance made assistance difficult. The Sacred Heart's Madeleine Sophie Barat sent a major shipment to the Missouri mission in 1819, including "clothing, an assortment of writing paper for letters and classroom use and of colored paper for the manufacture of the highly prized flowers, books, seeds, and, last and largest, the piano—to delight, and at times nearly to madden, all who dwelt in the convent" (Callan 1957, 319). The piano was a major contribution toward the music department, and the nuns were grateful for other classroom materials and books; however, shipments did not come often, and such shipments might help very little because of the expense entailed, as seen in a later letter from Barat to Duchesne. On 9 July 1819, she wrote, "Any time now, a case is being sent off from Amiens, containing a roll of black material, books, globes, and various other articles which you will find listed in the inventory. Every house wants to send you things, but we are afraid of sending what will cost higher customs' duty than their own value" (1850, 1:180).

Eugenie Audé left the Missouri convent to open a convent and school in Louisiana on 4 August 1821. One week later, Duchesne wrote to Barat that she had packed for Audé "all that could be spared, and much that could not . . . into boxes and satchels" (qtd. in Callan 1957, 346). On 15 August, she explained that "as to books, she took all the duplicates we had, a copy of the Constitution, and one of each of the books and note-books we use in the classes. She will have copies made, just as we have had the novices and pupils do here" (347).

The already overworked nuns spent long hours in translating and copying the texts that came from France. New recruits were highly prized, but Duchesne often had to produce much of the reading expected of them:

> As I could not get an orthodox abridgement of Sacred History, I made one from a large Catholic Bible, English translation, and the novices are copying this and learning it by heart. I also translated or summarized from English books the history of America and Roman history, and I made an outline of Ancient history. All this has furnished material for teaching the classes.... We have had to make copies of the arithmetic and geography books in use in this country, printed in English. I hope you approve of these methods—books are so scarce and the children cannot buy them—no one has any money. (qtd. in Callan 1957, 348)

The nuns often resorted to "resumés and dictation, the children's exercise books frequently serving as their only textbooks in some subjects." After 1840 the Society used standard American schoolbooks in Missouri and eastern states (Callan 1937, 747–48).[7]

The Ursuline convent outside Boston, taught primarily by English-speaking nuns for English-speaking students, also used standard American texts. The 1833 *United States Catholic Almanac* lists its texts for the junior division as follows: "Walker's Dictionary, Murray's Grammar and Exercises, Woodbridge's Geography and Atlas, Tyler's History, Questions to do, Goodrich's History of the United States, Polite Learning, Smith's Arithmetic, Tooke's Pantheon, Jamieson's Rhetoric and Logic, and Questions to do, Blair's Chemistry and philosophy, and McIntire on the Globes" (94). The senior class used "Rollin's Ancient History, Ferguson's Roman Republic, Russell's Ancient Europe, Russell's Modern Europe, Robertson's Works, and History of the United States by Ramsau and Marshall" in addition to books for French, Latin, Spanish, and Italian (94).[8]

Literacy with a Special Focus

Most members of European communities had come to the United States with the dream of teaching American Indians and sometimes the enslaved.

Both groups were exotic to Europeans and deemed ripe for Christianizing. But, once settled in the United States, few of the original members spent their lives in this way. Later, numerous religious communities would create teaching missions among the Indians, but in the early decades of the nineteenth century, the needs of European American parishioners kept the nuns occupied primarily among these groups. As will be seen in chapter 5, some nuns did create schools for African Americans, but political pressure often made these short-lived. The Ursulines had included Indian girls in their Quebec boarding school and free women of mixed race in their New Orleans schools and academies, but enslaved children were more often catechized than taught reading and writing, especially where laws mandated an exclusion of literacy for the enslaved and free African Americans. The Sisters of Mercy began a school for African Americans in Charleston in 1835, but opposition from clergy of other religions led to its closure. In addition, the Sisters of St. Joseph began an antebellum (1845) school for African Americans in St. Louis, but this, too, closed at the request of the bishop and mayor after repeated threats and mobs surrounding the convent (Coburn and Smith 1999, 53–54; Dougherty et al. 1966, 123). In both cases, the sisters were allowed to continue teaching religion but without the benefit of literacy instruction.

The nuns opened schools for other specific purposes in the early nineteenth-century United States. One of the most notable with regard to literacy, St. Joseph Institute for the Deaf, continues its mission today. When seeking nuns from Europe for his St. Louis diocese, Bishop Joseph Rosati had specifically requested that nuns open a school for the deaf. In 1836, six religious of St. Joseph arrived and opened schools and academies for girls in Carondelet, outside St. Louis, and in Cahokia, Illinois. The following year, two nuns who had studied methods for teaching the deaf with the Sisters of St. Charles in France joined the original nuns. They brought with them a copy of Charles-Michel, Abbé de l'Épée's instruction manual for teaching the deaf, *La Véritable Maniere d'Instruire les Sourds et Muets*. The Abbé de l'Épée, an internationally known teacher of sign language, had developed his system based on his observations among members of a deaf community. He subsequently opened schools for teaching the deaf across France, where the St. Joseph teachers of the deaf had been educated. As the Abbé de l'Épée's was the system used across France in the early nineteenth century, and because the early nuns brought with them a copy of his book, we may assume the nuns primarily used de l'Épée's method when teaching the hearing impaired.

It is also safe to assume that most early literacy efforts involving the deaf in the United States used this method, as not only did the Carondelet school use it but most other early successful schools for the deaf did so as well. For example, Thomas Hopkins Gallaudet, who has become synonymous with deaf education in the United States, had traveled to de l'Épée's Paris school to prepare for instructing the deaf. He returned with Laurent Clerc, one of the French teachers from de l'Épée's school. Gallaudet and Clerc founded the first permanent school for the deaf in the United States in Hartford, Connecticut, in 1817; the school served most of New England, and Gallaudet and Clerc often shared their knowledge with others in the region who were interested in providing education for the deaf (Best 1943, 390–93). The Josephites created the Carondelet school, where they taught numerous students from the South and Midwest in addition to assisting other communities of women religious in opening schools for the deaf. This method was clearly the most used in the United States in the first half of the century. The de l'Épée text, then, provides one way of understanding how instruction was provided for deaf students in the early nineteenth-century United States.

Although de l'Épée was best known for his development of the manual sign system that he implemented in his schools, his book includes instruction for both manual and oral methods: part 1 for teaching manual sign language and part 2 for teaching oral speech. Both parts provide the detailed step-by-step methodology typical of the religious communities' early pedagogical guides for teachers and assume a reading knowledge on the part of students. The narrative that has come to be accepted in the St. Joseph community is that the early nuns taught manual sign language and introduced the oral method much later, so it is unclear if nuns taught both methods in the early days.

The following example from a section titled "On the Articles and the Signs that Agree with Them" illustrates the detailed instruction for teaching students to recognize articles and various iterations to convey number and gender manually:

> Here is the way we proceed with this article. We make the Deaf and Dumb observe the joints of our fingers, our hands, the wrist, the elbow, etc., etc., and we name them articles or joints. We then write on the table that le, la, les, de, du, des join the words the way our articles join our bones (grammarians will excuse us if this definition does

not agree with theirs), from then the movement of the right index, which extends and recoils several times forming a hook, becomes the rational sign we give to all articles. We express gender by putting the hand to the hat for the masculine article le and to the ear where the coiffure of a woman ends for the feminine article la. The plural article les is expressed by the repeated movement of the four fingers of one or two hands forming a hook. The apostrophe is indicated by making an apostrophe in the air with the right index finger. It is necessary to add the sign of the masculine if the apostrophe is followed by a masculine substantive, and on the contrary the feminine sign if the substantive which follows is a feminine noun. (de l'Épée 1794, 14–16)

The text devotes 154 pages to a detailed, systematic manual display of the language. Similarly, part 2 explains step-by-step teaching of spoken language. For example,

> I write it and I pronounce forcefully cha pointing out to the Deaf and Dumb the face that we all make naturally when we strongly pronounce this word in order to scare a cat [*chat* in French], then I put his finger in my mouth and I make him notice 1. the strong impetus I give to the air in pronouncing this syllable, as is the case when pronouncing the letter s; 2. that the middle of my tongue nearly touches my palate; 3. that it [the tongue] extends and strikes my molars; 4. that it leaves enough room for the air to directly exit my mouth so it is not forced to descend perpendicularly, as it does when I pronounce the letter s. The Deaf and Dumb perceives very clearly the difference because when he puts his hand in front of my mouth, the air begins to strike it directly as I pronounce the syllable cha. I then put my finger in his mouth and, as I make him do what I myself have done, he pronounces cha and then ché, chi, cho, chu, but after some more or less long time, he always comes back to sa, sé, si so, su if he himself does not have his finger in his mouth to direct the movement of his tongue. It is only by habit that he will learn to do without this trick. (179–80)

As was typical of instruction in the schools of European-based congregations, the script presents a meticulously outlined procedure that reduces confusion about how to proceed and likely created uniformity in the various schools for the deaf.

The Sisters of St. Joseph found a successful and appreciated teaching mission in their work with the hearing impaired. They also became important in nursing and hospitals, as they had been in France. The Josephites continued to establish successful schools and academies for hearing students as well. The St. Joseph Institute for the Deaf continues in operation today, a highly respected educational academy for the hearing impaired.

Difficult Transition

Many of the European women religious migrating from a more affluent society with uniform religious and moral codes suffered from unfulfilled expectations and material hardships. They were unprepared for the many differences they would experience in America. Paschala Noonan has pointed out the advantages for U.S.-born sisters: "The language and customs of the country were their own. As American Catholics, they had already weathered the prejudices which cropped up periodically because of their religion. They were at ease with the practice of laity assuming responsibility for preserving the faith when the clergy were not available. They were imbued with a spirit of freedom and independence, and (for those in the West) even the youngest accepted austerities of frontier life" (1997, 31). Because they came with a good education, prepared to teach, those migrating from Europe held an advantage over many of the early members of U.S. foundations in that respect. However, for European nuns, especially those settling outside French cultures, their inexperience in all of the factors mentioned by Noonan created difficulties.

The dire poverty the nuns faced in Missouri was relieved, somewhat, by shipments of food from the New Orleans Ursulines, by school materials sent from France, and in later years by their more successful convents and academies in Louisiana. Their poverty complicated the problems they suffered from a lack of "lay" members, however, to whom they had been accustomed in France, who could relieve the "choir" nuns from domestic and manual labor in order that they might focus on teaching. In September 1825, Duchesne wrote Barat:

> The religious most essential to the good of this house is Sister Regis Hamilton. She has to take on all the heaviest and most unpleasant employments, one after another, because she is so solidly virtuous and courageous. But she is greatly needed for the classes, being the only

> one having a good English pronunciation—a thing so highly prized here that nothing else is considered comparable to it. What I tell you is true of the other houses and may prove to you, notwithstanding Monseigneur Du Bourg's opinion, that good coadjutrix Sisters, well trained and courageous, humble and ready to supervise the kitchen, would be quite as useful to us as choir nuns and would give the latter a chance to devote their time to the classes. (qtd. in Callan 1957, 426)

As seems typical of Louis DuBourg, he had few concerns for the teachers' heavy burdens added to full-time teaching, but Duchesne makes numerous references to the hardships this placed on teaching choir nuns.

Language and cultural differences also made life even more difficult for those who settled in English-speaking areas with large numbers of Protestants. The three communities who make up the majority of material for this chapter were ultimately successful in their mission; however, French nuns who settled in French-speaking areas found greater comfort and easier success in their new communities. Even the English-speaking Ursulines, who built their convent and academy outside Boston, found great success with parents and students in a mostly Protestant area. However, for non-English-speaking nuns who settled in English-speaking areas, language differences continued to create problems. They had trouble understanding and speaking English, but even American French speakers gave some pause. Callan explains that "their conversation, spiced with gay repartee, reminded Philippine [Duchesne] of happy gatherings she had known in distant Grenoble, but their French, though quite correct, was spoken with a somewhat languid drawl and often interspersed with expressions borrowed from Spanish or English, which she did not always understand" (1957, 260). Duchesne would suffer because of her difficulty with English most of her life.

Cultural differences also created problems for those coming from a Catholic background. Nuns had to contend with what some saw as a lack of religious fervor and problematic mixing of religions. On 20 December 1835, Duchesne expressed such a concern to Barat: "The academy in St. Louis is not increasing in numbers and the pupils give the religious much cause for anxiety on account of the impiety and ingratitude of some of the non-Catholic girls, and the inconstancy of the parents who withdraw their children just when the religious are hopeful of good results" (qtd. in Callan 1957, 585). In October 1818, she had seemed stunned that some of her students "have never heard of our Lord, of His birth or His death, nor of hell, and they listen open-mouthed to our instructions. I have to say to them continually, 'Yes this is really true'" (278). The nuns teaching outside traditionally French areas seemed bewildered at the lack of knowledge and reverence for what were Christian commonplaces in France and that the same degree of respect they were afforded in their native country did not materialize in their adopted home, especially where Protestants were numerous. But the concern seems to have included schools in which Catholics were a majority. Although the schools in French Louisiana flourished quickly, Duchesne worried about the many Protestant students in those schools as well. From Grand Coteau in January 1830, she wrote, "I am ashamed to say it, but one does not dare to speak to them of God. The study of the catechism is not insisted upon, through fear of losing pupils.... To tell you the truth, the mixture of religions produces an indifference that is deplorable" (503). Many American Protestants would have been surprised at the ignorance of Christian knowledge, also finding it deplorable, but Protestants would have had a very different context for perceiving such indifference from what the European nuns' mission afforded them.

On the other hand, Duchesne constantly reevaluated her opinions in her efforts to be fair and compassionate. In September 1821, she wrote Barat concerning young women who were considering a religious life:

> Girls are free in this country at the age of eighteen . . . and at eleven or twelve out here they are as well developed in body and soul as are those in France at fourteen years. Thinking over the obligation I have of helping my religious daughters in every way, I have sometimes judged myself blameworthy in not urging them more to use holy practices of penance. But when I see these children of fifteen and sixteen years baking bread, milking cows, cleaning the dormitory, doing the cooking, and having at most only one community recreation period a day because they help in the parish school, I am afraid of killing them if I add anything more. It seems to me the corporal penances can be introduced later on, when the work is divided among a larger number and when their physical strength is more robust. (qtd. in Callan 1957, 351–52)

In supervising those of such a vastly different culture, Duchesne repeatedly struggled as to how much of her French expectations were appropriate.

Language and religious expectations were not the only problems for Duchesne. She found morals in her new home scandalous, telling Barat in

1818 of the "conduct comparable to pagan bacchanalia: girls scantily clad, holding a bottle of whiskey in one hand and a man with the other, dancing every day of the year and never doing any work," and she spoke of "problems because of the independent and restless spirit of the people" (qtd. in Callan 1957, 277). As late as 1830, twelve years after her arrival, Duchesne admitted to Barat, "I can never deal easily with the parents of our children. The Americans do not understand me" (523).

European communities also faced difficulties with ecclesiastical superiors. Promises that enticed them to the United States were often broken. The Poor Clares opened convents and schools in the early part of the century in Cincinnati, Pittsburgh, and Detroit, but disputes with ecclesiastical superiors led them to close those schools. The Ursuline nuns had come to New Orleans expecting to convert Indians and enslaved peoples but worked primarily among Creoles. The Sacred Heart nuns had expected to work with Indians. Duchesne's life-long dream had been to work among the Indians. Even as she arrived in New Orleans, she began to worry that Bishop Louis DuBourg's intentions had been different from the promises he had made to lure the nuns to his diocese. DuBourg, in order to entice the nuns, "had stressed the need of missionaries to bring the light of the gospel to the savage natives of America" (Callan 1957, 267), but that did not happen. Eventually, long after DuBourg's tenure, the nuns would open missions to the Indians, but Duchesne was seventy-two years old by that time. Although she traveled to the Indian mission and finally realized her dream for a few months, her European superior, Madeleine Sophie Barat, concerned for the hard life for her among the Indians at her advanced age, ordered her back to Missouri to complete her life among European Americans.

Additionally, DuBourg's promise that the nuns would locate in St. Louis was broken. Despite protests from the nuns and from many in the St. Louis community, DuBourg decided they would locate in St. Charles, Missouri, a small outpost without the population necessary to financially sustain the academy the nuns would open. In an October 1818 letter to Barat, Duchesne called it "the remotest village in the United States," one "frequented only by those trading with the Indians, who live not very far away from here" (qtd. in Callan 1957, 277). DuBourg had also taken charge of 7,000 francs the nuns had intended for necessities upon their arrival in the United States but retained the money. Duchesne wrote to Barat in November 1818, "Among all the things we shall need and those I have already asked for, the essentials are such as may keep us alive, as here on earth the soul depends on the body.

LITERACY IN CONVENT SCHOOLS

... We look on potatoes and cabbage as you in France regard rare delicacies. There is no market. The gift of a pound of butter and a dozen eggs is like a fortune received" (qtd. in Callan 1957, 280). But DuBourg refused the nuns their own money. On the other hand, DuBourg's replacement, Joseph Rosati, was extremely supportive of the religious women in his diocese, including the Sacred Heart nuns and the Sisters of St. Joseph, helping them as much as possible, even at his own expense.

Yet, many French women saw advantages to joining the missionary efforts in the New World. Few single women outside convent life would have had access to the adventure and personal fulfillment these women found in their travels to the United States. The incentive for the earliest European religious who had come to the New World seems to have been not only an assurance of their own salvation but also adventure and spiritual reward for converting Indians and enslaved peoples. As Emily Clark notes, their letters teem with "adventure and the exotic from a perspective rare in eighteenth-century sources" (1999, 2). Such excitement is even more rare in an eighteenth-century woman's writing, and early nineteenth-century women read the accounts of earlier missionaries and sought the same experiences. For example, in letters to her father, Marie Madeleine Hachard includes accounts of the great excitement as the nuns traveled from city to city across France to reach their departure ship: "The whole city was at the door of our inn to see us board the coach. It was raining very hard, but this did not prevent the people from being on the street from five in the morning until eight, waiting for us," and at the next location, "all the people of the city were there to see us depart." Her pride is clear: "Perhaps you will not believe that your daughter would one day incite the curiosity of entire cities" (qtd. in Clark 2007, 20). The adventure continued during the nuns' Atlantic voyage, when corsair ships menaced the nuns' vessel (53–54), when they dined in "an exquisite French manner" with the governor during a stop in St. Domingue (55–56), when they were introduced to "Monsieurs Mosquitos" (56), and, after her arrival in New Orleans, when instructing "the blacks and savages" (74). Such celebrity, such mysterious and exotic experiences, would have been completely impossible for most French women. This tradition continued into the nineteenth century, with missionaries' letters circulating across France and the models created by such early women missionaries as Marie Guyart and Hachard fueling wishes of other young women to follow in the missionary work of New France.

Despite their hardships, all three European-based communities gained new members, and their material circumstances gradually improved. After 1840, these three communities slowly adjusted their school curricula to include instruction more typical of schools belonging to U.S.-based communities, adding more science classes, for example. The Sacred Heart's St. Louis academy included "elements of astronomy, chemistry, and botany; and Natural Philosophy" as part of its 1844 core curriculum (*Metropolitan Catholic Almanac* 1844, 104). By the 1840s and 1850s, all three communities were gaining sufficient American-born recruits to solve the language problem and help to assuage the cultural differences. Despite early difficulties, all three of these communities, who founded communities in the young United States prior to 1840, continue their convents and academies today.

5.
Literacy, Benevolence, and the Paradox of Good Works

Catholic sisters in the nineteenth-century United States dispelled some of the prejudicial attitudes and treatment directed at their religious communities and their religion through a performative rhetoric of good works that helped to change the conversation surrounding them from sexual innuendo, violence, and corruption of important nineteenth-century domestic ideals to an appreciation for the sisters' civic involvement.[1] Many of the sisters, nonetheless, held their own prejudicial attitudes in a country rife with bigoted outlooks related to religion, gender, and race. This chapter examines the many efforts of Catholic women religious to provide aid and comfort to others—especially as educators, nurses during outbreaks of disease and war, and caregivers for orphans—and places the sisters' work alongside another major benevolent effort, the antislavery movement, to highlight the complexity of benevolent workings and attitudes, especially with regard to literacy. The nineteenth century roiled with contentious issues, many that we have accepted in fairly simplistic terms, much as we have accepted the Protestant literacy myth. However, reality is often much more complex than the easy narratives we construct.

The primary purposes of most of the religious communities were spiritual, educational, and benevolent, but the sisters clearly believed their service to education could make a difference in prejudicial attitudes, reducing the hostility to Catholics and to their religion. For example, the initial paragraph of the *Rules of the Society and School of Loretto, Kentucky* gives the "Intention of the Institute":

> The glory of God and the attainment of one's personal sanctification is the primary and essential purpose of the Society: but the special object must never be lost sight of by those belonging to this Society

which is to devote one's self completely to the education of females and implanting in them the principles of our holy religion instilling in the minds and hearts of Catholics entrusted to our care its teachings and leading their conduct to virtue but, in the case of Protestants committed to us, removing the prejudices that may have been instilled in them against our religion. (1820, 1)

Their ecclesiastic superiors often acknowledged the effectiveness of the sisters' educational mission in reducing prejudice. In 1813, the Reverend Charles Nerinckx wrote the Propaganda Fide concerning the Sisters of Loretto:

During their first year, if I mistake not, [the sisters] have gathered abundant fruit into the barns of the Householder so that there is hope for much fruit in the years to come, especially since non-Catholics are not excluded from the school provided they voluntarily agree to abide by the rules. Various young ladies take advantage of this. *Consequently their prejudices are either destroyed or lost and they either become less hostile to the true religion or they actually favor it.* (qtd. in Wolff 1982, 2; emphasis added)

Similarly, in an 1832 letter to Archbishop James Whitfield, Bishop John England extolled the virtues of the Ursuline sisters for his Charleston diocese:

Their parents are greatly desirous of obtaining the best and most complete opportunities for their instruction. Though for the most part Protestant, they hold in great esteem the qualifications of these nuns, and I am sure that they will confide their children to them; and thus their prejudices will be removed and many conversions will follow; or at least the way will be opened through the good ladies educated by the nuns to exercise a very powerful influence on the whole mass of society. (qtd. in Guilday 1969, 1:527)

And in their "Report in Summary of the Establishment of the Sisters of Charity in Kentucky, United States of America," Bishops Benedict Joseph Flaget and Jean Baptiste David wrote, "The principal effect of all these means is to make [the boarders] lose entirely the prejudices that they have shared against the Catholic religion. Later, they defend it in their families, showing in themselves the falsity of all the charges against it" (1814, 5).

The sisters may have dispelled some prejudice among those in their schools, as demonstrated by students' diaries and memoirs. However, those attending the sisters' schools, by virtue of the fact that their parents allowed them to attend, would not have been among the most hostile to the sisters and their religion. As seen in chapter 2, Protestant ministers and the print media more likely promoted, rather than dispelled, prejudicial attitudes, often by capitalizing on fear of the growing number of Catholic institutions. But some newspapers highlighted the more positive educational features of the sisters' schools. For example, in 1838, the *Christian Register and Boston Observer* ran a series of articles titled "Spread of Catholics in the United States." The newspaper devoted two columns to "Female Religious Orders," providing a factual account of the communities of Catholic women religious in North America with a somewhat positive perspective, noting that "they instruct [poor families] gratis" and that "they receive and instruct orphans and have a school for unfortunate children . . . the number of which is enormous" ("Spread of Catholics No. 12" 1836, 1). The columns outlined the sisters' many schools that taught orphans, emphasizing the hundreds of poor children who benefited. While the *Christian Register* "believe[d] that there are great faults essentially connected with and incidental to their institutions," it nevertheless held that "nobler objects than these cannot be contemplated by the human mind; holier offices cannot be performed by the followers of Christ" ("Spread of Catholics No. 11" 1836, 1). Although the sisters got some good press in Protestant periodicals for their teaching, positive accounts usually surfaced in newspapers such as the *Christian Register*, a Unitarian newspaper whose subscribers were likely more tolerant of Catholics than other Protestant sects. References to the sisters' schools more often came from rigidly anti-Catholic periodicals, such as the *Cincinnati Journal*, which warned Protestant parents not to send their children to Catholic schools as "there is no end to the wiles of Jesuits" ("Designs of the Papists" 1831, 1).

The Cholera Years

The sisters also engaged in other works of benevolence, especially during times of great need; such work brought them into contact with those outside the convents, lessening secrecy and often promoting goodwill for them among Protestants. Early in the century, the sisters became acknowledged for their works of mercy on behalf of the diseased, especially during the cholera epidemic that swept the country. Charles F. Rosenberg calls cholera "the classic epidemic disease of the nineteenth century, as plague had been of the fourteenth" (1962, 1). Historically a disease confined primarily to India and its vicinity, cholera became in the nineteenth century a recurring pandemic. Arriving on the North American continent initially in the early 1830s, cholera produced two other major outbreaks in the United States, one in 1848 and another in 1866. Its sudden onset and gruesome symptoms instilled widespread fear. Newspapers reported, often in extras as well as in regular editions, the alarming progress of the disease and its grisly symptoms, which included "diarrhea, acute spasmodic vomiting, and painful cramps" with subsequent dehydration that left the victim's face "blue and pinched, his extremities cold and darkened, the skin of his hands and feet drawn and puckered" (Rosenberg 1962, 2–3). The disease often advanced rapidly, destroying its victim within days or even hours of initial symptoms. The fear instilled by the disease caused many who could to flee infected areas. Little help was offered victims. Anxiety about contagion was so great that it became "impossible to rent even the meanest sort of building for use as a cholera hospital. It was equally difficult to hire nurses to work in them" (Rosenberg 1962, 82). Thus, in major cities where the need for hospitals to care for cholera patients was so great, only the hospitals run by Catholic sisters provided established institutions with experienced personnel to treat victims (95, 119n44). In rural areas, sisters often entered the homes of cholera patients to relieve their suffering.

Under these circumstances, when the sisters went into their communities to care for the sick and dying, even as others fled or refused to help for fear of contamination, local and national newspapers praised the sisters' work, noting their self-sacrifice for those whom others had abandoned. Even Protestants normally disparaging of all things associated with Catholicism expressed admiration for the sisters' work. The *Alexandria (Virginia) Gazette* commended the sisters who came forward when "a sufficient number could not be found possessing courage enough to assist in burying the dead" and, nonetheless, "hastened to relieve the sufferers, and laboured assiduously, night and day, in alleviating their distresses" ("Cholera" 1833a).

As newspapers reported progress of the disease, they often also followed the sisters' movements. For example, the *Niles Weekly Register* of Baltimore, an influential publication nationally, reported,

> We understand fourteen of the sisters of charity, from St. Joseph's nunnery in Emmitsburg, passed through Baltimore last week on their way

to Philadelphia, whither they have gone for the purpose of attending the sick in the present season of affliction Shou and distress in that city produced by the cholera. Such a display of sympathy for the afflicted, and of a disposition to endeavor to relieve the distressed, is charity indeed, and is worth more than whole burnt offerings, or rivers of oil presented in sacrifice. ("Sisters of Charity" 1832a)[2]

Medical journals addressing the disease often reiterated that "none but the *sisters of charity* could be found willing to fulfill the divine command of healing the sick" ("Dr. Shew's Lectures on Cholera" 1849, 35).

Because the nation was absorbed with the cholera crisis, articles surfaced across the country, not just in locations in greatest peril, with newspapers reprinting reports from exchanges and often adding their own commentary. For example, the piece quoted above from the *Niles Weekly Register* also appeared in the *New York Spectator*, the *Salem (Massachusetts) Gazette*, the *Boston American Traveller*, the *Norfolk Advertiser and Independent* (Dedham, Massachusetts), the *Portland (Maine) Eastern Argus*, the *Alexandria Gazette*, the *New-Hampshire Sentinel*, and the *Portland (Maine) Advertiser*.

Columns addressing the sisters' good works often doubly and triply praised them by printing original favorable reports from exchanges as well as their own commentary. For instance, in November 1832, the *Vidalia Whig and Illinois Intelligencer* responded to a piece from the *Nantucket Massachusetts Inquirer*. The *Whig* claimed to honor all charity but especially that which "works without display, and with reference only to the good intended," and acknowledged that such charity "overcomes a multitude of prejudices." After an introduction offering "voluntary admiration" for such works, the *Whig* reprinted a request from the *Nantucket Massachusetts Inquirer* seeking the names of two Sisters of Charity who had contracted the disease and died while attending victims in Baltimore. The Massachusetts paper regretted that none of the reports of the sisters' deaths had included the names and history of these "ministering angels" and "apostles of charity" so that "a local habitation and name may be associated with the brightest, we had almost said the only example, of benevolence recorded in the annals of the cholera." Following the *Inquirer* piece, the *Whig* printed a letter to the editors of the *Baltimore American*, which had also printed the *Inquirer* article. The letter from the Reverend A. J. Elder detailed the history of the Sisters of Charity, including their many locations, their benevolent works with orphans and poor children, their hospital work, and their selfless response to requests for nursing in hospitals and almshouses during the current cholera epidemic. Reverend Elder then narrated the sad deaths visited on the "heroic band" of sisters, naming the two who had contracted and died of cholera in Baltimore while caring for cholera victims. Thus, the sisters, singled out for their benevolence in the original article, were lauded again in response to praise from both earlier newspaper reports ("Sisters of Charity" 1832a).

The sisters were repeatedly extolled because they "hastened to the relief of the sufferers." When sisters perished, their deaths were widely acknowledged with phrases such as "martyr" to "pure and disinterested charity" and "a sacrifice to [their] benevolent exertions" ("Cholera" 1833b; "Cholera" 1833c).[3] The praise continued in the form of poetry, so popular in the nineteenth century. One poem, "On the Death of Sister Mary Frances," printed and reprinted, honored the "Mins'tring angel," "Philanthropy's fair vot'ry" and "dauntless maid," attesting to her "worth on high" ("Poetry from the Baltimore Chronicle" 1832). Another verified the "Heaven-sent Sisters" whose "dauntless courage" can "waken rapture . . . refined" ("To the Sisters of Charity" 1834).

After the epidemic had subsided, numerous mayors and city councils publicly acknowledged the work of the sisters. The mayor of Baltimore, with the Board of Health, expressed appreciation to the sisters "whose benevolent conduct has been of such essential utility in alleviating the horrors incident to the fatal epidemic, which a short period since, raged in our city." Calling the sisters' work "the purest system of unostentatious charity that could have been devised," the mayor named individually all the sisters involved in this service, acknowledging clearly that the sisters' work was unremunerated: "our warmest gratitude, and deepest obligation, for those services which were without compensation: thereby, leaving us doubly debtors"[4] ("Mayor's Office" 1832).

The sisters were similarly honored in Philadelphia, where the Board of Managers of the Philadelphia Almshouse publicly resolved

> that this body entertain a deep, lasting and grateful sense of the general devotedness—the serene and Christian kindness, and the pure and unworldly benevolence which have prompted and sustained the Sisters of Charity . . . during the trying period of pestilence and death, and afterwards in the midst of constant suffering and disease. . . . The

LITERACY, BENEVOLENCE, AND GOOD WORKS

invaluable services of these amiable women have been productive of lasting benefit to this institution, in the admirable and energetic measures which they have introduced for the relief and comfort of the sick and afflicted, and entitle them to the warmest thanks and gratitude of the whole community, which has been benefited by their labors. ("The Sisters of Charity and the Cholera" 1833)

When the sisters declined to accept engraved silver plate in gratitude for their service, this, too, received national attention:

These Angels of Mercy, hearing that the city authorities of Philadelphia were about to present each of them with a piece of plate, with appropriate inscriptions, for their labors in the cholera hospitals, during the spread of the pestilence, have addressed a letter to the Mayor, informing him that they are unwilling to receive any guardon [sic] for the perils which they voluntarily braved, other than the reward of an approving conscience. They remark, in their letter, public approbation of their conduct. If their exertions have been useful to their suffering fellow beings, and satisfactory to the public authorities, they deem it a sufficient reward, and indeed the only one which it would be consistent with their vocation to receive. Here, we perceive that mercy which droppeth, like the gentle dew from Heaven upon the earth beneath. Unostentatious—kind—from the heart. They look at the absent places of their departed sisters, who have dropped—flowers untimely nipped—into honorable graves, and the spirit of worldly pride is hushed, in the memory of virtues which they live but to emulate—of a sad but glorious fate, which they would if need should be, most willingly share. How touching the picture! The gentle "Sisters" are treading a path over which He walked, as an example, who comforted the afflicted—bound up the broken hearted—visited the sick and the suffering—weeping with those who wept! They have coveted no man's silver nor gold—but have performed unostentatious deeds of goodness, which they blush to find have gained them fame. ("Reprinted from *Providence Journal*, 'Sisters of Charity'" 1832)

The "angels" were now likened to Christ himself.

Even many who were normally critical of Catholics publicly acknowledged the sisters' good deeds. Methodist bishop Oscar Penn Fitzgerald praised the sisters' work with the ill: "Should I reach heaven and not meet there the Sisters of Mercy and the Sisters of Charity whom I have met in the hovels of want, the abodes of sickness, and the chambers of death . . . I should feel that I was in the wrong place" (qtd. in Stern 2007, 180). Even vocal Catholic critic and editor of the *Philadelphian* Ezra Stiles Ely[5] praised the sisters (Rosenberg 1962, 64), and the *New Orleans Whig* reported that "while the affrighted inhabitants are flying in all directions, the priests and nuns are flocking in all the infected places and braving the danger with heroic courage" (qtd. in Rosenberg 1962, 269). A common account is this 1836 one reminding readers that

> when the Malignant Cholera prevailed to some extent in our country, be it remembered to the credit of the Sisters of Charity, and to that of the sisters of some other orders, and to their honor as Christians, they voluntarily appeared at the bedside of the sick and dying, and gave them their sympathy and care, when fear seized many and paralyzed the humane affections of friends and other philanthropists, who feebly felt the divine principle of Christian love, and fled before the wasting pestilence, leaving the victims to the charity of these guardian spirits alone. ("Spread of Catholics No. 12" 1836)

The Catholic hierarchy acknowledged such sympathy. In an 1834 letter to the archbishop of Vienna, the Reverend Martin Henni noted "the large number of impartial newspaper articles praising [the sisters] and the priests who remained in the city to minister while others fled in panic" (qtd. in Metz 1996, 213). Such praise continued with subsequent cholera epidemics during the remainder of the century. The sisters thus became associated in the minds of many with benevolent, heroic response to national catastrophes. The mysterious, dangerous women hidden behind convent walls became visible angels of mercy, their stories of humility and charity surfacing repeatedly.

Controversy initiated by prejudicial ministers with regard to the cholera crisis catapulted the traditionally private sisters into public discussion, allowing them to defend themselves where they had previously been silent. In 1832, when cholera swept the city of Louisville, the Sisters of Charity of Nazareth had offered their "gratuitous" services on behalf of the stricken, asking only that the city cover their expenses. The city's board immediately requested the sisters' help, agreeing to pay "traveling expenses, board,

LITERACY, BENEVOLENCE, AND GOOD WORKS

and lodging for any who came to Louisville from Nazareth" (qtd. in Doyle 2006, 101), their motherhouse, some forty miles south. When, after the epidemic had abated, a local minister named the sisters mercenaries, taking as evidence city accounts that listed the seventy-five dollars paid the sisters for "services," Mother Catherine Spalding wrote a stinging letter to the mayor and city council reminding them of their invitation and the agreed-upon terms:

> Gentlemen,
>
> At that gloomy period, when the cholera threatened to lay our city desolate, and nurses for the sick poor could not be obtained on any terms, Rev. Mr. Abell in the name of the society of which I am a member, proffered the gratuitous services of as many of our Sisters as might be necessary in the then existing distress, requiring merely that their expenses should be paid.
>
> This offer was accepted, as the order from your honorable board, inviting the Sisters will now show. But when the money was ordered from your treasury, to defray those expenses, I had the mortification to remark that instead of the expression "the expenses of the Sisters," the word "services" was substituted. I immediately remonstrated against it, and even mentioned the circumstances to the Mayor, and another gentleman of the Council, and upon being promised that the error should be corrected, I remained satisfied that it had been done until a later ascertion [sic] from one of the pulpits of the City, leads me to believe that it stands uncorrected on your books, for the same books were referred to, in proof of the ascertion.
>
> If so, gentlemen, pardon the liberty I take in refunding you the amount paid for the above named expenses, well convinced that our Community for whom I have acted in this case would prefer incurring the expenses rather than submit to such an unjust odium. Gentlemen, be pleased to understand we are not hirelings; if we are in practice the Servants of the poor, the sick and the orphan; we are voluntarily so, but we look for our reward in another and better world. (Spalding 1834)

The notion of sisters' rendering "services" to be paid for must have evoked reminders of the very rhetorical slurs about nunneries that the sisters were trying to undo; Spalding clearly would not readily permit the good images the sisters had worked to establish to be undermined.

Other Benevolent Acts

When cholera swept the country again beginning in the late 1840s and returned in 1866, the sisters continued to care for those sick and dying of this disease, as well as for victims of yellow fever, smallpox, malaria, and a host of other diseases, gaining positive press for their actions; but they were often left with children orphaned by these scourges, children no one wanted or felt able to care for. Thus, the sisters opened orphanages for destitute children, another service widely acknowledged and appreciated. For example, the *Cincinnati Chronicle and Literary Gazette* reported in 1830 on St. Peter's Orphan Asylum, calling it "one of the most interesting charities in our city." The newspaper noted that the Sisters of Charity are "supporting and educating eight destitute orphan children, besides teaching about one hundred and fifty day scholars. Most of these are charity pupils.... No effort, we are assured, to inculcate the doctrines of the Roman Catholic church among the Protestant children placed in the asylum." Another paper admired the motherly demeanor of Mother Catherine Spalding, who founded an orphanage in Louisville after the 1832 cholera epidemic, creating a touching image: "She came up the street with a small child in one arm, a baby cradled in her apron and a toddler clinging to her skirt" (qtd. in Doyle 2006, 102).

The sisters' good works brought them directly into contact with wealthy merchants and local officials as they sought support for the children they housed and instructed. They became visible to the general public, as well, when their groups of children left the orphanages. The sisters recognized the positive perceptions that public display of the children in their care might contribute in garnering support, both public and private. For example, Sister Margaret George, a Sister of Charity, wrote her superior, "Our children—such as they are able—go to the Cathedral twice every Sunday. This keeps them before the public who love to see them and encourages them to contribute to their support" (qtd. in Metz 1996, 230).

The sisters also gained appreciation for their general service on behalf of the poor. When the Sisters of Mercy opened a laundry on Fourth Street in Cincinnati to provide employment for poor women "of good character," the *Cincinnati Daily Commercial* reported on the operation:

> Eminently practical in all their operations, they seem disposed to follow St. Paul's rule, and show their faith by their works rather than by prayer.... As their charity is bestowed alike upon Jew and Gentile,

orthodox and heterodox, so they have equal claims upon all denominations of christians and those of no denomination at all. . . . They employ destitute women and pay them current rates for their work as well as a sewing room in which those able and willing to work with the needle are employed. ("Sisters of Mercy" n.d.)

The sisters often received praise for their work with those whom most others refused to assist. For example, the *New York Daily Times* noted their efforts in prisons and with the mentally ill:

The Roman Catholic Order of the Sisters of Charity has especially dedicated itself to the care of the inmates of these establishments. What energy, what patience, what watchfulness, what courage do not these women—of the young, beautiful, and high-born—display in their self-imposed task. And in the most violent paroxysms of the lunatics, when every other authority has failed, their terror and rage are hushed beneath the voices and in the presence of these angels of mercy and benevolence. ("Sketches from Life School" 1852)

To support their work, many of the sisters held fairs at which they offered for sale a variety of goods and culinary treats made by the sisters and outside supporters. The fairs helped to sustain their benevolent institutions financially but also called public attention to their good work. Newspapers across the country carried notices of the annual fairs held in support of the sisters' institutions. Thus, readers gained knowledge about and were prompted to consider and support the sisters' work. A typical newspaper report reminded readers of the sisters' many benevolent acts, of their "heroic . . . administering [of] relief to the wretched victims of indigence and crime, pining under the hand of disease, in hospitals and prisons," and of their "training of nearly four hundred destitute children, daughters of indigence and penury, in the principles and habits of virtue and usefulness," as well as of their "irksome employment of training the youthful female mind in the rudiments of letters, in the principles and practices of virtue and religion, and in the acquisition of all other useful knowledge" ("Sisters of Charity" 1828).

By midcentury, despite nativist sentiment toward Catholics and immigrants in general, insults against the sisters and their convents began to diminish, as a broader population came to know the sisters through their educational mission and other benevolent acts. But, later in the century, the sisters became most renowned and favorably perceived for their efforts during the Civil War.

War Service

The Ursuline nuns in Quebec and Three Rivers had nursed both British and colonial soldiers during the Revolutionary War, as well as those from both sides in the War of 1812. The New Orleans Ursuline convent had become the center of relief efforts during the 1814 Battle of New Orleans, after the British general Edward Pakenham had supposedly promised his soldiers "booty and beauty" upon the capture of the city. Many of the city's women and girls clustered inside the convent chapel of Our Lady of Consolation for protection. Whether the nuns would have been able to safeguard the women and girls, or themselves, from such intentions had the British been victorious is questionable, but the convent was clearly seen as *the* place of refuge for the city's women. Following the Battle of New Orleans, the Ursulines cared for the sick and wounded soldiers for several months. These and other members of Catholic religious communities served the war-wounded in numerous places and in a variety of battles and wars. But attitudes changed most dramatically as the sisters became widely recognized for their assistance to wounded soldiers during the American Civil War. During and after the war, recognition of their good works became ubiquitous in news media, lectures, autobiographies, and fiction.

Because they had opened and operated some of the earliest U.S. hospitals, "on the eve of the Civil War, then, the only source of any kind of trained nurses—male or female—existed primarily in the twenty-eight Catholic hospitals, which were run by several different women's religious communities" (Maher 1999, 38).[6] Both in hospitals and in their work during epidemics, they had gained experience with contagious diseases, significant because during the Civil War more soldiers perished from disease than from wounds. Mary Denis Maher cites the "practical nature of their nursing work, learned in a community setting where the written regulations were demonstrated, passed down to newer members, and inculcated in the beginnings of their hospitals" as making the sisters "unique as a group of women when they served the sick and wounded in the Civil War" (39–40). Maher credits the "tradition, organization, commitment, [and] hospital and nursing experience" (40) as setting the sisters apart from any other group of women in the country. She claims that "because of their religious training [they] were used to being assigned demanding tasks within the convent and institutional structures, and working and learning easily from each other," and asserts that surgeons often requested sisters' help regardless of previous nursing experience. Sisters' daily lives had accustomed them to work congenially with others, to live and work in often difficult material circumstances, and to relate to soldiers in a nonsexual manner (100). According to Carol K. Coburn and Martha Smith, "One in five Civil War nurses were nuns" (1999, 65).

The sisters' hospital and nursing experience placed them in demand, but their convents and grounds often positioned them within the thick of battle. The convent and academy of the Sisters of Charity of St. Joseph at Emmitsburg, Maryland, for example, lay within a few miles of Gettysburg. The Union army camped on the spacious convent grounds, and the sisters fed the hungry soldiers. After the Battle of Gettysburg, the sisters went onto the battlefield to assist wounded soldiers and turned their academy into a hospital to care for casualties of both sides. The sisters' close contact with soldiers and their superiors during difficult times such as these helped to diminish prejudicial attitudes, especially because of the credibility and respect military officers and war veterans had with the public at large.

The sisters often became personally acquainted with influential military generals, surgeons general, and other government officials, both north and south. According to Mary Ewens, "Sister Anthony O'Connell of the Cincinnati Sisters of Charity was personally acquainted with Generals Grant, Sherman, Sheridan, McClellan, and Rosecrans, as well as Jefferson Davis" (1981, 236). The sisters were often given special passes and official letters of protection for themselves and their property. Even the hated General Benjamin Butler, whom New Orleans residents called "the Beast," held affection for the sisters. In a letter to Sister Maria Clara and the Donaldson, Louisiana, Daughters of Charity, he apologized for damage to their property: "No one can appreciate more fully than myself the holy, self-sacrificing labors of the Sisters of Charity. To them our soldiers are daily indebted for the kindest offices. Sisters of all mankind, they know no nation, no kindred, neither war nor peace. Their all-pervading charity is like the boundless love of 'Him who died for all,' whose servants they are, and whose pure teachings their love illustrates" (qtd. in Maher 1999, 142). Similarly, Lucius E. Chittenden, great-grandson of Vermont's first governor and himself U.S. senator and register of the U.S. Treasury during the Lincoln administration, proclaimed, "Of all those who assisted with the wounded, those of some Catholic sisters were most efficient. I never knew when they came or what was the name of their order. [Because of the sisters] these scenes which were altogether the most painful I have ever witnessed . . . have a beautiful side" (qtd. in Maher 1999, 143). Similarly, at a ceremony in Springfield, Illinois, honoring President Ulysses S. Grant and placing a statute of Abraham Lincoln in its Oak Ridge Cemetery, Grant "insisted that two nuns unveil the statue, in acknowledgement of the country's debt to sisters for their wartime services to the wounded" (Kolmer 1978, 644n11). Such highly placed, influential military officers and government officials acted as models for others in appreciating the sisters' work and in dispelling prejudice.[7]

Newspapers praised the sisters' work. For example, the *Atlanta Daily Register* reported from the General Hospital in Montgomery, Alabama, that

> it is attended by the Sisters of Charity—those dear souls whose whole life is a systematized sacrifice of self on the altar of the good of others. An abnegation of personal comfort, a tender ministration to the sick and suffering, a Samaritan like charity characterize this holy Sisterhood. . . . Their lives of abnegation have their reward even in this world. The grateful prayers of those whose wounds they have dressed, whose fevered brows they have cooled, whose sufferings their mild ministrations have alleviated, must constantly go up to God as a sweet incense from the altar of their charity.—The hand that pens these lines must be cold in death when I cease to feel a tender gratitude for Sister Prudentia. Long may she and her noble Sisters live to scatter the blessings of charitable lives on suffering humanity. ("Correspondence" 1864, 1)[8]

Popular testimonials and memoirs following the war became ubiquitous, often including praise for the sisters. U.S. Sanitary Commission leader Mary Ashton Livermore noted the sisters' professional and businesslike manner in her very popular account of the war, when she quoted one of the surgeons with whom she worked:

> "Your Protestant nurses are always finding some mare's-nest or other," said one of the surgeons, "that they can't let alone. They all write for the papers, and the story finds its way into print, and directly we are in hot water. Now the 'Sisters' never see anything they ought not to see, nor hear anything they ought not to hear, and they don't write for the papers—and the result is we get along very comfortably with them." (1887, 224)

Livermore later recalled,

> I am neither a Catholic nor an advocate of the monastic institution of that church. Similar organizations established on the basis of the Protestant religion, and in harmony with republican principles, might be made very helpful to modern society, and would furnish occupation and give position to large numbers of unmarried women, whose hearts go out to the world in charitable intent. But I can never forget my experience during the War of Rebellion. Never did I meet these Catholic sisters in hospitals, on transports, or hospital steamers, without observing their devotion, faithfulness, and unobtrusiveness. They gave themselves no airs of superiority or holiness, shirked no duty, sought no easy place, bred no mischiefs. Sick and wounded men watched for their entrance at night. They broke down in exhaustion from overwork, as did the Protestant nurses; like them, they succumbed to the fatal prison fever, which our exchanged prisoners brought from the fearful pens of the South. (177–78)

Other popular testimonials by women cited the sisters' work. In 1866, Kate Cumming, who had devoutly nursed soldiers during the war despite her family's objection, wrote, "A very nice lady, a member of the Methodist Church, told me that she would go into the hospital if she had in it a brother, a surgeon. I wonder if the Sisters of Charity have brothers, surgeons, in the hospitals where they go? It seems strange that they can do with honor what is wrong for Christian women to do. Well, I cannot but pity those who have such false notions of propriety" (1959, 178). Cumming set Catholic sisters apart from other Christians, but she acknowledged the value and honor in their work. Like Catharine Beecher before them, Livermore and Cumming observed the positive advantages of organizations that provided active, honorable, and rewarding career opportunities for unmarried women to benefit society; like Beecher, they lamented the lack of such avenues for Protestant women.[9]

Women were not the only ones wistful for a Protestant sisterhood. The *New York Times* expressed similar sentiment. After praising the work done by the Catholic sisters, both in America and in Catholic countries, the *Times* asked, "Does not all this suggest to our great Protestant churches the necessity of establishing some order of holy women, whose labor shall be akin to that of the sisters of Charity, or rather, . . . to that of the angels?"

Remarkably, the *Times* followed this praise and question with, "If we cannot have such an order, we earnestly hope, for the sake of suffering humanity, that the Catholic Church will devote itself more than ever to enlarge the numbers and extend the beneficent labors of the sisters" (qtd. in Misner 1988, 238). Only three decades after the animosity created by Maria Monk and her cohorts, only one decade past the nativist riots against Catholics, the *Times* called for more sisters.

Many soldiers commended their sister-nurses in public lectures and memoirs after the war. In his popular dramatic stage presentations, John Wallace "Captain Jack" Crawford, who had become well known as a Union scout, praised the sisters at length:

> On all God's green and beautiful earth there are no purer, no nobler, no more kind-hearted and self-sacrificing women that those who wear the somber garb of Catholic Sisters. During the war I had many opportunities for observing their noble and heroic work, not only in the camp and hospital; but on the death-swept field of battle. Right in the fiery front of dreadful war, where bullets hissed in maddening glee, and shot and shell flew madly by with demoniac shrieks, where dead and mangled forms lay with pale, blood-flecked faces, yet wear the scowl of battle, I have seen the black-robed Sisters moving over the field, their solicitous faces wet with the tears of sympathy, administering to the wants of the wounded and whispering words of comfort into the ears soon to be deafened by the cold, implacable hand of death.

Crawford continued with dramatic images of sisters splattered with blood kneeling over soldiers, "binding gaping wounds from which most women must have shrunk in horror" and enumerating the many ways the sisters offered comfort. Crawford claimed that many veterans "of the Blue and Gray" remembered the "soothing touch," the "sympathetic-eyes," the soft-spoken words of encouragement and cheer. Not atypically, Crawford qualified, "My friends, I am not a Catholic, but I stand ready at any and all times to defend those noble women, even with my life, for I owe that life to them" (qtd. in Barton 1898, 299–301).[10] The common acknowledgment that a speaker was not Catholic only served to give his or her claims more credibility.

In *Rebel Private, Front and Rear*, William Fletcher wrote of the change to his anti-Catholic prejudice: "The most of the dressing was done by Sisters of Charity. It was my first experience, and I was in love with the women and the uniform at once and have not gotten over it yet; for there is a feeling of gratitude uppermost when and where my eyes behold them." As Fletcher explained, he was brought up in the "Methodist and Baptist ways" and learned there was

> no place in heaven for a Catholic; but my opinion changed, after falling in love and my religious efforts ceased feeling: "If there was a God, he was a just one, and if He in justice consigned the sisters to hell, there was no use of my trying." But the sisters were onto their job and were thrown more in a motherly contact with the boys when the most of them were pining for a mother's or sister's care. (1954, 78)

Another veteran noted the protective stance another soldier took in stopping disparaging comments from some Protestants: "I don't know what Catholics are, what they believe, nor what they do; but since I was attended, in my sickness, by the Daughters of Charity at Richmond, I swore never to allow anyone to speak against their church in my presence" (Louis-Hippolyte Gache qtd. in Rousey 19).

Such public appreciation from the nursed continued for decades. The *Galveston News* reported the grateful tributes paid the sisters by those they had tended during the Civil War as late as 1878: "Twice each year are the portals of the Ursuline Convent thrown open to delegates, commissioned respectively by the Confederate veterans and the G.A.R., to decorate Mother St. Pierre's humble grave in the Convent cemetery. Why this honor, conferred with bared heads and respectful mien, as to a departed comrade, the memory of whose service to God and country even death itself cannot obliterate?" The article continues, "[Mother St. Pierre] and her self-sacrificing daughters nobly performed the task assigned to them, bringing into requisition everything that was needed, even their own beds and bedding; nay, more, their own clothing was torn to serve as bandages.... Mother St. Pierre's courage never once failed during those awful hours of strife and carnage" (qtd. in Semple 1925, 77, 79). Official documents recognized the sisters' work as well. The surgeon general's circular #4 cited the sisters as an example of efficient hospital management: "Twenty-eight Sisters of Charity were on duty, and I must bear evidence to their efficiency and superiority as nurses. The extra-diet kitchen is under the care of a sister and one is detailed by the superior of each ward. They administer medicine, diet, and stimulants, are under the orders of the ward surgeon, and are responsible to him alone. They have been beloved and respected by the men" (qtd. in Maher 1999, 108). The appreciation of soldiers and of their loved ones who were grateful for the kind attention the soldiers received, as well as public acknowledgments by influential military and political leaders, led many who had feared and detested the sisters and their religion to reconsider their previous prejudices.

Standard press notices, such as announcements for the sisters' fairs, continued, now often praising the sisters' good works at length. When the New York Sisters of Mercy held their 1865 fair, the *New York Times* opined:

> We are glad to see that the attention of the public is at last directed to this almost unknown institution. But little of the charity and self-devotion of the sisterhood is known to the world, for their deeds are performed in the abodes of the poor, in the prison cell and in the camp hospital. Subjoined are some statistics taken from the annual report, which show that this is one of the most useful and practical of our charitable institutions.

The *Times* continued with a listing of the sisters' good works during the past year, including "sick poor visited and relieved, 7,063; visits paid to the sick, 23,471; persons instructed and consoled in hospitals, 22,613," and enumerating other benevolent exercises such as "persons visited at Sing Sing and City Prison," "persons prepared for the scaffold," and the like. The *Times* finished by encouraging readers to participate: "Our citizens will be assisting in a really laudable work" ("Fair for the Sisters of Mercy at Palace Garden" 1865).

Other positive portrayals surfaced in influential places after the war. In 1868, James Parton, admired editor, historian, biographer, and husband to the wildly popular writer Fanny Fern, wrote a twenty-page article for the *Atlantic Monthly* titled "Our Roman Catholic Brethren." The piece can only be described as flattering to Catholics. Among many aspects of praise were those for Catholic sisters. Describing a New York City school run by the Sisters of Charity, Parton explained the "marvelous economy" of Catholic schools because "these pious sisters . . . only require the necessities of life." According to Parton, the bishop was able to run the model school for more than a thousand children for "eight thousand dollars . . . possibly ten thousand," an admirable amount because a similar school "would cost the city of New York eighteen thousand dollars." Parton follows with such rosy descriptions as this one of the sisters' school: "It happened to be a snowy day on which I visited the school, and no one went home to dinner. But when dinner time came, an apparatus containing a hot dinner for the sisters was brought round to them from their home near by, and they all sat down together in a nice little room to enjoy it, with the musical accompaniment of twelve hundred romping girls" (Parton 1868, 449). Such a positive article in one of the nation's most popular magazines by one of the country's most respected authors could only have enhanced affirmative attitudes toward Catholics; it also demonstrates how decidedly public opinion had changed after the war.

Favorable evocation of the sisters became ubiquitous. For example, the term "Sisters of Charity" surfaced in stories and poems in *Godey's Lady's Book* and other popular magazines of the time. In a *Godey's* piece, "Little Miss Stoddard," the respected Doctor Robertson praises a character as follows: "'Charity!' Not an unfitting name for the sober, pleasant faced little lady, for, with her spry step, quiet voice, and soothing air, she reminds me of those best of all nurses—the Sisters of Charity—I sometimes encounter in my professional rounds among the poor" (Janvrin 1863).

Even children's magazines referenced the sisters. In *Merry's Museum for Boys and Girls*, one author recalls observing cows imprisoned in boxcars, lowing in the hot sun and deprived of water. Wishing he could leave his train to somehow assist the suffering animals, he watched as two little girls, hearing the lowing, brought water to the cattle: "I wish I could have told those tender-hearted children how beautiful their compassion made that hot, noisy place, and what a sweet picture I took away with me of those two little Sisters of Charity" ("Merry's Monthly Chat" 1869). The phrase is used twice in this story meant for children, an astonishing change from the instruction children had received in schoolbooks.

In the early twentieth century, a monument in honor of the sisters who served as nurses during the Civil War was erected in Washington, D.C. Titled *Nuns of the Battlefield*, the granite and bronze memorial near Dupont Circle was "erected on government land and sanctioned by Congress" (Szpila 2012, 42). The inscription reads, "They comforted the dying, nursed the wounded, carried hope to the imprisoned, gave in his name a drink of water to the thirsty."[11]

The Catholic sisters recognized their value in service to their religion. Entered into their record in reference to their work, the Emmitsburg Sisters of Charity wrote,

LITERACY, BENEVOLENCE, AND GOOD WORKS

> In 1832, the city of Boston, the Athens of America, has seen its frozen prejudices gradually melt away before the kindly sun of charity. The dark night of intolerance has passed by, and the enlightened citizens in that capital have not scrupled to entrust the charge of their Orphan Asylum and Benevolent School, in which three hundred children are gratuitously educated, to an association, whose religious principles have for centuries formed the theme and terror of the pious bigot and gloomy fanatic—thus much has been written by the public press—. ("Annals . . . at St. Joseph's" n.d., 261)

The sisters reminded their superiors of the delicate nature of their role as well as their important contributions. For example, when disagreeing with a decision he had made, Mother Catharine Spalding wrote Bishop Joseph Flaget in 1841:

> We zealously and cheerfully spent the energies of our youth in the fields, looms, spinning rooms, kitchens, etc. . . . rejoicing that we could thus, by our humble labors, in the most servile and lowest occupations, contribute our mite to the support of the seminaries and churches in your diocese. . . . With due humility and a deep sense of the overruling care of Heaven, allow us to call to your mind, the numbers of respectable families added to the church, by the education and religious impressions, which individuals receive at Nazareth. . . . You know far better than we do the immense weight of prejudice which has been removed by Nazareth's humble efforts, aided by the blessing of God.

On occasion the sisters' superiors did formally acknowledge their work. After the Civil War, in 1866, the Second Plenary Council declared, "We discharge a grateful duty in rendering a public testimony to the virtue and heroism of these Christian Virgins, whose lives shed the good odor of Christ in every place, and whose devotedness and self-sacrifice have, perhaps more than any other cause, contributed to effect a favorable change in the minds of thousands estranged from the Faith" (qtd. in Evans 1959, 93).

The sisters, clearly, did not destroy all prejudice, as some of that prejudice continues. However, their consistent good works softened and changed negative attitudes among many, helping to reshape popular prejudice and demonstrating how a nineteenth-century marginalized group of women who were denied a public voice entered into and changed civic discourse surrounding them. Whether the New Orleans Ursuline Sisters sheltering the helpless and nursing the wounded, the Sisters of Mercy tending the victims of yellow fever, the Sisters of Charity of Nazareth opening their doors to victims of plague and war, the Sisters of Charity of Emmitsburg providing solace at the horrendous Battle of Gettysburg, or the dozens of other groups of Catholic women religious across the country who ventured into their communities to offer comfort and instruction, the sisters of the nineteenth-century United States helped to change the common depiction of Catholic sisters in many minds from that of victims of or accomplices to licentious priests, of prostitutes and murderers of infants, to honored and gentle benefactors of the helpless and needy.

A Paradox of Benevolence

The struggle for who would populate and lead the United States was fought in many arenas, with the battle over literacy instruction an important one. The significance placed on the power of literacy in the early nineteenth century can be seen in efforts to offer or deny literacy and to control its delivery. As literacy continued to be associated with morality, and increasingly with social prestige and integrity, it also became a legal and cultural means of excluding many, either completely or by degrees. Exclusion based on religious grounds was diminished after the Constitution allowed for religious freedom but continued to some extent, if not based on law then certainly by social practice.

Proponents of education often differed on how broadly literacy should be afforded. While earlier arguments had addressed the dangers of providing literacy to the masses, by the early nineteenth century most people were coming to accept literacy as desirable (Graff 1979, 23). There were, of course, many qualifiers to this general belief. Literacy had become accepted as a manner for establishing standard values and cultural practices, a way to control dangerous societal elements. The powerful saw control of literacy as the means for determining the direction of the country and of acculturating children to proscribed roles, usually according to class and sex (and race, in its absence). Who had the right to literacy, whose tenets would be included in the curriculum, and how much literacy individuals might receive remained contested issues as various groups sought to control literacy efforts in the service of their own beliefs. Although schooling had become accepted as a means for controlling and shaping the lower classes to societal norms, literacy for the enslaved, and even for free African Americans, continued to be opposed by many. Even in the New England colonies, where literacy has been most closely associated with religion and the Bible and where abolitionists were strongest, African Americans were denied literacy.

That paragon of religion, Cotton Mather, had addressed the issue as early as 1706. In *The Negro Christianized*, Mather evoked Abraham's assurance that his servants should "know the way of the Lord" in warning masters to ensure religious instruction for servants (9). However, his recommended instruction came in the form of an oral catechism, not literacy. Mather enticed masters by explaining that, "were your Servants well tinged with the Spirit of Christianity, it would render them exceedingly Dutiful unto their Masters, exceedingly Patient under their Masters, exceedingly Faithful in their Business, and afraid of speaking or doing anything that may justly displease you." He then offered a catechism meant to teach docility and obedience without literacy:

> Tell them; That if they Serve God patiently and cheerfully in the Condition which he Orders for them, their condition will very quickly be infinitely mended, in Eternal Happiness.
>
> Show Them, That it is God that has Caused them to be Servants; and that they serve Jesus Christ while they are at Work for their Masters. (32)

Mather includes "A Shorter Catechism for the Negroes of a Smaller Capacity" and "A Larger Catechism for the Negroes of a Larger Capacity" (36), but both were to be taught orally. Following catechetical instructions, he includes the Ten Commandments, the fifth commandment admonishing the enslaved to "show all due Respect unto Every One, and if I have a Master or Mistress I am to be dutiful unto them" (41).[12]

While those in the North rarely prohibited literacy among African Americans by law, they showed little support for their education and often opposition. Schools for African Americans, where they existed, were nearly always run primarily by and at the expense of African Americans. In Connecticut, one of the leading states in education for white citizens in the first half of the nineteenth century, outrage erupted when Prudence Crandall admitted a young black woman to her private school. White students withdrew, and Crandall then opened her school to African American girls specifically, but opposition was fierce, including threats and acts of vandalism; Crandall and one of her students were jailed. Opposition was so strong that the Connecticut legislature passed a Black Law in 1833 to ensure that schools open to African Americans from outside the state required permission of the town to operate.

Attitudes in general were not favorable to African Americans' literacy. As Lawrence Cremin states, in the work of Horace Mann, appointed secretary of the newly created Massachusetts Board of Education in 1837 and often seen as the father of the common school, "the sense that common schools should embrace all *races* as well as classes and denominations" is absent (1957, 25).[13] And the Reverend Hiram Ketchum, anti-Catholic leader of the American Bible Society and crusader for requiring the adoption of the King James Bible as a textbook in all schools, "refused to accept contributions to send Bibles to Negroes" (Beals 1960, 76).

Even abolitionists disagreed over the necessity of literacy for African Americans. While Lydia Maria Child and William Lloyd Garrison supported literacy efforts by and for African Americans, their attitudes were rare among abolitionists; most called for religious instruction for the enslaved but rarely sought literacy on their behalf. In the American Deep South, where African Americans were seen as a danger to security and to a way of life, numerous states made explicit laws forbidding the teaching of reading or writing to African Americans, both free and enslaved. The laws stipulated punishment for the teachers of such individuals, usually monetary fines for white offenders and corporal punishment for black people; retribution for those trying to learn to read and write was generally left to owners. Many African Americans did learn to read and write, some clandestinely, some because kind white individuals believed in their right to learn, others because literacy made them more useful to masters who wanted their assistance in such matters as record keeping or in other creative or supervisory practices.

However, many sought to restrict literacy efforts among African Americans. Officials often spoke openly about the dangers of literate African Americans, claiming that it would make them discontent with their positions, that it would facilitate flight among the enslaved, and that the enslaved would be more susceptible to the propaganda of antislavery publications. The fear of the latter escalated after pamphlets such as African American David Walker's 1829 *Appeal to the Coloured Citizens of the World* began appearing in the South. Fear of literacy among African Americans was similarly amplified because slave conspiracies and rebellions were usually led by literate individuals, such as Gabriel (Prosser) in 1800 near Richmond, Virginia, and Nat Turner in 1831 in Southampton County, Virginia, the connection between literacy and rebellion appearing evident for owners and officials.

Still, religion was so important to early nineteenth-century Americans that many slaveholders felt the pressure to catechize the enslaved. After all, one of the chief arguments on behalf of southern slavery was that Africans who came to the United States were better off than the pagans left behind because they were Christianized and, therefore, had access to eternal salvation. Plantation missions gained popularity in the South, but as Albert J. Raboteau has noted, "first and last the plantation mission had to prove that it represented no threat to slavery" (2004, 157) as the plantation owner controlled missionaries' access to the enslaved on their land. Prominent southern advocates for religious instruction among the enslaved, then, such as leader of the Plantation Mission movement and Presbyterian clergyman Charles Coldcock Jones,[14] reassured plantation owners. To this end they emphasized parts of the Bible that commanded obedience and separated religious instruction from literacy, as had Mather more than one hundred years earlier. In *The Religious Instruction of the Negroes in the United States*, Jones comforted slaveholders that "Christianity and the embracing of the Gospel does not make the least alteration in civil property, or in any of the duties that belong to civil relations; but in all these respects, it continues persons just in the same state as it found them" (1842, 21). Similarly, in his *Essay on the Management of Slaves, and Especially, on Their Religious Instruction*, influential state governor and president of the South Carolina Agricultural Society Whitemarsh B. Seabrook attested that "no Christian will deny the importance of religious instruction to slaves" (1834, 15), but in his detailed plan for teaching religion, instruction was to be simple, in the vein of Mather, with "Sabbath-schools to be taught orally" (21). To that end, all popular catechisms and calls for broader religious instruction followed similar methods. For example, William Capers's very popular *Catechism for the Use of Methodist Missions* drew from Ephesians to instruct, "Servants be obedient to them that are your masters according to the flesh, with fear and trembling, in singleness of your heart, as unto Christ" (1853, 20–21). And Jones's *Catechism of Scripture Doctrine* bade the enslaved "to count their Masters 'worthy of all honour,' as those whom God has placed over them in this world; 'with all fear, they are to be subject to them' and obey them in all *things*, possible and lawful, with good will and endeavor to *please them well*, . . . and let Servants serve their masters as faithfully behind their backs as before their faces" (qtd. in Raboteau 2004, 162–63). Thus, religious instruction generally enforced antiliteracy codes and "promote[d] subservience to the slave system" (Conwill 1998, 203).[15]

The acceptable degree of literacy and education, especially for women and the poor, was also contested in a patriarchal and socially stratified culture. The degree of literacy offered by the Catholic sisters differed, as it did in other academies and schools, according to the ability to pay. As seen in chapters 3 and 4, day schools generally accommodated large numbers of children with a high student-to-teacher ratio and offered religious instruction, basic literacy, and sometimes rudimentary instruction in math, history, or geography. But access did not depend completely on ability to pay. Cultural presumptions influenced what the poor were taught as well. Beth Daniell and Peter Mortensen cite the "nuanced relationship . . . between the possession of certain literacies by certain people at a certain historical moment" (2007, 25). Such a relationship was not subtle in the early nineteenth century. Few in either the convent schools or other schools saw the need for educating beyond children's current station in life. For the poor, this meant primarily religious instruction, which molded children to accepted conventions and beliefs about their role in society, some basic literacy, and training for manual labor.

Even affluent girls and young women found restrictions on the degree and kind of literacy offered. Latin and Greek, the languages of the "classics," were generally reserved not just for the affluent but for well-to-do boys and young men. Girls in convent academies might be taught Latin, but primarily for pronunciation with just enough understanding to participate in Catholic services. A rigorous study of the classics in Greek and Latin was absent. French and other modern languages were seen as more appropriate for affluent women. The number of years in school, too, differed for girls. Two to four years beyond an elementary education was considered optimal. However, for most girls, education rarely extended to foreign languages and academic subjects.

An Extensive Network of Schools Assisted by Slavery

The sisters expanded their mission through frugality and mutual support. Priests and professors at Catholic colleges willingly educated early sisters to prepare them for teaching. The sisters also offered support to other existing and beginning communities of religious women. For example, the New

Orleans Ursulines acted as the gateway/reception point for missionary nuns from Europe, playing host to the Poor Clares at the end of the eighteenth century, as well as to the Sisters of the Sacred Heart and the Sisters of St. Joseph of Carondelet in the nineteenth century. Newly arrived sisters rested from their long voyages at the convent and prepared for their inland journeys. The Ursulines later sent numerous shipments of food and other staples to their new nun-friends upon learning of their impoverished conditions.

Sisters often accommodated others as they opened new missions in the same city. In 1830, when the Sisters of Charity of Emmitsburg traveled to New Orleans to assume a school for African Americans, the woman whose school they expected to acquire had changed her mind. The sisters therefore stayed with the New Orleans Ursulines, whom they praised for their "gracious acceptance" and ongoing friendship, until they could open their own orphanage on Poydras Street ("Annals . . . at St. Joseph's" n.d., 256–57). When Sisters of the Good Shepherd came to the United States from Angers, France, in 1842, they lived nine months with the Sisters of Loretto in Louisville until their home was built. Convents often provided refuges for other nuns in more urgent situations as well. After the burning of the Ursulines' Mount Benedict convent and academy, the homeless nuns found shelter at other Catholic convents.

European congregations had long assisted others in their preparation for teaching. Because of their long tradition of education, the European Ursulines often helped others to become teachers. For example, Louise de Marillac, founder of the Sisters of Charity, "sent sisters to Ursulines to learn to teach; then they taught others" (Charpy n.d., 129). The tradition continued in the United States. The Sisters of Loretto helped the newly formed Sisters of the Holy Cross learn art and music at their motherhouse (Bede [1923] 1926, 47). When the Sisters of St. Joseph of Carondelet arrived in St. Louis, they lodged with the Sisters of Charity and received instruction in English at the Sacred Heart convent (Coburn and Smith 1999, 43). The list of incidents of assistance among communities is lengthy.

While the sisters' efforts and mutual assistance served them well in extending their mission, their complicity with the U.S. slavery system was instrumental in the success of many congregations. Although the sisters became known for their benevolence, leading frugal lives themselves to educate and help others, caring for the diseased when others fled, taking in unwanted orphaned children, and performing many other works of mercy, the majority of early U.S. Catholic women religious in the South held bondmen and bondwomen. The New Orleans Ursulines had brought "a Moor to wait on us—as it is the custom of the country" (qtd. in Clark 2007, 33), and their contract with the Company of the Indies required the company to provide eight others. The nuns became one of the largest holders of enslaved Africans and African Americans in New Orleans, contributing greatly to their ability to provide benevolent and educational missions.

Other communities held far fewer bondpeople than did the New Orleans Ursulines, but their release from many of the manual duties entailed in early nineteenth-century America, as well as the economic benefits the enslaved provided, clearly undergirded the accomplishments of many of the early sisters. Some of the communities received slaves upon the entrance of more affluent postulants. The Sisters of Loretto took ownership of the rustic cabins in which they lived and had begun their school, as well as adjacent property, when one of the original sisters "sold her man slave, Tom, willed to her by her deceased father" (Barrett n.d., 31). The money she thus received also allowed for improvements to the cabins—"putting in lofts, laying planks on the upper joists, making a kind of attic where the Sisters could sleep, and where the boarders' beds could be put in the daytime and pulled down and laid on the floor at night for rest" (31–32).

When the Sacred Heart nuns arrived in Missouri, they were dismayed at the manual labor that required so much of their time and energy. In France, lay members had taken on this work. The nuns were cloistered and expected to stay within their residence while others left to purchase necessary food and materials. Philippine Duchesne wrote Madeleine Sophie Barat, "We do not want slaves and we have no money to buy them, yet we scarcely know how to get along without them, especially as we are cloistered and do not go about. No one wants to hire out as a domestic servant; all want to be on the same social level" (qtd. in Callan 1957, 328). However, in a few years one father paid two years' academy tuition with a slave.

Not all sisters' communities in the U.S. South participated in the slavery system. For example, the Oblate Sisters of Providence, a black community founded by a migrant from Cuba and refugees from the St. Domingue Revolution, did not own bondpeople and accepted some freed slaves into their community, even though they had belonged to privileged groups in their native lands. Nor did the Irish Sisters of Mercy in Charleston, South Carolina, participate in slavery, perhaps because they also were sensitive to the immorality and abuses of slavery due to their Irish heritage. And the Sisters of St. Joseph, who came to the United States later than the other communities included here, never held enslaved peoples. However, the majority of communities in the South seem to have accepted the custom of the territory and failed to question the inconsistencies between their moral and benevolent aspirations and the horrible abuses of the U.S. slavery system.[16] They instead appear to have believed in their own "kindnesses" to the enslaved peoples they kept—religious instruction, institutional marriage, efforts to keep families together—and did not rise above the "custom" of their social surroundings.

The white sisters sometimes assisted African American women's communities, as when the Sisters of Charity instructed Marie Therese Duchemin in English at St. Joseph Academy in Emmitsburg that she might take charge of English instruction at the Oblates' St. Francis Academy. According to Roger Baudier, the Sacred Heart nuns assisted the Sisters of the Holy Family in their initial formation (1939, 397). Charles Nerinckx, who helped to found the Sisters of Loretto, arranged for admission of black women to the congregation in 1824, "for the special education of the blacks, whose neglected condition in servitude no one more sincerely deplored" (Maes 1880, 510). It appears that these sisters would have been separate, or somewhat separate, from the white sisters; regardless, his policy was reversed by his successor when Nerinckx died shortly after the women entered the congregation.[17] Subsequently, women of color in this area of Kentucky expressed interest in beginning a community similar to that of the Oblates. Bishop Joseph Benedict Flaget wrote Father Louis Deloul about the matter,

> Kindly let me know by yourself, or by one of your seminarists, if this community of women of color is prospering, if there is appearance that it will go on increasing in piety and in number of subjects. Several free negresses of Louisville would be quite pleased to know what is taught in that school and the price of the pension etc. etc. Try to send me a prospectus of the said establishment, if there is one. The negress who was at the head of your ménage at the time of the last council belonged if I remember correctly to that family. How edifying was her conduct! And what an advantageous idea did she not give me of her community. (Flaget 1842)

I have found no evidence that such a community was founded in Louisville.

Philippine Duchesne had wished to admit people of color, or at least to found a separate community for them. In an 1830 letter she wrote:

> We had a visit recently from one of our mulattoes from St. Ferdinand. She longs with her whole heart to enter with us, but we may not accept her as a religious. This has suggested to me the idea of offering our house out there for the use of colored girls, either like the Sisters of St. Martha, or like the St. Michael nuns in Paris, who were founded for girls whose parents complained of them. . . . Could not we, too, gather together colored girls who want to leave this world and set aside for them one or two of our own nuns until they would be able to continue on their own as a community or congregation according to their special calling? (qtd. in Callan 1957, 529)

Except for Nerinckx's brief attempt at Loretto, however, none of the white communities accepted black women as members of their congregations. According to Mary Christina Sullivan, a biracial woman became a member of Les Dames de la Retraite in Charleston, South Carolina, adding tension to that created by the Sisters of Mercy's school for African Americans. As noted in chapter 4, the community seems never to have received approval as a religious community, however, and the group moved from location to location for a few years, finally landing in Florida, where information about them ceases (1940, 70).

A number of convent communities began schools for black children, but these were often short-lived in the early part of the century because of local opposition. The Charleston Sisters of Mercy opened a school for African American children in 1835, but residents' hostility forced its closure, and although Philippine Duchesne had wished to include African Americans in the community's schools, the local bishop opposed such inclusion.[18] According to James Hennesey, Elizabeth Seton taught African American children at Emmitsburg, and "the first mission to be established by the Sisters of St. Joseph outside their mother house at Carondelet, Missouri was a school for blacks on Third Street in St. Louis" (1983, 145). Hennesey credits the Sisters of Charity of Nazareth and the Sisters of Loretto for establishing schools for African Americas. However, the extent of teaching beyond catechetical instruction is difficult to determine. The most successful efforts on the part of African American literacy came from the Oblate Sisters of Providence. Diane Batts Morrow explains that "issues of race and incidents of racism affected the Oblate Sisters of Providence from their beginning," noting opposition from both lay and religious individuals. However, the sisters maintained their successful convent and academy in the antebellum South, a remarkable accomplishment (2002, 146).

LITERACY, BENEVOLENCE, AND GOOD WORKS

While the white sisters devoted themselves to literacy efforts for women, sometimes including African Americans and the enslaved, their "benevolent" work on the part of African Americans seems not to have included concern for their freedom, many sisters comfortably accepting the holding of enslaved peoples. Andrew Stern claims that many southern Catholics supported slavery in an effort to ally with Protestants and lessen religious animosity toward Catholics (2007). Some scholars have suggested that the proslavery attitude of many U.S. Catholics stemmed in part from abolitionist attacks against Catholicism.[19] In their opposition to slavery, abolitionists often equated members of the Catholic Church with enslaved African Americans and the church with slave masters. Lyman Beecher repeatedly equated the two. In 1834, just before the Charlestown convent burning, Beecher regularly held in his sermons that "the Catholic Church holds now in darkness and bondage nearly half the civilized world. . . . It is the most skillful, powerful, dreadful system of corruption to those who wield it, and of slavery and debasement to those who live under it" (qtd. in Beals 1960, 36). Angelina and Sarah Grimké often spoke of the two forms of slavery, usually with the Catholic Church as the standard by which to measure the horrors of American slavery. In *An Epistle to the Clergy of the Southern States*, Sarah suggests that if the horrors of the Catholic Church "could be fully and fairly brought to view and compared with the details of slavery in the United States, the abominations of Catholicism would not surpass those of slavery" ([1836] 1989, 112). Similarly, Angelina chided those who condemned Catholics "for denying the Bible to the common people" because U.S. slaveholders were "doing the same thing" (*Appeal* [1836] 1989, 56). And Jane Grey Swisshelm spoke of the "alliance between Romanism and slavery" (Walker 1978, 164); as Peter F. Walker suggests, Swisshelm presented "priests and slaveholders [as] cut from the same cloth" (164). Newspapers often printed such equations. The influential Republican Party newspaper, the *Boston Daily Atlas and Bee*, warned, "We are unalterably, sternly opposed to the encroachments of political and social Romanism, as well as to its wretched superstition, intolerance, bigotry and mean despotism—as much so as we are to the monster institution of human slavery and for the same reasons" (qtd. in McGreevy 2003, 9).

Because most abolitionists were vehemently anti-Catholic, apparently sincerely seeing Catholics and their church in such terms of domination, the easy association between the two surfaced repeatedly, increasing animosity on both sides. Those opposed to Catholicism had always warned that the religion was inimical to republican government, and for abolitionists the charge became associated with slavery. For example, Ray Allen Billington reports the following Know-Nothing resolution at Norfolk, Massachusetts:

> Whereas, Roman Catholicism and slavery being alike founded and supported on the basis of ignorance and tyranny; and being, therefore, natural allies in every warfare against liberty and enlightenment; thereby, be it
>
> Resolved, that there can exist no real hostility to Roman Catholicism which does not embrace slavery, its natural co-worker in opposition to freedom and republican institutions. (1938, 425)

Especially in the early nineteenth century, most Americans' concern for the welfare of the enslaved, or for free African Americans, was minimal, with interest in their literacy even more rare. But Catholic sisters' lives of benevolence and mission of education might lead us to expect greater opposition to slavery on their part. I have found no evidence of such disapproval.

As shown above, many abolitionists, who were generally well educated and espoused the importance of literacy, took little interest in literacy among African Americans and made every effort to squash literacy efforts on behalf of enslaved and free black individuals alike by religious groups outside their own faith, especially those of Catholics. Even as they expressed disdain for the American treatment of black people, most abolitionists held staunchly to their own prejudices based on religion. Wendell Phillips, an exception, publicly denounced abolitionists' crusade against Catholics, but most of the famed abolitionists from whom we expect kindness and acceptance were the most vitriolic persecutors of Catholics and their schools. The anti-Catholic press was primarily associated with abolitionists. Arthur Tappan, cofounder and first president of the American Anti-Slavery Society, founded the *New York Journal of Commerce*, the nation's leading anti-Catholic newspaper, with his brother Lewis and Samuel F. B. Morse, their compatibility based on their hatred of Catholics, not on their concern for the enslaved.[20] The Tappan brothers supported numerous antislavery causes, but Morse did not support abolition, though he often took up the cause of American Indians. However, the three united in their ruthless persecution of Catholics. Morse wrote the popular anti-Catholic book *Foreign Conspiracy against the Liberties of the United States*,[21] along with numerous tracts and diatribes, and Arthur Tappan funded many anti-Catholic causes.

He paid for the seminary study of Elijah P. Lovejoy, often seen as martyr to the abolitionist cause, and helped to launch Lovejoy's anti-Catholic newspaper, which increased hostility in the St. Louis area greatly. In his *St. Louis Observer*, Lovejoy repeatedly railed against "the stealthy cat-like step, the hyena grin, with which the 'Mother of Abominations' was approaching the Fountain of Protestant Liberty" (qtd. in Lovejoy, Lovejoy, and Adams 1838, 115) and campaigned relentlessly against the Catholic Church. All three bitterly opposed Catholic schools, but they differed on literacy for African Americans. Tappan seems to have supported literacy for African Americans. As Morse maintained that slavery was deemed by God, he opposed literacy for the enslaved, and the antislavery Lovejoy, rather than supporting literacy for African Americans, felt they should be "returned" to Africa. The three represent some of the complexities among abolitionists rarely acknowledged today.

While the major Protestant churches broke apart over the slavery issue, the Catholic Church did not.[22] The hierarchical nature of the church helped to keep it intact. In 1839 Pope Gregory XVI banned Catholics' participation in the slave trade but fell short of condemning their ownership of slaves, permitting Catholics who held enslaved peoples in the U.S. South to do so in good conscience. Much of the Catholic leadership in the early United States came from southern culture. John Carroll, the first U.S. bishop and leader of the early church in the United States, belonged to a wealthy Maryland family whose affluence was based partly on the slave/plantation system. Other leaders of the U.S. church also benefited from and accepted slavery. While some lay Catholics and Catholic leaders opposed slavery, any organized opposition to slavery among U.S. Catholics paled in comparison with its support or acceptance on the part of others.

While religion and moral precepts shaped literacy for most citizens in the nineteenth-century United States, they had little positive influence on African Americans' literacy. However, women's literacy was especially swayed by religious beliefs. Ironically, the two religious groups of women educators examined in this study, Protestant and Catholic, saw themselves as advancing religious and moral principles as well as literacy but found themselves in opposition to one another. The sisters and the "pioneer" New England women, both of whom worked unceasingly for women's education, saw their work as part of a messianic mission. Leading women educators in the early nineteenth century seem to have followed the direction of their religious leaders for the most part. They also represented their times: even though both groups supported literacy for women, sometimes in unique and progressive ways, they became rivals rather than supporters of richer literacy for all women. The proprietor schools for women became more typical for the North, the convent academies flourishing primarily in the South. The women in both cases, for the most part, supported the established culture in which they lived. Their efforts highlight the very complex entanglement of literacy with religion. We could benefit by learning more about such influence, in these groups as well as in other religious groups who contributed to literacy efforts but have been largely ignored because of our grand narrative. We have readily accepted rather simplistic stories about literacy and benevolence in the early nineteenth century. But the story is much more involved than our traditional tales of Protestant promotion of literacy and common schools, of benevolent sisterhoods, and of worthy abolitionists.

Conclusion

Nancy Cott has pointed out that "no other avenue of self-expression besides religion at once offered women social approbation, the encouragement of male leaders (ministers), and, most important, the community of their peers" (1977, 141). Given this context, it is not surprising that women joined the drive to evangelize students in large numbers. As it became important that women be educated to properly form the leaders of the new Republic, that formation most importantly required shaping to the correct religious beliefs and moral values. Thus religious leaders increasingly supported women's education. Cott refers primarily to Protestant white women; however, her claims apply even more appropriately to Catholic women. Protestant ministers gave moral support and advice to women of their faith, facilitating funding for Protestant schools for women either directly or indirectly by rousing antagonism for and fear of Catholic convent academies; but Catholic priests, bishops, and faculty at Catholic colleges willingly instructed young Catholic sisters for the classroom and encouraged well-educated women to join the sisters' communities.

Many illiterate or barely literate women gained educational opportunities previously unthinkable. The teaching profession offered a means of independence for both Protestant and Catholic women; however, Catholic women gained a degree of autonomy and security unavailable to their Protestant rivals. Living in community with other learners who were focused on teaching provided welcome support for the women who embarked on a lifetime teaching profession. They lived without daily interference from men, and they inaugurated a career that permitted lifelong learning with security in old age. Sharing religious purpose and a common objective permitted them to expand their mission quickly. As shown in earlier chapters, Protestant women such as Catharine Beecher and Mary Ashton Livermore clearly understood the positive attributes of the manner in which the sisters operated, a system most single Protestant women could only dream of.

CONCLUSION

While a large number of students in Catholic academies were Protestant, Catholics avoided the Protestant schools for women, primarily by choice, although most could ill afford the steep tuition and board. Those who could afford an academy education chose Catholic academies and schools rather than those unfriendly to their religion. In contrast to Protestants, Catholics avoided overt campaigns against Protestant and "common" schools prior to 1840, as they had little control over powerful avenues of information and feared reprisals in a country where they were an out-of-favor faction.

The competition among religious groups that propelled women's education in the nation's early years continued as the country moved westward. David Tyack has shown that by midcentury, "founding schools was an established part of the missionary program on the frontier" (1966, 456), including the "anti-Catholic hysteria (which was a staple item in the fund-raising literature of the missionary societies)" (450). In Oregon, for example, Protestant ministers tried to impose the New England Protestant model for schools, helping to write laws and becoming superintendents of schools. George Atkinson, "known as the father of the common school in the state" (456), had been commissioned by the American Home Missionary Society to create "'churches, schools, whatever would benefit humanity'—temperance, virtue; the industrial, mental, moral and religious training of the young, and the establishment of society upon sound principles by means of institutions of religion and learning" (qtd. in Tyack 1966, 456). Atkinson protested against the "three bishops, twenty-seven priests, thirteen sisters, and two schools" in his province. When sisters began building another school, his failed efforts to convince Oregon City officials to build one for countering the Catholic institutions where "fickle Protestants were sending their daughters" prompted him to open a private girls' school himself. As Tyack explains, "It was a commonplace among evangelical ministers that the Catholics intended to train 'Romish mothers' in their girls' schools" (460).

By 1840, Catholic women religious had opened 40 U.S. convent academies (Coburn and Smith 1999, 161) and far more day schools and orphanages, the convents themselves being major literacy sites for women. The number given by the 1840 *Metropolitan Catholic Almanac* is 119 convents, academies, day schools and orphanages operated by Catholic sisterhoods, in addition to numerous other homes and support services for women. The sisters also built and staffed many of the earliest hospitals, establishing firsts for women in many medical areas.[1]

CONCLUSION

The period addressed in this study represents the earliest years of the Catholic convents and schools in the United States. Although significant in number by 1840, their growth increased quickly after that time, reaching a peak in the 1960s, when "some 5.5 million youngsters, 14 per cent of the nation's school population, were enrolled in 10,633 Catholic elementary schools and 2,502 Catholic secondary schools, representing a $5 billion capital investment and an annual operating cost of $850 million" (McCluskey 1964, 1). Some 125,000 women religious belonged to Catholic sisterhoods.

Rosemarie Zagarri sees a "relatively small number of women" embracing "a more radical alternative for women in the early Republic" (5). However, the terms scholars have used to describe women's activities fail to capture the complex nature of Catholic women's roles—probably always, but certainly in the first half of the nineteenth century. They might be considered radical in their manner of communal living, in their going into communities to care for the victims of disease, in their creation and staffing of hospitals, and in their administration of very large convents, schools, orphanages, hospitals, and other social service institutions. Yet, as they chose to pursue what had been nontraditional opportunities, they also adhered to many societal norms. They often depended on men for advice and to maneuver the male-dominated world in which they lived. They maintained a "feminine" demeanor appropriate to the middle- to upper-class nineteenth-century woman, and they cultivated their academy students to grace their homes and social circles in a similar, acceptable manner. They educated orphans and lower-class students to fit the roles expected of them, making exceptions only for those students who showed intellectual and emotional promise as recruits for their convents or as governesses for the wealthy. A majority of the sisterhoods during this period held enslaved people.

As in most other schools for well-to-do girls, "education was first religious and moral, and only then intellectual and cultural. They were to develop habits of regularity, neatness, and order, with an emphasis on manners and deportment." The sisters followed "a curriculum in keeping with their aim of producing the ideal Christian woman" (Buetow 1970, 19). Women throughout the ages have had to work within the context of their situation. They often negotiate their surroundings by adhering to some societal standards while breaking others. To create change, such negotiation is often necessary. Such was true of early nineteenth-century American women.

As Kim Tolley has shown, claims about early women's academies are often inaccurate. The pioneer women often cited as establishing the earliest academies for girls actually offered basic, primary education in the early years. Sarah Pierce opened a school for girls in the dining room of her home in Litchfield, Connecticut, moving the school into another building in 1798 and incorporating it as an academy in 1827. Similarly, Catharine and Mary Beecher opened a school in 1823, calling it Catharine and Mary Beecher's School for Girls. "This small school, located over a harness shop on Main Street in Hartford, was clearly an entrepreneurial effort" (Tolley 2001, 232). Many of the sisters' academies, beginning as early as 1798, were very strong by the 1820s, with advanced curricula, including the sciences, state-of-the-art facilities, and large, comfortable boarding accommodations. The sisters were also clearly pioneers of women's education in the United States.

I hope scholars will continue questioning our grand narratives. The stories we have told about women's education have been based largely on happenings in Protestant New England. Such narratives have created a lens through which we see our history, an often limited one. Efforts at women's education were going on outside New England, in religious groups other than the Protestant ones in the East, and in groups marginalized in other ways, as Jacqueline Jones Royster and Shirley Logan have shown. Other groups may not fit the pattern we have created, but learning about them is important and makes out histories richer.

We might also question narratives about the overwhelming influence of the British on U.S. education and about resistance to French culture because of national allegiances. While some early opposition to Catholics in British America and the young United States related to hostilities between the British and the French and Spanish, anti-Catholicism clearly went beyond national antagonisms. As early geography schoolbooks (as well as nineteenth-century tracts and periodicals) demonstrate, American authors disdained all Catholic countries and peoples. But national antagonisms were not simple. By the beginning of the new Republic, Americans had received some support from the French in the Revolutionary War, and it was the British who became the enemy in that war and in the War of 1812. Thomas Jefferson had promoted the French culture in the late eighteenth century, and Americans became fascinated with the French in other ways. French was the foreign language well-bred girls and young women were most expected to know and French fashion that most aspired to, as shown by the major U.S. fashion periodicals that promoted their subscriptions and maintained popularity by including original French fashion plates.

CONCLUSION

The extent of French influence on women's education and on education in general may be worth examining more closely.

Although Mary Kelley attributes the curriculum in early women's academies to the British influence (2006, 21–23), the French affected American society in more ways than language and fashion. Because of the 1763 Treaty of Paris following the French and Indian War and, after 1803, the acquisition of the Louisiana Territory, large parts of the United States were mostly French-speaking, with education in those areas swayed primarily by French religious. There is good reason to believe that the French influenced girls' and women's education in the United States, as the Catholic academies obviously had an impact on other women's education. But there is evidence that other direct influences were in play.

François Fénelon and Madame de Maintenon greatly inspired ideas about women's education, Fénelon especially through his *Treatise on the Education of Girls* (1687) and Madame de Maintenon because of her educational philosophies and her school at St. Cyr. Fénelon was the earliest and most influential proponent of women's education for the late seventeenth and eighteenth centuries, but his work remained important throughout the nineteenth century as well. The European-based communities of women religious cite Fénelon and Madame de Maintenon specifically in their plans of study, and the Sacred Heart nuns explicitly claimed to model their schools on the educational philosophies of the two and on the school at St. Cyr.[2] Other Catholic women educators cite the two as well, especially Fénelon. But, both Fénelon and Madame de Maintenon were also popular among American Protestants. Fenelon's *Treatise* saw numerous, continuous printings in the United States, and American periodicals paid tributes to the two throughout the eighteenth and nineteenth centuries, citing their educational philosophy and curriculum. Fénelon's *Treatise* calls for much of what became popular in women's education during the national period: that vanity and arrogance not be condoned; that modesty and politeness be promoted; and that teachers act as models for students' imitation. He warns against severe or public punishment. Fénelon's instruction for the education of girls is a blueprint for education in Catholic convent academies, but its first and most fully developed argument is for the education of girls because they will be the mothers of future citizens, molding their moral character; it cites many of the reasons scholars now give for Republican Motherhood.

Nearly all Catholic academies taught rhetoric and elocution by the 1820s, and male Catholic religious taught rhetoric and composition to the early sisters in many areas. As I have shown elsewhere (2005), those college professors drew from their own French tradition: from Jesuits René Rapin and Dominique Bouhours, Oratorian Bernard Lamy, and Sulpicians, especially Fénelon; the Catholic schools avoided the virulently hostile George Campbell. Archives and catalogs in U.S. Catholic colleges and seminaries demonstrate that eastern Jesuit schools, such as Georgetown, Gonzaga, Holy Cross, and Loyola, focused primarily on a traditional classical model. However, in eastern Sulpician schools, such as St. Mary's College at Emmitsburg, Maryland, and in western Jesuit schools, such as St. Louis and Xavier, the French influence remained strong through most of the century. In fact, in many of these schools, rhetoric was divided into three categories: Latin (primarily Cicero and Quintilian), Greek (with the main focus on Demosthenes), and English (Hugh Blair). However, rhetoric was taught in French classes, as well, with the Abbé Girard's *Precepts of Rhetoric* a standard text in most schools, often supplemented by such authors as Nicolas Boileau-Despréaux. In his preface, Girard pays tribute to such earlier French influences as Fénelon and Charles Rollin. He draws examples from both classical and modern writers and speakers, but the examples come primarily from French rhetors, with a heavy influence on French religious.

Later in the century, nearly all Catholic colleges relied upon Jesuit Charles Coppens's *Art of Oratorical Composition* and Sulpician Oliver Jenkins's *Student's Handbook of British and American Literature* for more contemporary rhetoric. But to assume that only Catholic colleges used these texts may be an oversimplification. For example, in the popular collection he edited for use at Andover Theological Seminary and other seminaries, Edwards A. Park included extensive excerpts from Fénelon, with few excerpts from Campbell; he made clear that his highest admiration was for Fénelon:

> Dr. Edward Williams says in his Christian Preacher that they (Fénelon's *Dialogues*) are deservedly mentioned by many writers of eminence, with a sort of respect bordering on veneration; and no wonder, for such a union of the sublime and simple of learning familiarity, of judicious criticism and happy illustration; such unaffected humility and warm benevolence, delicate taste and solid sense; and above all, such reverence for sacred things, blended with a subject so often employed by human vanity and pride, are superior excellences very rarely found. (1845, ii)

CONCLUSION

And on Campbell's *Lectures*, Park comments, "Although imperfect, they have yet become a kind of professional classic for the preacher" (iv).

Some nineteenth-century "benevolent" actors might also present a cautionary tale for us. Though admirable in many ways, their assuredness in their own beliefs and acts of benevolence blinded them to their often malevolent acts. Most New England antislavery proponents were aggressively hostile to religious groups outside their own, especially Catholics, often encouraging and partaking in violence against those with whom they disagreed. Their belief in their own righteousness may have, in fact, slowed emancipation, as Stanley Elkins has suggested. The numerous antislavery societies in the South withered in the face of northern abolitionists' fierce attacks on the South and its people. As the Garrisonian faction won out over more moderate factions, Elkins claims, they may have prolonged the evils they were trying to eliminate. Similarly, many Catholic religious, in numerous ways demonstrating compassion for the diseased and suffering neglected by others, participated in the enslavement of people. Neither group seems to have seen their acts as improper in any way, their good intentions and deeds in one area not extended in others. These nineteenth-century abolitionist leaders, as well as Protestant and Catholic women religious who sought and provided education for women, all of whom inspire us in many ways, viewed their world and works through teministic screens. We all do.

APPENDIXES

NOTES

WORKS CITED

INDEX

APPENDIX A: CHRONOLOGICAL INDEX OF THE EARLIEST CATHOLIC WOMEN RELIGIOUS COMMUNITIES IN THE UNITED STATES

Carmelite Sisters

The American Carmelite sisters originated at Port Tobacco, Maryland, in 1790 when Mother Bernardina Matthews and her two nieces, natives of Maryland who had joined the Belgian congregation, along with Sister Clare Joseph Dickerson, left their monastery in Belgium to open a convent in the United States. Although the sisters operated an academy from 1831 to 1851, education was not part of their mission. The Carmelites were a cloistered group whose purpose was prayer and contemplation. Financial pressures and prompting from their bishop led the sisters to enter education for a number of years.

The Order of the Visitation of the Blessed Lady

Three Irish women, Alice Lalor, Ursula Sharpe, and Maria McDermott, formed a community they called the Pious Ladies and opened a school in Philadelphia in 1797. In 1799 the women moved to Georgetown at the Reverend Leonard Neale's behest when he became president of Georgetown College. There, they taught in the academy of the Poor Clares, a group of French religious who had come to the Americas to escape persecution. The Pious Ladies formed a separate community, known as the Order of the Visitation of the Blessed Lady, established Visitation Academy in 1802, and added the property of the Poor Clares to their own when members of the latter group found it safe to return to France. The sisters eventually adopted the European Visitandine religious rule and name; their early literacy efforts, however, resemble those of U.S. communities that lacked such affiliation and that created their own processes of literacy for member-teachers and for students.[1]

Ursuline Sisters

The Ursuline congregation was founded in Brescia, Italy, in 1535 by Angela Merici. French Ursulines first came to the New World in 1639, establishing a school in Quebec and subsequently creating teaching communities in other areas of Canada. In 1727, another group of French Ursulines settled in New Orleans, founding a school there. The Ursuline sisters' convent and academy became a part of the United States in 1803 with the Louisiana Purchase and is the oldest extant convent and school for women in the country. At least three other Ursuline communities arrived in the early nineteenth-century United States. Irish Ursulines from Cork, Ireland, established a convent and school in New York in 1812, but the foundation lasted only a few years. Later, three Irish Ursuline sisters, who had journeyed to the Ursuline convent in Quebec to prepare for teaching, began an academy in Boston, moving to the Boston suburb of Charlestown in 1827 and building Mount Benedict Academy. In 1834, at the behest of Bishop John England, three Irish Ursuline sisters from Cork, Sisters M. Charles Maloney, Borgia McCarthy, and Antonia Hughes, opened an academy in Charleston, South Carolina.

Sisters of Charity of St. Joseph (Emmitsburg)

The earliest religious order in the United States with no early ties to European orders and with all native U.S. initial members, the Sisters of Charity of St. Joseph at Emmitsburg, Maryland (now Daughters of Charity), founded in 1809, was led by Elizabeth Ann Seton, a convert to Catholicism who would become the first American woman canonized to sainthood. Other early members included Cecilia O'Conway, Maria Murphy, Mary Ann Butler, and Susan Clossy. The group was soon joined by Rose Landry White and Seton's sisters-in-law Cecilia and Harriet. Both Elizabeth Seton and White were widows with children. The community was initially near the Sulpician College and Seminary in Baltimore and later neighbored the Sulpician College and Seminary in Emmitsburg. The group joined with the European Sisters of Charity in 1850, taking the European community's rules and habit.

Sisters of Loretto

The Sisters of Loretto, founded in 1812 in rural central Kentucky, originally took the name Friends of Mary at the Foot of the Cross. Mary Rhodes, an educated Marylander, began teaching her brother's children and some neighborhood children in 1811 upon seeing their lack of educational opportunities while she was visiting Kentucky. She was soon joined by Christina Stuart and Ann Havern, and the three, with their cofounder and ecclesiastical superior, Reverend Charles Nerinckx, initiated their religious community with education as a primary mission. Nerinckx, a Belgian priest, wrote their early rules. The convent was near Jesuit and Sulpician establishments, members of both rendering support for the early sisters and their academies.

APPENDIX A

Sisters of Charity of Nazareth

Later in 1812, within fifteen miles of the Sisters of Loretto, Elizabeth (Betsy) Wells and Teresa Carrico, with Father Jean Baptiste David, took first steps at creating another religious community, the Sisters of Charity of Nazareth. The "Annals of the Community of the Sisters of Charity of Nazareth" describe them as "poor and illiterate but of good repute" (1); however, Mary Ellen Doyle, community historian, claims Wells was not entirely illiterate. Wells and Carrico were joined within weeks by Catherine Spalding and several months later by Mary Beaven, Harriet Gardiner, and Mary Gwynn. Spalding, an educated woman from Maryland, took the leadership role for the community and is generally accepted as its cofounder, along with David. The convent and school began on the grounds of St. Thomas Seminary but a short time later relocated, being renamed Nazareth and becoming affiliated with nearby St. Joseph College. Because of the need to prepare early members for their teaching role, the sisters' school did not open until 1814.

Society of the Sacred Heart

The Society of the Sacred Heart originated in France in 1800, founded by Madeleine Sophie Barat. In 1818, Philippine Duchesne led four other sisters from the community to the United States, opening the first free school west of the Mississippi upon their arrival outside St. Louis; later that year they opened an academy and boarding school. The sisters also opened convents and academies in Louisiana in 1821 and 1825, as well as a foundation and school in St. Louis in 1827. They are often seen as counterpart to the Jesuit order because of their close affiliation with the Jesuits at their founding and because their teaching methodology was fashioned on the Jesuit model.

Dominican Sisters of St. Rose

The Dominican Sisters of the United States were founded in 1822, within fifteen miles of the Sisters of Loretto and the Sisters of Charity of Nazareth, near Springfield, Kentucky. At the call of their parish priest and the superior of nearby St. Thomas College, Dominican Samuel Thomas Wilson, Mariah Sansbury, Mary Carrico, Severly Tarleton, and Judith McMan began a religious community of women with the purpose of educating children in their settlement. This community of sisters was one of the earliest to include boys in their schools. The early convent and school were located near St. Rose Dominican Priory.

APPENDIX A

Oblate Sisters of Providence

In 1829, two Baltimore women, Elizabeth Clarisse Lange, originally from Santiago de Cuba, and Marie Magdelaine Balas, an emigrant from the 1790s St. Domingue Revolution, founded the Oblate Sisters of Providence with Sulpician James H. Joubert; theirs was the first African American Catholic teaching congregation in the United States. Joining Lange and Balas shortly after were Rosanne Boegue, another émigré from St. Domingue, and Almaide Duchemin, a Baltimore native. Lange, Balas, and Boegue had been teaching children in the black community for some time when they formally joined as the Oblate Sisters of Providence. Under their new name, they continued their mission of teaching African American children.

Sisters of Charity of Our Lady of Mercy

The Sisters of Charity of Our Lady of Mercy, originally named Sisters of Our Lady of Mercy, were established in 1829 by Bishop John England and four young women, three of them Irish immigrants—Mary and Honora O'Gorman and their niece Teresa Barry—and Mary Elizabeth Burke, who was born in the United States (the O'Gormans and Barry had lived in Baltimore for a number of years). The five met in Baltimore while England was attending the first Provincial Council of Catholic Bishops and agreed to form a religious community modeled on the Sisters of Charity at Emmitsburg. The community began in Charleston, South Carolina, England's diocese. The group was later joined by Julia Datty, a refugee from the St. Domingue revolution and an accomplished teacher and administrator who contributed greatly to the sisters' early success. The sisters operated without a constitution until 1844.

Sisters of Charity of the Blessed Virgin Mary

Sisters of Charity of the Blessed Virgin Mary date their founding to 1833 Philadelphia. Irish women Mary Frances Clarke, Margaret Mann, Eliza Kelly, Rose O'Toole, and Catherine Byrne had joined in community in Dublin in 1831 to pray and teach, opening a small school. In 1833 the women moved to Philadelphia at the urging of a Catholic priest who told them of the great need for work among the Irish in Philadelphia. Here they met the Reverend Terence James Donaghoe, who encouraged them in their educational mission. The women opened a day school in late 1833 and an academy by 1838. In 1843 they moved to the Iowa territory with Donaghoe, expecting to teach Indians, but in fact they provided schools for children of U.S. miners and other settlers there. No record remains of their teaching prior to removing to Iowa.

APPENDIX A

Sisters of St. Joseph of Carondelet

The Sisters of St. Joseph of Carondelet derived from an early French congregation founded in Le Puy, France, in 1650. The congregation was disbanded during the French Revolution, but Mother St. John Fontbonne reestablished the order in 1807. A group of sisters from the congregation came to the United States in 1836, to the St. Louis area. Three of the sisters opened a school in Cahokia, Illinois; the remaining three initiated St. Joseph Academy at Carondelet, outside St. Louis. Later that year, they were joined by two sisters who had been instructed in teaching the hearing impaired and founded St. Joseph Institute for the Deaf.

The following groups, while influential in women's literacy, especially the Detroit sisters, were never formally acknowledged as religious congregations.

Les Dames de la Retraite

Les Dames de la Retraite came to New York from France, led by Madame Hery du Jarday. Du Jarday claimed affiliation with a community founded in 1678 Brittany at Quimper; however, she had apparently left under problematic circumstances and could provide no evidence of support from that community. According to Peter Guilday, the "unstable" du Jarday had caused "considerable alarm" among her superiors in Quimper, leaving in 1831 (1969, 2:142). New York bishop Jean Dubois declined to support her efforts to open a school because she lacked appropriate identification from the European community. Du Jarday's group moved to Philadelphia, opening a short-lived academy there, but soon left Philadelphia for Charleston. Volumes of the *United States Catholic Almanac* for the years 1833 through 1835 list the group's academies. The women resurfaced in St. Augustine and Pensacola, Florida, but left no trace after 1842. No record of their schools exists except for promotions.

Detroit Teachers

In 1804, four women, Angelique Campau, Monique Labadie, Elizabeth Williams, and Elizabeth Lyons, formed a teaching community in Detroit. Although their mentor, Reverend Gabriel Richard, called them sisters, the group was never formally recognized as a religious community.[2] As in other areas, the women were trained and supported by the local clergy, primarily by Father Richard and Reverend John Dilhet, who had been a professor in France. The priests taught the women to specialize in preparation for the academy they would open, supplying them "with first-class chemical apparatus" (Elliott 1901, 506); the group proceeded to train other women as teachers. Three of the four continued to teach in the Detroit area during their entire lifetime, Williams and Lyons "eventually enter[ing] religious houses" (Woodford and Hyma 1958, 84); in time, the fourth married but supported women's higher education in Detroit financially and in other ways for the remainder of her life. All had a profound impact on women's literacy in the Detroit area. According to J. A. Burns, by 1842 there were twenty Catholic schools in the Detroit diocese "not counting mission schools" (1908, 348).

APPENDIX B:
REPRESENTATIVE ACADEMIC RULES AND SCHEDULE

Following are the rules created for the schools of the Sisters of Loretto in 1812. They are typical of those for most early convent schools in the United States.

Rules for the School

1. No denomination is refused, if willing to observe the Rules of the School. The other denominations will not be forced on Sundays and Holidays to go to the Chapel and perform our Christian duties; but they must suffer to be friendly invited. In the School they are to be present at every exercise, and to behave, if not in a religious, at least, in a civil manner.
2. The Boarders are to rise at five O'clock in the summer, and at six in the winter. Being decently dressed, washed, &c. they begin their Prayers, directed by one of the Teachers, which will last till quarter before six. The beginning and the ending will be a Song. A short Meditation; so as to make the whole last some better than half an hour. Then one quarter for fixing beds, cleaning, &c. They are to make up their own beds, if able.
3. At six o'clock, Work-School till seven in the Winter, when Mass or Mass-Prayers. Mass in Summer is one hour sooner.
4. Winter and Summer at eight o'clock, School both for *interns* and *externs*, till half-past ten, when, if advisable, leisure for one quarter.
5. At a quarter before eleven, Work-School till twelve, when to the Oratory for one quarter, after which dinner and leisure till half-past one. In time of breakfast, dinner and supper, some reading. Nothing may be taken between meals: here some exception for younger and weakly.
6. At the beginning of the School, the intention will be directed with some prayer, and once or twice during School. At the end, a Prayer by way of thanksgiving, or a pious Song.

APPENDIX B

7. At half-past one, School as before noon, till half-past three, when a quarter leisure. Then half an hour writing. The residue Work-School till quarter before five; when one quarter chatechizing, or a lesson of instruction. After which, with the usual Prayer or Song, the School finishes that day for the *externs*; who still are allowed to remain longer, and to join the *interns*. The Winter, or some other circumstances, may require some alteration in this time; also for ciphering and arithmetic, a particular time may be determined.

   ***At three the hour of Salvation

8. After the Evening School, recreation or leisure for the *interns* till six. From six till seven, writing, ciphering, or reading. From seven till bed-time, the Rules as in the Community.
9. The youngest Teacher is to sleep in the same room with the Boarders, to keep a particular watch over them.
10. The Scholars are to ask pardon of one another whenever offence is given, and at the ending of the School at night. They also are to pay due honour and respect to their Teachers, Superiors, and Members of the Society: to every one, as also to one another, becoming kindness and civility. All manner of reproach strictly forbidden.
11. Faults are to be corrected, as good deeds and signal improvements are to be rewarded. If one should refuse to submit, she is to be dismissed the third time; and once dismissed, not to be admitted any more. Parents are requested to leave the full direction and authority over their children to the Teachers.
12. There will be writing half an hour before, and half an hour after dinner. A Dictamen twice a week—on Tuesday and Thursday in the afternoon. Every other week in the afternoon, on a Friday, a *Composition* or *Trial* will take place, to determine the improvement in reading, writing, &c. Their places will be made known, and fixed in the School on the following day. The Saturday is a vacation for the *externs*; the *interns* are to repair their clothes, &c. What time is over, they spend it in any useful exercise or piety.
13. None to be admitted for less than three months, for the appointed price, or other terms, if an Orphan. Those that come for first Communion only, are not under this Rule. The poorer class and Negroes will be provided by way of Sunday Schools.

14. An Assistant and Censor will be assigned, taken out of the improved Scholars.
15. None to be admitted that has any contagious complaint, and is to be dismissed when found out, until she be cured. They are to sleep single, as much as possible. All care must be taken to keep their heads, and the whole body neat and clean, for the sake of health and decency, by combing, washing, &c. When sick, so as not to be able to go home, care will be taken of them in the Infirmary, but parents are to look for the expenses, and choose the Doctor.
16. All immodesties in dresses and newfound fashions are most strictly forbidden; as much as possible they are to wear house-spun clothes on week-days, which are to be made plain and full, and in UNIFORM, if possible; of brown, on work-days; of white, on Sundays and Festivals.
17. Every second Sunday in the month is a day of general Confession and Communion. Confession will be heard the Saturday before.
18. NO VACATIONS for those that stay only three months; four days['] vacation if they stay six months; and eight days after one year's stay.—No allowance to be given for unnecessary absences; bad weather, sicknesses, and such like good causes, will excuse.
19. Their boundaries for play, recreation, &c. are to be fixed; a teacher or an assistant will be with them for natural necessities[,] rules and decorum of strictest kind.
20. No Books respiring vanity, immorality, &c. as romances, &c. are admitted in the School.—None of their letters to be sent abroad or received, without the examination of the *Sister Guardian* or a higher superior.
21. No Visits to be paid by interns; the first Monday in the month they may receive in the afternoon, from one till four o'clock, their near relations, provided they have good reasons, and not a bare visit; the whole with the knowledge and in the presence of the *Sister-Guardian*.
22. For books, paper, &c. the parents ought to provide. (Archives of Sisters of Loretto)

APPENDIX B

The schedule for St. Joseph Academy (and perhaps for the day schools initially) follows:

Regulations of the School of St. Joseph
+
Regulations of the School of St. Joseph
about 1812 in the writing of Mother Seton
to be preserved as document of the early times
And as comparison in times future.[1]

Sister Fanny [Jordan][2]

1st class of Grammar Monday and Thursday begins at ½ past 8 to ½ past 9.
2nd class every day—Tuesday and Friday from ½ past 8 to ½ past 9
Half of them sent alternately to writing
2nd class of spelling from ½ past 9 to ½ past 10, during which the 3rd class will alternately go to figures and writing—
3rd class of spelling from ½ 10 to ½ past 11, during which 2nd class will go alternately to figures and writing—
from ½ past 11 to ½ past 12. 2nd and 3rd class will read alternately English with Sister F[anny Jordan] and French with Sister Elizabeth [Boyle] any of either class not learning French will read to [Jane Frances] Gartland or Sister S[usan Clossey] if necessary.

Afternoon

2nd class of geography—during which French read alternately to Sr. Elizabeth [Boyle]
3rd class of geography—[Jane Frances] Gartland
2nd class of reading—Sister [Jane Frances] G[artland] Monday and Thursday
3rd class of reading—[Jane Frances] Gartland
Monday and Thursday 1st class parsing—
Tuesday and Friday 2nd and 3rd class parsing
while 2nd class parse 3rd class read French or repeat
    Cecil [O'Conway]
Writing and work
Sister Kitty [Mullen]—
—Externs and all who want the 1st sections of the Spelling Book
Arithmetic divided between Sister Martina [Quinn] and [Jane Frances] Gartland

APPENDIX B

(Sister [Margaret] George
and Sister Margaret the same person)[3]

3rd class of grammar every day heard while 1st class writes
Monday and Thursday 2nd class of grammar half sent alternately to writing—
1st class reading from ¼ past 10 to ¼ past 11
1st class of geography (repetition) on Tuesday and Friday
succeeds the hour of writing ¾ hour (on Tuesday and Friday)
4 may read French alternately during the repetition—
class of bookkeeping on Monday and Thursday succeeds the hour of writing
    ¾ hour
Sister Fannys 1st class of reading each one 5 minutes each to correct the other
    while 1st class are writing
Heathen Mythology and French vocabulary ¼ past 12.

Afternoon

Monday Tuesday and Friday a given quantity of French translation
Tuesday and Friday practical geography
Monday and Thursday Sister Fannys 2nd class of reading assist Cecilia
    [O'Conway] with work. (*Regulations* 1812)

APPENDIX C: SCHEDULE FOR PUPILS FROM THE URSULINE *RÈGLEMENTS*

Rise 6:00 Summer, 6:30 Winter

    6:45   Morning prayer

    7:00   Mass

Breakfast

    8:00   Classes begin

    10:00   Morning classes end

    10:15   Dinner

Recreation

    12:15   Classes resume

    2:00   Classes end

    2:15   Prayer

    2:45   Lunch

    3:00   Classes resume

    4:15   Catechism, public reading, private reading or work

Supper in silence

Recreation

    6:45   Prayer, examination

    8:25   Retire

NOTES

Introduction: Beyond the Protestant Literacy Myth

1. Edward Gordon and Elaine Gordon are more inclusive of religions other than Protestantism in their excellent 2003 work on literacy.

2. Catherine Clinton, in *The Plantation Mistress* (1982b, xv–xvi), and Elizabeth Fox-Genovese, in *Within the Plantation Household* (1988), have called this the New Englandization of American women's history.

3. In 1701, Jesuit and Recollect religious established a church in Detroit, and by the beginning of the nineteenth century, Sulpician Gabriel Richard had built academies for both boys and girls there (Elliott 1901, 505).

4. Earlier works on "American" and English education helped set the stage for the assumptions in these texts. Such influential texts as Bernard Bailyn's 1960 work *Education in the Forming of American Society: Needs and Opportunities for Study* (Chapel Hill: University of North Carolina Press) and Lawrence Cremin's *American Education: The Colonial Experience, 1607–1783* (New York: Harper and Row) of 1970 assume the importance of Protestantism in promoting literacy. Daniel P. Resnick and Lauren B. Resnick review influential scholars who have promoted the importance of Protestantism to literacy in their 1977 *Harvard Educational Review* article, "The Nature of Literacy: A Historical Exploration."

5. Gawthrop and Strauss cite Karl Holl, 1928, "Die Kulturbedeutung der Reformation," in *Gesammelte Aufsatze zur Kirchengeschichte*, 7th ed., 3 vols. (Tubingen: J. C. B. Mohr), 1:518; H. G Haile, 1976, "Luther and Literacy," *PMLA* 91:816–28; Barbara Konneker, 1975, *Die deutsche Literatur der Reformationszeit: Kommentar zu einer Epoche* (Munich: Winkler), 43; Elizabeth Eisenstein, 1979, *The Printing Press as an Agent of Change*, 2 vols. (Cambridge: Cambridge University Press), 1:333; and Stone (1969, 77–78), as scholars who have concluded or assumed that literacy advanced primarily because of Protestantism following the Reformation.

6. Although some Catholics did become literate, the difficulties of gaining more than the most basic literacy were extreme. According to *The Oxford Companion to Irish History*, "Official figures suggest that in the 1820s between 300,000 and 400,000 children attended hedge schools, the number of schools rising to 9,000 by 1824" (Connolly 2002, 249); however, education in these clandestine

schools must have been rudimentary. Edmund Burke described the penal laws as "a machine as well fitted for the oppression, impoverishment and degradation of a people, and the debasement in them of human nature itself, as ever proceeded from the perverted ingenuity of man" (qtd. in Woodham-Smith 1989, 27).

7. New England Protestants would later demonstrate their hostility toward Catholic nuns and the literacy they provided girls and burn the Ursuline convent and academy in Charlestown, Massachusetts, outside Boston in 1834; the academy was probably the most prestigious academy for girls and young women in New England at the time.

8. The primary purposes of most of the religious congregations were spiritual, educational, and benevolent, but the sisters clearly believed their service to education could make a difference in prejudicial attitudes, reducing the hostility to Catholics and to their religion. For example, the *Rules of the Society and School of Loretto, Kentucky* (Sisters of Loretto) reads:

> The glory of God and the attainment of one's personal sanctification is the primary and essential purpose of the Society: but the special object must never be lost sight of by those belonging to this Society which is to devote one's self completely to the education of females and implanting in them the principles of our holy religion instilling in the minds and hearts of Catholics entrusted to our care its teachings and leading their conduct to virtue but, in the case of Protestants committed to us, removing the prejudices that may have been instilled in them against our religion. (1820, 1; Wolff 1982, 85)

9. The nuns saw the American Indians as eager to learn, and the Indians did come to the convent regularly and in large numbers for instruction, especially in winter, remaining "two or three hours at a time, always occupied in learning their prayers or the Christian doctrine" (*Glimpses* 1897, 43); however, the Indians were fed twice daily (after mass and later after instruction) before leaving, probably a major incentive during the winter when food was scarce. Many were absent in summer. Even during the winter chase, some parents withdrew seminarists from the boarding school for lengthy periods of time so that they could accompany them on hunts. The degree to which the American Indians wanted to learn European, Christian ways is difficult to determine. Probably some did while others did not. Some of the seminarists accepted the new life and married into the French community, one marrying a Three Rivers governor; on the other hand, the nuns also reported "wild" young Indians who could be happy only in nature, outside cities.

10. Greer's purpose is to demonstrate literacy patterns in Canada and to dispel arguments such as that of Lionel Groulx, who claims that the French colonial administration, hand-in-hand with the church, contributed to education

in Canada, and argues further for the decline of literacy rates after the British conquest. Greer studies parish registers of four French Canadian communities, determining that in three of the four, women's signature rate surpassed that of men. The Ursuline nuns had established schools in the three communities where women's signature rate was higher.

11. Many of the communities of sisters were encouraged by their superiors to begin providing schooling for boys toward midcentury, as the need was so great. While some communities refused to change their policy in this regard, some slowly began educating boys as early as the late 1830s.

12. Marriage records were signed by the persons posting bond to assure the court that no lawful cause obstructed the marriage, usually the prospective groom and a male relative of the bride. As the future bride was not asked to sign, the records are not useful for determining the relative rates of literacy. U.S. Census records did not include information on literacy until 1840, and that census, especially, and subsequent ones that tried to interpret literacy levels are highly problematic.

13. In an age of ready-made clothing and easily accessible art prints and decorative tapestries, we sometimes forget the importance for nineteenth-century Americans of the ability to sew for both basic needs and to provide decorative artwork for the home; similarly, our appreciation of the importance of musical knowledge and ability for personal and group pleasure and entertainment may be diminished by the availability of recorded music.

14. As Jacqueline Jones Royster, Shirley Wilson Logan, David Gold, and Catherine Hobbs have begun to demonstrate, literate practices in the South, especially among southern women and African Americans, have been overlooked partly because their practices often necessarily included different patterns from those we have come to expect. Christie Anne Farnham's *The Education of the Southern Belle* provides valuable information on southern academies for girls; however, she fails to include the numerous Catholic academies for girls. While similar in some ways to the academies that Farnham describes, the Catholic academies differ in numerous important ways.

15. Catherine Clinton's argument that northern women found greater independence and opportunities for living outside traditional marriage than southern women did fails to take into account the many southern women who lived together in religious communities (1982b, 56 and 85).

1. Literacy, Religion, and Schoolbooks

1. In the late eighteenth and early nineteenth century the term "schoolbook" was most often used for texts intended for the lower grades; the term "textbook" usually referred to books used in colleges and sometimes academies. Prior to midcentury the term was most often hyphenated: school-book.

2. According to Paul Leicester Ford, in his history of the *New-England Primer*, Rogers was met by his wife and children on the way to his execution, not at the execution, and exhortations attributed to him in the primers were actually those of Robert Smith. *Foxe's Book of Martyrs* reads "in presence of Mr. Rochester, comptroller of the queen's household, Sir Richard Southwell, both the sheriffs, and a great number of people he was burnt to ashes, washing his hands in the flame as he was burning" (qtd. in Ford 1962, 266). Later, Foxe relates that "his wife and children, being eleven in number, ten able to go, and one sucking at her breast, met him by the way, as he went towards Smithfield" (qtd. in Ford 1962, 266). The wife and children are mentioned separately from the crowd at his burning.

3. While the difference might seem minor today, nineteenth-century Protestants and Catholics felt differently. A good example of tension over the two versions is the 1859 Boston Eliot School Rebellion, when Catholic students tried to recite their own version of the commandments at morning exercises.

4. Morse was father of another leading figure in the anti-Catholic press, painter and inventor of the telegraph Samuel F. B. Morse.

5. Callcott reports the typical increase of history as an independent subject in secondary schools as 33 percent by 1825, 77 percent by 1830, and 92 percent by 1860 (58).

6. Copies of William Grimshaw's texts were found in the archives or on lists of texts taught in the early nineteenth century at the Archives of St. Joseph Province House (Sisters of Charity at Emmitsburg), Emmitsburg, Md.; the Archives of Sisters of Loretto, Nerinx, Ky.; and the Archives of Sisters of Charity of Nazareth, Nazareth, Ky.

7. Carey's publishing house was much larger than its Catholic interests. He followed the publication of the Douay Bible with a Protestant Bible; both efforts proved highly profitable for Carey. Also financially lucrative was his publication of Guthrie's *Geography*, discussed above. In addition, he revised other schoolbooks to make them less hostile to Catholics. Carey's most successful agent was the Protestant clergyman, author, and book agent Mason Locke "Parson" Weems.

8. The early Philadelphia publication houses that would become Lippincott also provided Bibles, prayer books, and other materials used in some schools. Grigg and Elliott, an early Quaker publishing house absorbed by Lippincott, published the Grimshaw history texts.

9. Born in Dublin, Carey had been imprisoned by the British for publishing a radical newspaper defending the rights of the Irish. He immigrated to the United States after his release from prison at the recommendation of many friends concerned about his safety.

10. Carroll assured Carey that "I know your accuracy too well, not to be assured, that they [mistakes and inaccuracies] have fallen under your notice, & will be corrected by you" (1793).

11. One southern mayor posted a note in the *New-York Daily Advertiser* thanking benefactors in that city for a "gift" intended for prisoners in the Savannah jail: "Your donation of SchoolBooks is accepted, with our thanks for your good intentions, but as the greatest number of our sufferers had received at least the elements of education, your books, catechisms and pamphlets, will be distributed among the children of the Free School, or some other charitable institution" ("City of Savannah" 1820, 2).

12. New England names remained powerfully influential on American education well into the nineteenth century. In 1837, Dwight family member Edmund Dwight assured the appointment of Horace Mann as first secretary of the Massachusetts Schools Board, even though Mann had virtually no experience for the position, and James G. Carter, who had piloted the bill establishing the board through the legislature, was the presumed shoo-in. In his position as secretary, Mann greatly influenced the direction of education for the entire country.

2. *The Religious Nature of Early Women's Literacy*

1. I use these women as examples because they are the most cited by scholars as *the* pioneers in women's education in the United States. See, for example, Thomas Woody (1929), Shirley Nelson Kersey (1981), S. Alexander Rippa (1969), Woodystine Goodsell (1931), and Kathryn Kish Sklar (1973).

2. The tract societies often published pamphlets without dating, so as to inexpensively reprint materials they expected to use repeatedly. Catholic clergy were clearly concerned about appearances. As early as 1801, faculty minutes of the Sulpician St. Mary's Seminary recorded,

> The Superior expressed his strong wish that women, even domestic, not come into the interior of the house; that is, to shut the mouths, as much as possible, of slanderers who do not fail to use that chance to spread things unfavorable to us. So this is the unanimous decision: 1) the Gentlemen will not have their rooms taken care of by women domestics. 2) No women will be admitted to any upstairs room, except for confession, and even then only if the confession cannot be heard elsewhere. 3) As for the new school building, care must be established from the very beginning to have those two rules observed; if a contrary custom became established, it would be more difficult to do away with it afterwards. ("SMS Faculty" 18 November 1801)

See also entries for 21 September 1810, 11 April 1817, and 10 September 1850.

3. *Awful Disclosures* names the Sisters of Charity as the religious community in charge of the Montreal convent in which Monk supposedly experienced the narrative she recounts; however, the Montreal convent was actually an institution of the Ursuline sisters.

4. McGreevy names Theodore Dwight, of the influential anti-Catholic family, specifically for arranging the publication (2003, 23).

5. Hale made this claim regarding twenty seminaries in the November issue. By December, she reported that "probably, twelve of the fifteen Catholic female Seminaries [were located] in the valley of the Mississippi" (Hale 1834a, 561).

6. Catholics and Protestants had long been in conflict about the validity of Bible translations. Catholics adhered to the Douay translation; Protestants insisted upon the King James Version.

7. Lyman Beecher's initial foe had been the liberal Congregationalists who formed the Unitarian community. He and other New England Congregationalist leaders forced these "dissenters" out of the church. Their anger at the Ursuline academy was surely increased as the Unitarians made up much of the student population of the Catholic academy.

8. Their attitudes toward conversion echo those at the Litchfield Academy. As Sizer and his colleagues have described, "In [Lyman] Beecher's mind, as well as in the beliefs of Sarah Pierce and John Pierce Brace [Pierce's nephew and Litchfield headmaster], conversion followed a series of steps from the soul's awakening to its neglect of God, to a renunciation of worldly interests and a turning to God, to an acceptance of one's former state of sinfulness, to repentance, and—finally—to total submission to God's will" (1993, 58).

9. Anne Firor Scott has suggested that "as far as it can be determined, Emma Willard and her young contemporary, Catharine E. Beecher, were the first to grasp the possibilities inherent in such networks and the first to experiment with institutional links among women going beyond a single community" (1978, 696); however, both Willard and Beecher followed upon the systems established by the Catholic sisters.

10. Willard had actually criticized boarding schools as late as 1819 in her *Plan for Improving Education*, which she delivered before the New York Legislature ([1819] 1918). Sklar also claims that teaching was not a woman's profession in 1830, naming Catharine Beecher "the first to envision teaching as a profession dominated by . . . women" (1973, 97), but Catholic sisters had been making teaching a profession in the United States for decades.

11. Responding to concerns about how low-paid teachers would care for themselves in sickness, Lyon suggested,

> Let them do just what they would have done, if they had not received a superior education, let them do what other unmarried females, in good standing in society, but without property, do in case of sickness. Most of these, in time of health just live along, coming out even at the end of the year, & no more. And they may be very happy in living on mutual acts of kindness, & perhaps those who by their good deeds, lay up a large store in

the hearts of others, are made as comfortable in time of sickness, & feel as little solicitude as any other females who are dependent on their own exertions. (qtd. in Green 1979, 113)

12. Edward Beecher later published a prominent anti-Catholic text, *The Papal Conspiracy Exposed*.

13. Sarah Pierce's school was not a boarding school. Students boarded with families in Litchfield; one of those families was the Beecher family. Catharine Beecher, who attended Pierce's school, describes it in the following manner:

Her school house was a small building of only one room, probably not exceeding 80 ft. by 70, with small closets at each end, one large enough to hold a piano, and the others used for bonnets and over garments. The plainest pine desks, long plank benches, a small table and an elevated teacher's chair, constituted the whole furniture. When I began school there, she was sole teacher, aided occasionally by her sister in certain classes, and by her brother-in-law in penmanship. At that time the "higher branches" had not entered female schools. Map-drawing, painting, embroidery and the piano, were the accomplishments sought, and history was the only study added to geography, grammar, and arithmetic. (qtd. in Vanderpoel and Buel 1903, 179)

3. U.S.-Based Convents and the Literacy Experience

1. Upheavals threatened the colony prior to the Anglican establishment. When Virginia established the Anglican Church as the state church, Virginia Puritans moved into Maryland and gained control of governance, abolishing the Act of Toleration and establishing the Congregational Church. Lord Baltimore regained control of the colony and reenacted toleration, but shortly thereafter Anglicans came into control of the colony and again repealed the Act of Toleration.

2. The earliest Catholic convents and other Catholic institutions were established outside New England, as Catholics rarely settled in that area. The New England states were last to disestablish religion: New Hampshire in 1817, Connecticut in 1818, Maine in 1820, and Massachusetts not until 1833 (Lambert 2003, 225).

3. The Carmelites founded the earliest permanent community of Catholic women religious in the United States in 1790. This study begins with the Pious Ladies, however, who joined in community in 1797 Philadelphia and moved to Georgetown in 1799, founding Visitation Academy in 1802. The Carmelites were a contemplative cloistered order, teaching only later and under pressure, as teaching was not their mission.

4. Kentucky was not atypical. Common schools were becoming "common" only in more populated areas of the country by this time. Near the turn of the century, land grants had provided for academies in frontier areas, yet inadequate income from the land and a complete lack of other public support prevented continuous schooling in most cases. Those districts that did institute academies required tuition that made attendance unaffordable for most students and the academies essentially private in nature. Free public common schools were nonexistent; educational opportunities for girls were especially rare.

5. Kentucky superintendent of public instruction B. B. Smith wrote Bishop Flaget with regard to assistance from education taxes:

> In case no such understanding should satisfy the Roman Catholic Community and they should altogether decline any participation in the benefits of the proposed System, as one of the Board of Education, I shall be prompt to move the Legislature to relieve our Roman Catholic Fellow Citizens, from the burden of the neighborhood tax from the advantages of which they may feel themselves excluded; on condition that some security be given for the education of every child of Roman Catholic parents, between the ages of 7 and 17 years; it seeming to me reasonable that the state should insist that no portion of its population should grow up in ignorance. (n.d.)

Some support continued until the 1960s.

6. St. Joseph College was considered by many the best in the South. Among those who attended the school were James Speed, attorney general under President Lincoln, and a number of southern governors.

7. David apparently did this out of necessity. He expressed anger at the Emmitsburg community, from whom he had requested sister-teachers who could train those at Nazareth, for neglecting his request.

8. I received this information from Knecht in an e-mail dated 11 May 2015.

9. Woodson calls the sisters' academy a "center for enlightenment of colored women" (1919, 140).

10. The convent of the Oblate Sisters of Providence was an exception, having established a dowry of $400. Morrow suggests that the archbishop, who set the dowry, "undoubtedly intended to bolster the community's financial self-sufficiency" (2002, 50–51). The dowry could be waived.

11. A sign of the prestige of these academies can be seen by the attention given them by notable political leaders; many presidents visited the Georgetown Visitation Academy. President John Quincy Adams presided at closing ceremonies in 1828; others who visited or participated in ceremonies include Andrew Jackson, John Tyler, James K. Polk, Zachary Taylor, James Buchanan, and Ulysses S. Grant. Henry Clay gave premiums at the first Nazareth graduation. Daughters of Jefferson Davis, Zachary Taylor, and southern governors attended that school.

12. McNeil phrases this as "educat[ing] them with as much care and daily regularity as our pay boarders" (1996, 198), quoting an 1820 letter from Seton to Filicchi found in Kelly (1981, 230). However, care and daily regularity does not necessarily equate to curriculum.

13. In 1834, the Oblates charged $80 annual board with $4 per month tuition. This might be compared with the basic charge of $160 at the Visitation Academy and $147 at the Sisters of Charity's St. Joseph Academy in Emmitsburg (Morrow 2002, 110).

14. Carroll's manual is titled *On Education Book 1st*, but if she created a second manual or more, they have not been found. The manual is not paginated.

15. The Archives of the Sisters of Loretto seem to have contained the most extensive collection of extant books from the early days. Declan Carroll's 1937 dissertation lists *Keith on Globes*; *Geographical, Historical and Commercial*; *Modern Geography*; Echard's *Roman History*; Rollin's *Ancient History* (in eight volumes and translated into English); a variety of history books by Grimshaw; Hunt and Noyes's *History of the Revolutions in Europe*; *Chateaubriand's Travels*; *Guide to Classical Learning*; *Elemens de Politesse*; Comley's *English Grammar*; and several French/English dictionaries. The precarious nature of archives is demonstrated in the fact that Sister Kate Misbach, the archivist when I visited, could not locate a record of the books. As Carroll's dissertation is meticulously researched, I have no doubt she found the books.

16. The Archives of St. Joseph Province House (Sisters of Charity at Emmitsburg), Md., contain a few early texts. One 1802 copy of *Lecons de Fenelon* bears the name of Annina Seton, the daughter of Elizabeth Seton. *Lecons* is intended for children, with fables, historical stories, dialogues, and moral promptings. The archives also contain an 1803 fourth edition of Lindley Murray's *Murray's English Reader*. Murray's texts were likely used in many of the schools. In addition, the archives hold an 1831 copy of Reverend J. L. Blake's *Natural Philosophy*, a comprehensive examination with chapters on gravity, motion, mechanics, astronomy, hydrostatics, water, pneumatics, and optics (RB 11-5-24).

17. For a fuller account of Carroll's fascinating literary guide for teachers, see Powell (2012).

18. See early books and papers, 11-5-24a-4, ASJPH. Another title, *A Devout Life—St. Francis de Sales*, celebrates the patron of the Sisters of Charity; the classic *Paradise Lost* was also included.

19. Elizabeth Seton warned her daughter and the older students at the academy that "reading romances and attending the theater could distort their values" (McNeil 1996, 197).

20. The definitions of politeness and courtesy seem to have been assumed to have general understanding.

21. Bishop Martin J. Spalding explained that the sisters moved "for greater convenience and retirement" (1844, 233).

22. Bracketed information appears in original.

23. According to Maes, as the original site was "so dear to the sisters because of its manifold associations with their early struggles and sufferings," and since they were "unwilling to have old Loretto desecrated by indifferent men for worldly purposes, the sisters set fire to the convent and chapel after they had removed the rest of their household to the new place" (1880, 576).

4. *Literacy in Convent Schools of European-Based Congregations*

1. Sister Joan Marie Aycock, archivist at the New Orleans Ursuline convent while I was conducting this study, told me that when members of her community die, all letters and personal effects are destroyed to protect the sisters' privacy. The Sisters of St. Joseph did not arrive until the late 1830s, and difficult material circumstances took most of their time; they left less information regarding their impressions prior to 1840. Additionally, there were many fewer communities for this category—those who came well prepared to teach with explicit manuals for proceeding—than for those who initiated teaching communities without a history and established methodology for teaching.

2. Other short-lived communities taught in the United States during this period but provide less material for this chapter. Irish Ursulines taught in New York from 1812 to 1815, and Belgian Poor Clares created a school in Pittsburgh from approximately 1828 to 1830. According to Burns, Poor Clares also opened schools in Cincinnati for a short time but moved, some to Pittsburgh, others to Detroit. Disagreements with their bishop and ecclesiastical superior over administrative and property issues led to the closing of those schools as well (1908, 329, 338, 346). A group calling itself Les Dames de le Retraite, but without support from the European community, lasted a few years; little information about their schools or pedagogies remains. The Sisters of the Blessed Virgin taught briefly in Philadelphia before moving permanently to Iowa in the 1840s. Few records remain of their literacy efforts before they removed to Iowa.

3. The tradition had a long history. Marie Tranchepain, who led twelve religious women in community to New Orleans, had been inspired by Guyart's letters (Clark 1999, 8–9, 16). Subsequently, Marie Madeleine Hachard, one of the women accompanying Tranchepain, had not professed final vows and was therefore free to write of her adventure to her father, Jacques Hachard, who published the letters in France. Hachard's letters, too, influenced French girls to consider a missionary life in the New World.

4. Other communities assured continued learning as well. In the Sisters of St. Joseph community, Sisters Celestine Pommerel and Julie Fournier (a

novice, later Sister St. John), who had studied methods for teaching the hearing impaired in France, taught other members to teach sign language for the deaf, that tradition expanding to numerous schools taught by women religious.

5. Irish Ursulines established Mount Benedict Academy, not the French Ursulines who had established the Ursuline Academy in New Orleans.

6. For an interesting theorization of the rhetorical nature of needlework, see Goggin (2002).

7. The importance of good transcribers of textbooks may be seen in Duchesne's letter to Barat, 8 October 1821, as she outlines the strengths of each of her teachers: "Sister Xavier has a good memory and translates both languages fluently. That is a great help in getting our French books into English" (Callan 1957, 350).

8. American expectations also surface in other details of the promotion, such as accountability to parents:

> To accelerate the advancement of the Young Ladies in their respective classes, every means is resorted to, which is calculated to act upon the youthful mind, in order to excite and maintain therein, a laudable emulation: such as distinction of places; daily marks; weekly repetitions; privileges granted to application and merit; honorable mention made every month of those whose assiduity in their studies, and excellence in good conduct, deserve approbation; premiums distributed at the end of the year, &c. (*United States Catholic Almanac* 1833, 91)

5. Literacy, Benevolence, and the Paradox of Good Works

1. Ewens suggests that Catholic sisters may have been more effective than male religious in altering prejudicial attitudes toward Catholics (1981, 101).

2. The press commonly used the term Sisters of Charity when reporting on the sisters' good works. Although the various Sisters of Charity communities furnished many of the nurses during the war, numerous other communities of sisters became actively involved as well.

3. See also *Saratoga Sentinel*, 2 July 1833, 2; *Charleston Courier*, 3 July 1833, 1; *Worcester National Aegis*, 3 July 1833, 2; and *Boston American Traveller*, 5 July 1833, 2.

4. The mayor "tender[ed] the sincere and grateful thanks of the Board of Health and myself" to

> Sisters *Barbara, Claire, Loecadia, Julia* and *Euprozene*, at hospital No. 2—to Sisters *Mary Paul, Domtella, Mary Jane* and *Mary James*, at hospital No. 3—to Sisters *Ambrosia*, superior of the infirmary; and also, to *Henrietta, Dorothea, Hillaria, Octavia, Delphine* and *Chrysostom*, of that

institution,—to Sisters Felicity, superior to the orphan's asylum; and also to *Camilia, Bernerdine, Marcelliva Brozilia* and *Alphonso*, of that institution for their unwearied attention to the sick of cholera; and although they will receive no pecuniary remuneration from us, yet I humbly hope, their reward is registered in heaven. ("Mayor's Office" 1832)

5. Ely famously created the Christian Party and in a speech on 4 July 1827 called for "Christian freemen to elect Christian Rulers." Ely felt "true" Christians could control offices by joining together. A Presbyterian himself, he cited Presbyterians, Baptists, Methodists and Congregationalists, with perhaps Germans in Ohio and Pennsylvania and Reformed Dutch in New York. He did not include Catholics as "true Christians."

6. Many European sisters had a long history of caring for the sick. More recently, they had nursed wounded soldiers in the Crimean War. Twenty-four of Florence Nightingale's thirty-eight nurses came from Catholic or Anglican women religious communities. According to Mary McAuley Gilgannon, "whatever semblance [Nightingale's nursing group] possessed of being a cohesive body" came from the Irish and English Sisters of Mercy (qtd. in Maher 1999, 29).

7. That Chittenden's remark was often attributed to Lincoln probably only increased the effect. For other praise among high-ranking military and government officials, see Maher (1999).

8. See also *Charleston Mercury*, 24 July 1861, 1, and 14 November 1863, 2; *Arkansas True Democrat* (Little Rock), 15 August 1861, 2, and 21 November 1861, 2; *Savannah Republican*, 4 September 1861, 2; *Dubuque Herald*, 16 April 1862, 4; *Daily Missouri Republican*, 19 April 1862, 2; and *Chicago Daily Tribune*, 9 May 1862, 3.

9. Various versions of this appeal had been heard since Sarah Josepha Hale's call for Protestant women to save the West from Catholicism. More typical were calls such as this in the *New York Daily Times*: "What is especially needed for this penitentiary hospital is a body of Christian women to visit the sick. Why are there not Protestant 'Sisters of Charity'? So far as we know, the only ladies who have attempted to do good among these poor creatures have been Roman Catholic. We honor them for it" ("The Prison-Hospital" 1852).

10. The 1886 biographical sketch of Crawford by Leigh Irvine in *The Poet Scout: A Book of Song and Story* depicts his difficult background working in the coal mines to support his family, unable to attend school; during the war, as he recuperated from serious wounds at Philadelphia's Saterlee Hospital, a Sister of Charity had taught him to read and write.

11. The communities represented by the monument are as follows: Sisters of St. Joseph, Carmelites, Dominicans, Ursulines, Sisters of the Holy Cross, Sisters of the Poor of St. Francis, Sisters of Mercy, Congregation of the Sisters

of Our Lady of Mercy, Daughters of Charity of St. Vincent de Paul, Sisters of Charity of Nazareth, Sisters of Providence of Saint Mary-of-the-Wood, and Congregation of Divine Providence.

12. Popular early spellers often naturalized the word "slavery," including it in chains of common words with long *a* sounds; Noah Webster, himself a staunch Congregationalist, included the word in all his "Blue-Backed Spellers."

13. Mann was not sensitive to non-Protestant groups either. Despite the strong feelings of many religious groups, Mann felt "if the word of God—personified in the King James Bible—were taught without comment, how could that conceivably be sectarian?" (qtd. in Cremin 1957, 13).

14. Jones was patriarch of the Georgia family made famous in the twentieth-century publication *The Children of Pride*.

15. For a more complete account of slavery and religion in the United States, see Raboteau (2004) and Genovese (1974, 159–284).

16. Clark found no concerns about their practice among the New Orleans Ursulines. Similarly, Doyle found that Mother Catherine Spalding of the Sisters of Charity of Nazareth "viewed [the enslaved] much like children, to be cared for materially and spiritually, assigned tasks, supervised, and then trusted, rewarded, or penalized according to performance" (2006, 122). I have found no evidence of concern among the communities who practiced enslavement.

17. Maes cites an 1824 Nerinckx letter: "Two days ago, twelve young ladies offered themselves at Loretto for the little veil, amongst them our three blacks, who received nearly all the votes! Their dress is to be different, also the offices and employment, but they keep the main rules of the society; they will take the vows, but not the perpetual ones, before twelve years of profession. Their rules are set apart" (1880, 510). Nerinckx's reference to "our blacks" is to three children who had been adopted by the society at his encouragement in preparation for this moment.

18. According to Duchesne,

> Monseigneur Du Bourg has said positively that we may not admit [Negroes and mulattoes] to either of our schools, and he has appointed one day a week for the instruction of the colored people; otherwise, he says, we should not hold the white children in school. He told us of an experience he had in the college in Baltimore, which shows how difficult it is to overcome race-prejudice in this country. He consulted the Archbishop of Baltimore on the matter and was told that this attitude would have to be maintained as the last safeguard of morality and manners in this country. (qtd. in Callan 1957, 277)

19. For fuller accounts of Catholicism and slavery, see McGreevy (2003, 43–67). See also Raboteau (2004, 87–90), Hennesey (1983, 143–57), and Fitz (1999).

20. Other, smaller contributors were Nathan and David Hale, nephews of Revolutionary War hero Nathan Hale, and Gerard Hallock.

21. The book was composed of a series of attacks Morse had published in the *New York Journal of Commerce*.

22. For example, in 1844 the Methodist Church split over the status of Bishop James A. Andrew, a slaveholder, but this came after decades of internal conflict. Southern Methodists created the Methodist Evangelical Church South. The Presbyterian General Assembly broke apart in 1838 but reunited in 1869. In 1844 Georgia Baptist slaveholder James E. Reeve applied to be a missionary but was refused because such admission would violate the church's policy of neutrality over slavery. Later (upon challenge from Alabama) the board ruled that it could not be party to any arrangement that suggested its approval of slavery. The Southern Baptist Convention was founded the following year; the two churches remain separate today.

Conclusion

1. For example, Sister Mary Bernard of the Sisters of St. Joseph became the first nurse to specialize in nurse anesthesia. Some of the sisters' hospitals evolved into the significant research hospitals we recognize today. For example, Mayo Clinic began as St. Mary's Hospital, a hospital of the Franciscan sisters (American Association of Nurse Anesthetists 2014).

2. The sisters' mandate to educate upper-class girls in their academies makes sense in light of their adhering to the model at St. Cyr, which had been founded to provide education for daughters of nobility.

Appendix A: Chronological Index of the Earliest Catholic Women Religious Communities in the United States

1. Two communities preceded the Visitandines in the D.C. area, the Carmelites and the Poor Clares. The Poor Clares, French noblewomen who had come to America to escape the French Reign of Terror, returned to France in 1804. Other small groups of Poor Clares opened schools for brief periods in Cincinnati, Pittsburgh, and Detroit but formed no permanent communities in the United States until 1875, and records of their earlier schools are not extant. The Carmelites also created an early convent in Port Tobacco, Maryland (1790); however, they initiated a school under pressure from religious leaders and out of economic necessity. Education of young women and girls was not a part of their original mission, and they discontinued their school when they found it feasible. A group of Trappistines settled in New York from 1812 to 1815.

2. In an 8 October 1821 letter to Madeleine Sophie Barat, Philippine Duchesne explained the failure of the Detroit community to become a formal religious community after she had a visit from Father Richard:

Monseigneur Flaget wants them to make their novitiate under a superior who knows religious life, before they bind themselves by perpetual vows. He wanted to send someone from one of the orders in Kentucky, either the Sisters of Charity, who have a modified rule, or the Penitents, who resemble the Trappists. They had not enough money to undertake this long journey, and besides, Father Richard and his nuns are Canadians, and they do not want to merge with Americans, so nothing has come of it at all. They want to be trained by a French religious, and Father Richard is asking us to send them a superior. I told him it is impossible just now. (qtd. in Callan 1957, 352)

Appendix B: Representative Academic Rules and Schedule

1. According to Regina Bechtle and Judith Metz, editors of *Elizabeth Bayley Seton: Collected Writings* (in which these regulations appear), this notation was written by Revered Simon Bruté (Seton 2006, 3b:124n1).

2. Bechtle and Metz completed the names in brackets in this document.

3. According to Bechtle and Metz, "In another hand the following note is added on the side: 'Mother writes Sr. George because she first called Sr. Margaret [that] a long time ago—'" (Seton 2006, 3b:126n5).

WORKS CITED

AOSP	Archives, Oblate Sisters of Providence, Baltimore, Md.
ASCN	Archives of Sisters of Charity of Nazareth, Nazareth, Ky.
ASJPH	Archives of St. Joseph Province House (Sisters of Charity at Emmitsburg), Md.
ASL	Archives of Sisters of Loretto, Loretto, Ky.
ASMSU	Associated Archives at St. Mary's Seminary and University, Baltimore, Md.
ASSH	Archives, Society of the Sacred Heart, Canadian and United States Province Archives, St. Louis, Mo.
ASSJ	Archives, Sisters of St. Joseph of Carondelet, St. Louis Province, Mo.
DLB	Duplicate Letter Book, Archives of Sisters of Charity of Nazareth, Nazareth, Ky.
FHS	Filson Historical Society, Louisville, Ky.
UNDA	University of Notre Dame Archives, South Bend, Ind.

"An Act against Jesuits and Popish Priests." (1700) 1894. In *The Seventh Assembly, Second Session. 25 July 1700. The Colonial Laws of New York from the Year 1664 to the Revolution*, 428–30. Albany: J. B. Lyon.

American Association of Nurse Anesthetists. 2014. "History of Nurse Anesthesia Practice." http://www.aana.com/ceandeducation/students/Documents/history-nap-student.pdf.

"Annals of the Community of the Sisters of Charity Established at St. Joseph's, Frederick Co., Md. Compiled by Sister Bernard Boyle." N.d. ASJPH.

"Annals of the Community of the Sisters of Charity of Nazareth." N.d. ASCN.

Barat, Madeleine Sophie. 1850. *Letters of Saint Madeleine Sophie Barat to Our Religious*. 2 vols. Surbiton, Surrey: Anchor Press Rashpern Ltd.

Barksdale, Hamlett. 1914. *History of Education in Kentucky*. Frankfort: Kentucky Department of Education.

Barrett, M. Matilda. N.d. *One Hundred and Fifty Years: Part 1, 1812–1890*. N.p. ASL.

WORKS CITED

Barth, Pius J. 1945. *Franciscan Education and the Social Order in Spanish North America, 1502–1821.* Chicago: n.p.

Barton, George. (1897) 1898. *Angels of the Battlefield: A History of the Labors of the Catholic Sisterhoods in the Late Civil War.* Philadelphia: Catholic Art Publishing Company.

Baudier, Roger. 1939. *The Catholic Church in Louisiana.* New Orleans: n.p.

Baym, Nina. 1991. "Women and the Republic: Emma Willard's Rhetoric of History." *American Quarterly* 43 (1): 1–23.

———. 1992. *Feminism and American Literary History: Essays.* New Brunswick, N.J.: Rutgers University Press.

Beadie, Nancy. 2001. "Academy Students in the Mid-Nineteenth Century: Social Geography, Demography, and the Culture of Academy Attendance." *History of Education Quarterly* 41:251–61.

Beals, Carlton. 1960. *Brass-Knuckle Crusade: The Great Know-Nothing Conspiracy, 1820–1860.* New York: Hastings House.

Bede, Brother. (1923) 1926. *A Study of the Past and Present Applications of Educational Psychology in the Catholic Schools of the Diocese of Louisville.* Baltimore: St. Mary's Industrial School Press.

Beecher, Catharine E. 1835. *Essay on the Education of Female Teachers; Written at the Request of the American Lyceum and Communicated at Their Annual Meeting, New York, May 8th, 1835.* New York: Van Nostrand and Dwight.

———. 1846. *The Evils Suffered by American Women and American Children: The Causes and the Remedies.* New York: Harper and Bros.

Beecher, Catharine E., and Harriet Beecher Stowe. (1869) 2002. *The American Woman's Home.* Edited by Nicole Tonkovich. New Brunswick, N.J.: Rutgers University Press.

Beecher, Edward. 1835. *The Papal Conspiracy Exposed, and Protestantism Defended, in the Light of Reason, History and Scripture.* New York. M. S. Dodd.

Beecher, Lyman. 1835. *A Plea for the West.* Cincinnati: Truman and Smith.

———. 1961. To Catharine Beecher. In *The Autobiography of Lyman Beecher,* edited by Barbara M. Cross, 2:167–69. Cambridge, Mass.: Harvard University Press.

Best, Harry. 1943. *Deafness and the Deaf in the United States, Considered Primarily in Relation to Those Sometimes More or Less Known as "Deaf-Mutes."* New York: Macmillan.

"Bethlehem Academy." 1959. *Loretto Magazine* 1 (1): 20. ASL.

"The Bible a New School Book for Roman Catholics." 1817. *Religious Intelligencer* (Boston), 15 February, 657; 22 February, 613; 8 March, 644; 15 March, 657.

Billington, Ray Allen. 1938. *The Protestant Crusade, 1800–1860: A Study of the Origins of American Nativism.* New York: Rinehart and Company.

Bingham, Caleb. 1794. *The American Preceptor.* Boston: Manning and Loring. Early American Imprints, Series 1.

Bizzell, Patricia, and Bruce Herzberg. 2001. *The Rhetorical Tradition: Readings from Classical Times to the Present.* Boston: Bedford/St Martin's.

Boas, Louise Schutz. 1935. *Woman's Education Begins: The Rise of the Women's Colleges.* Norton, Mass.: Wheaton College Press.

Bodine-Reed, Cheryl A. 2013. "A Comparative Analysis of the Education of Middle-Class and Upper-Class Women in Paris and Saint Louis (1863–1882)." PhD diss., St. Louis University.

Brainard, Ezra. 1893. *The Life and Work in Middlebury Vermont of Emma Willard.* New York: Evening Post Job Printing Company.

Brouillet, Eliza McKenny. 1890–91. "Memoirs of Eliza McKenny Brouillet." D-M-5b,c. ASSJ.

Bruckner, Martin. 2006. *The Geographic Revolution in Early America: Maps, Literacy, and National Identity.* Chapel Hill: University of North Carolina Press.

Bruté, Simon. (1836) 1978. "Bishop Bruté's Report to Rome in 1836." In *Documentary Reports on Early American Catholicism*, edited by Philip Gleason, 177–233. Translated by Thomas T. McAvoy. New York: Arno Press.

Buetow, Harold A. 1970. *Of Singular Benefit: The Story of Catholic Education in the United States.* London: Macmillan.

Burns, J. A. 1908. *The Catholic School System in the United States: Its Principles, Origin, and Establishment.* New York: Benziger Brothers.

———. 1969. *The Growth and Development of the Catholic School System in the United States.* New York: Arno Press.

Butler, Frederick W. 1817. *A Catechetical Compend of General History, Sacred and Profane; from the Creation of the World, to the Year 1817, of the Christian Era, in Three Parts.* 4th ed. Hartford: Cooke and Hale. Early American Imprints, Series 2.

———. 1819. *Sketches of Universal History, Sacred and Profane, from the Creation of the World, to the Year 1818, of the Christian Era, in Three Parts.* 2nd ed. Hartford: Cooke and Hale. Early American Imprints, Series 2.

———. 1821. *A Complete History of the United States of America Embracing the Whole Period from the Discovery of North America Down to the Year 1820.* Elizabethtown, N.J.: Mervin Hale. Early American Imprints, Series 2.

Button, H. Warren, and Eugene F. Provenzo Jr. 1983. *History of Education and Culture in America.* Englewood Cliffs, N.J.: Prentice-Hall.

Byrne, Patricia. 1986. "Sisters of St. Joseph: The Americanization of a French Tradition." *U.S. Catholic Historian* 5 (3/4): 241–72.

———. 1995. "A Tradition of Educating Women: The Religious of the Sacred Heart and Higher Education." *U.S. Catholic Historian* 13 (4): 49–79.

Callan, Louise. 1937. *The Society of the Sacred Heart in North America.* London: Longmans, Green, and Co.

———. 1957. *Philippine Duchesne: Frontier Missionary of the Sacred Heart, 1769–1852*. Westminster, Md.: Newman Press.

Callcott, George H. 1970. *History in the United States, 1800–1860: Its Practice and Purpose*. Baltimore: Johns Hopkins Press.

Campbell, Joan. 1987. *Loretto in Louisiana: The Legacy of La Fourche*. Nerinx, Ky.: Sisters of Loretto.

Capers, William. 1853. *Catechism for the Use of Methodist Missions*. 3rd ed. Charleston, S.C.: John Early.

Carey, Mathew. 1898–1900. "Selections from the Correspondence of the Deceased Mathew Carey." *Records of the American Catholic Historical Society of Philadelphia*, 9:352–55; 10:222–25; 11:67, 213, 338; 12:96–105; 13:237–47. Philadelphia: American Catholic Historical Society of Philadelphia.

Carpenter, Charles. 1963. *History of American Schoolbooks*. Philadelphia: University of Pennsylvania Press.

Carr, Jean Ferguson, Stephen L. Carr, and Lucille M. Schultz. 2005. *Archives of Instruction: Nineteenth-Century Rhetorics, Readers, and Composition Books in the United States*. Carbondale: Southern Illinois University Press.

Carroll, Columba. N.d. "Course of Literary Studies." ASCN.

———. N.d. *On Education Book 1st: Boarding Schools for Young Ladies*. ASCN.

Carroll, Declan. 1937. "The American Sisters of Loretto: Pioneer Educators." Lexington: University of Kentucky Press. ASL.

Carroll, John. (1785) 1978. *Report for the Eminent Cardinal Antonelli Concerning the State of Religion in the United States of America*. In *Documentary Reports on Early American Catholicism*, edited by Philip Gleason, 152–54. New York: Arno Press.

———. 1793. To Mathew Carey. 3 August. "Selections from the Correspondence of the Deceased Mathew Carey." *Records of the American Catholic Historical Society of Philadelphia*, 9:372 (1898). Philadelphia: American Catholic Historical Society of Philadelphia.

Carter, Karen E. 2011. *Creating Catholics: Catechism and Primary Education in Early France*. Notre Dame: University of Notre Dame Press.

A Catechism, or Short Abridgement of Christian Doctrine Newly Revised for the Use of the Catholic Church in the United States of America. 1816. Georgetown, D.C.: Wm. Duffy. Early American Imprints, Series 2.

The Catholic Calendar and Laity's Directory. 1834. Baltimore: Fielding Lucas Jr.

Ceplair, Larry, ed. 1989. *The Public Years of Sarah and Angelina Grimké: Selected Writings, 1835–1839*. New York: Columbia University Press.

Challoner, Richard. (1737) 1786. *The Catholick Christian Instructed in the Sacraments, Sacrifice, Ceremonies, and Observances of the Church. By Way of Question and Answer*. Philadelphia: Christopher Talbot.

Charpy, Elizabeth. N.d. *A Way to Holiness: Louise de Marillac*. Dublin: Mount Salus Press Ltd. ASJPH.

Chiniquy, Charles. N.d. *The Priest, the Woman, and the Confessional*. 44th ed. Toronto: Gospel Witness. UNDA.

Chittenden, Lucius E. 1891. *Reactions of President Lincoln and His Administration*. New York: Harper and Brothers.

"Cholera." 1833a. *Alexandria (Va.) Gazette*, 27 June, 2, reprinted from the *Bardstown (Ky.) Herald*. America's Historical Newspapers.

"The Cholera." 1833b. *Philadelphia Inquirer*, 28 June, 2. Early American Newspapers.

"The Cholera." 1833c. *Albany Argus*, 2 July, 1. Early American Newspapers.

"Cholera." 1835. *United States Catholic Miscellany*. 21 February, 269. Early American Newspapers.

"City of Savannah, Police Office." 1820. *New-York Daily Advertiser*, 3 March, 2. Early American Newspapers.

Clark, Emily. 1997. "'By All the Conduct of Their Lives': A Laywomen's Confraternity in New Orleans, 1730–1744." *William and Mary Quarterly*, 3rd ser., 54:4.

———. 1998. "A New World Community: The New Orleans Ursulines and Colonial Society, 1727–1803." PhD diss., Tulane University.

———, ed. 2007. *Voices from an Early American Convent: Marie Madeleine Hachard and the New Orleans Ursulines, 1727–1760*. Baton Rouge: Louisiana State University Press.

Clinton, Catherine. 1982a. "The Education of the Planter Daughter in the Early Republic." *Journal of the Early Republic* 2 (1): 39–60.

———. 1982b. *The Plantation Mistress: Woman's World in the Old South*. New York: Pantheon.

Coburn, Carol K., and Martha Smith. 1999. *Spirited Lives: How Nuns Shaped Catholic Culture and American Life, 1836–1920*. Chapel Hill: University of North Carolina Press.

Cogliano, Francis D. 1995. *No King, No Popery: Anti-Catholicism in Revolutionary New England*. Westport, Conn.: Greenwood Press.

Connolly, S. J., ed. 2002. *The Oxford Companion to Irish History*. 2nd ed. Oxford: Oxford University Press.

Constitutions and Rules of the Society of the Sacred Heart of Jesus. (1800) 1890. N.p.: Rochampton. ASSH.

Constitutions of the Sisters of St. Joseph of Carondelet. (1693) 1860. St. Louis: Sisters of St. Joseph of Carondelet. ASSJ.

Constitutions of Ursuline Religious. (1705) 1812. Translated from the French. Dublin: R. Coyne, Capel-Street. Archives, Ursuline Sisters of Louisville, Louisville, Ky.

Conway, Jill K. 1974. "Perspectives on the History of Women's Education in the United States." *History of Education Quarterly* 14 (1): 1–12.
Conwill, Giles. 1998. "Black Catechesis: Catching the Flame and Passing It On." In *Taking Down Our Harps: Black Catholics in the United States*, edited by Diana L. Hayes and Cyprian Davis, 199–231. Maryknoll, N.Y.: Orbis Books.
Coppens, Charles. 1880. *A Practical Introduction to English Rhetoric: Precepts and Exercises*. New York: Schwartz, Kirwin and Fauss.
Corcoran, Miriam. 1966. "A Survey of the Educational Ministry of the Sisters of Charity of Nazareth: The Written Component of the Video Production of the Same Title." ASCN.
"Correspondence of the Knoxville and Atlanta Register." 1864. *Atlanta Daily Register*, 30 March.
Cott, Nancy. 1977. *The Bonds of Womanhood: "Woman's Sphere" in New England, 1780–1835*. New Haven: Yale University Press.
"Council Minutes, 1818." 1818. ASJPH Council Minutes 3-3-5. ASJPH.
Cremin, Lawrence A. 1957. "Horace Mann's Legacy." In *The Republic and the School: Horace Mann on the Education of Free Men*, edited by Lawrence A. Cremin, 3–28. New York: Teachers College, Columbia University.
Crumlish, John Mary. 1945. "The History of St. Joseph's Academy, Emmitsburg, Maryland, 1809–1902." MA thesis, Catholic University of America. ASJPH.
Cumming, Kate. 1959. *Kate: The Journal of a Confederate Nurse*. Edited by Richard Barksdale Harwell. Baton Rouge: Louisiana State University Press.
Curtis, Sarah A. 2000. *Educating the Faithful: Religion, Schooling, and Society in Nineteenth-Century France*. DeKalb: Northern Illinois University Press.
Daniell, Beth, and Peter Mortensen. 2007. "Introduction—Researching Women and Literacy: Usable Pasts, Possible Futures." In *Women and Literacy: Local and Global Inquiries for a New Century*, edited by Beth Daniell and Peter Mortensen, 1–41. Mahwah, N.J.: Lawrence Erlbaum.
David, Jean Baptiste. 1813. To Simon Bruté. 7 September. DLB-XXIV, 82–83.
———. 1814. To Pere Duclaux. 14 September. DLB-II, 104–7.
———. 1824. To Rose White. DLB-III, 4–6.
———. 1827. To Simon Bruté. 27 November. DLB-XXIV, 75–77.
———. 1828. To Simon Bruté. 27 January. DLB-XXIV, 80.
Davies, Benjamin. 1813. *A New System of Modern Geography, or, a General Description of the Most Remarkable Countries throughout the Known World*. 3rd ed. Philadelphia: Johnson and Warner. Early American Imprints, Series 2.
De Castell, Suzanne, and Allan Luke. 1983. "Defining 'Literacy' in North American Schools: Social and Historical Conditions and Consequences." *Journal of Curriculum Studies* 15:373–89.
De l'Épée, Charles-Michel. 1794. *La Véritable Maniere d'Instruire les Sourds et Muets, Confirmee par une Longue Experience*. N.p. ASSJ.

WORKS CITED

DePalma, Michael John. 2008. "Austin Phelps and the Spirit (of) Composing: An Exploration of Nineteenth-Century Sacred Rhetoric at Andover Theological Seminary." *Rhetoric Review* 38 (3): 379–96.

———. 2012. "Rhetorical Education for the Nineteenth-Century Pulpit: Austin Phelps and the Influence of Christian Transcendentalism at Andover Theological Seminary." *Rhetoric Review* 31 (1): 1–20.

DePalma, Michael John, and Jeffrey M. Ringer. 2015. *Mapping Christian Rhetorics: Connecting Conversations, Charting New Territories.* New York: Routledge.

"Designs of the Papists." 1831. *Cincinnati Journal*, 22 July, 1.

Detiege, Audrey Marie. 1976. *Sr. Hentiette Detille, Free Woman of Color.* New Orleans: Sisters of the Holy Family.

Dixon, Henry. 1736. *The English Instructor, or the Art of Spelling Improved.* Boston: J. Draper and D. Henchman. Early American Imprints, Series 1.

Dolan, Jay P. 1985. *The American Catholic Experience: A History from Colonial Times to the Present.* Garden City, N.Y.: Doubleday.

Donohue, Francis J. 1940. "Textbooks for Catholic Schools prior to 1840." *Catholic School Journal* 40 (3): 65–68.

Dougherty, Dolorita Marie, Helen Angela Hurley, Emily Joseph Daly, St. Claire Coyne, and others. 1966. *Sisters of St. Joseph of Carondelet.* St. Louis: B. Herder Book Co.

Doyle, Mary Ellen. 2006. *Pioneer Spirit: Catherine Spalding, Sister of Charity of Nazareth.* Lexington: University Press of Kentucky.

"Dr. Shew's Lectures on Cholera." 1849. *Water-Cure Journal*, 1 February, 35. American Periodicals.

Duffy, John, Julie Nelson Christoph, Eli Goldblatt, Nelson Graff, Rebecca S. Nowacek, and Bryan Trabold. 2014. *Literacy, Economy, and Power: Writing and Research after "Literacy in American Lives."* Carbondale: Southern Illinois University Press.

Dwight, Nathaniel. 1795. *A Short but Comprehensive System of the Geography of the World; by Way of Question and Answers.* Hartford, Conn.: Elisha Babcock. Early American Imprints, Series I.

Dwight, Timothy. 1836. *Open Convents; or, Nunneries and Popish Seminaries, Dangerous to the Morals, and Degrading to the Character of a Republican Community.* New York: Van Nostrand and Dwight.

"Early Annals, 1812–1842." N.d. ASCN.

"Early Schools." RG-Special 5. ASL.

Eastman, Carolyn. 2010. *A Nation of Speechifiers: Making an American Republic after the Revolution.* Chicago: University of Chicago Press.

Eiting, Mary Leander. N.d. "Biographical Sketches." Vol. 2. ASCN.

Elkins, Stanley M. 1968. *Slavery: A Problem in American Institutional and Intellectual Life.* Chicago: University of Chicago Press.

Elliott, Richard R. 1901. "Two Centuries of Catholicity in Detroit." *American Catholic Quarterly Review* 26 (July): 499–523.

Ellis, John Tracy. 1969. *American Catholicism*. Chicago: University of Chicago Press.

Elson, Ruth Miller. 1964. *Guardians of Tradition: American Schoolbooks of the Nineteenth Century*. Lincoln: University of Nebraska Press.

Ely, Ezra Stiles. 1828. *The Duty of Christian Freemen to Elect Christian Rulers*. Philadelphia: W. F. Geddes.

Emerson, Ralph. 1834. *Life of Rev. Joseph Emerson, Pastor of the Third Congregational Church in Beverly, Ms. and Subsequently Principal of a Female Seminary*. Boston: Crocker and Brewster.

Entich, John. 1800. *Entich's New Spelling Dictionary, Teaching to Write and Pronounce the English Tongue. With Ease and Propriety*. Wilmington: Reprinted by Peter Brynberg. Early American Imprints, Series 2.

Evans, Mary Ellen. 1959. *The Spirit Is Mercy: The Sisters of Mercy in the Archdiocese of Cincinnati, 1853–1958*. Westminster, Md.: Newman Press.

Ewens, Mary. 1978. *The Role of the Nun in Nineteenth-Century America: Variations on the International Theme*. New York: Arno Press.

———. 1981. "The Leadership of Nuns in Immigrant Catholicism." In *Women in American Religion*, vol. 1, edited by Rosemary Radford Ruether and Rosemary Skinner Keller, 101–49. San Francisco: Harper and Row.

"Fair for the Sisters of Mercy at Palace Garden." 1865. *New York Times*, 9 May. Proquest Historical Newspapers.

Farnham, Christie Anne. 1994. *The Education of the Southern Belle: Higher Education and Student Socialization in the Antebellum South*. New York: New York University Press.

Fell, Marie Leonore. 1971. *The Foundation of Nativism in American Textbooks, 1783–1860*. New York: J. S. Ozer.

"Female Academy of Bethlehem." 1837. *United States Catholic Almanac*. Baltimore: James Myres. ASCN.

Fenning, Daniel. 1786. *Universal Spelling-Book or, A New and Easy Guide to the English Language*. Falmouth, Maine: Printed and sold by Thomas B. Wait at his office in Middle Street. Early American Imprints, Series 1.

Fenton, Elizabeth. 2006. "Birth of a Protestant Nation, Catholic Canadians, Religion, and National Unity in the Early U.S. Republic." *Early American Literature* 41 (1): 29–57.

Fiske, Fidelia. 1866. *Recollections of Mary Lyon, with Selections from Her Instructions to the Pupils in Mt. Holyoke Female Seminary*. Boston: American Tract Society.

Fitz, James. 1999. "U.S. Catholic Religious and Slavery: A Seldom Told Story." *Review for Religious* 58 (4): 342–63.

WORKS CITED

Fitzgerald, O. P. 1903. *Fifty Years—Observations—Opinion—Experiences*. Nashville: Publishing House of the M.E. Church, South.

Flaget, Joseph Benedict. (1815) 1978. *Report of the Diocese of Bardstown to Pius VII, April 10, 1815*. In *Documentary Reports on Early American Catholicism*, edited by Philip Gleason, 305–19. New York: Arno Press.

———. 1815. To Louis Deloul. 10 April. FHS, folder 8.

———. 1841. To Deloul. 20 July. FHS, folder 8.

———. 1842. To Deloul. 10 September. FHS, folder 8.

Flaget, Joseph Benedict, and Jean Baptiste Mary David. 1814. "Report in Summary of the Establishment of the Sisters of Charity in Kentucky, United States of America." DLB-XXIV.

Fletcher, William. 1954. *Rebel Private, Front and Rear*. Austin: University of Texas Press.

Ford, Paul Leicester. 1962. *The New-England Primer; a History of Its Origin and Development with the Reprint of the Unique Copy of the Earliest Known Edition and Many Facsimile Illustrations and Reproductions*. New York: Teachers College, Columbia University.

"For the Gazette." 1801. *New York Gazette*, 31 October, 2. Early American Newspapers.

Fox, Sister Columba. 1925. *The Life of the Right Reverend John Baptist Mary David (1761–1841), Bishop of Bardstown and Founder of the Sisters of Charity of Nazareth*. New York: U.S. Catholic Historical Society.

Foxe, John. (1563) 2007. *Foxe's Book of Martyrs*. London: Forgotten Books.

Fox-Genovese, Elizabeth. 1988. *Within the Plantation Household: Black and White Women of the Old South*. Chapel Hill: University of North Carolina Press.

Frances, Catharine. 1936. "The Convent School of French Origin in the United States, 1727 to 1843." PhD diss., University of Pennsylvania.

Franchot, Jenny. 1994. *Roads to Rome: The Antebellum Protestant Encounter with Catholicism*. Berkeley: University of California Press.

Fraser, Antonia. 1984. *The Weaker Vessel*. New York: Knopf.

Gallegos, Bernardo P. 1992. *Literacy, Education, and Society in New Mexico, 1693–1821*. Albuquerque: University of New Mexico Press.

Gannett, Cinthia, and John Brereton, eds. 2015. *Traditions of Eloquence: The Jesuits and Modern Rhetorical Studies*. New York: Fordham University Press.

Gawthrop, Richard, and Gerald Strauss. 1984. "Presentation and Literacy in Early Modern Germany." *Past and Present* 104:31–55.

"General Directions, 8th Rule." N.d. *Annals of the Community of the Sisters of Charity Established at St. Joseph's, Frederick Co., Md. Compiled by Sister Bernard Boyle*, 197. ASJPH.

Genovese, Eugene D. 1974. *Roll, Jordan, Roll: The World the Slaves Made*. New York: Pantheon Books.

WORKS CITED

Gilgannon, Mary McAuley. 1962. "The Sisters of Mercy as Crimean War Nurses." PhD diss., University of Notre Dame.

Gleason, Philip, ed. 1978. *Documentary Reports on Early American Catholicism.* New York: Arno Press.

Glimpses of the Monastery: Scenes from the History of the Ursulines of Quebec during Two Hundred Years, 1639–1839. 1897. 2nd ed. Quebec: L/J. Demers & Frere.

Goggin, Maureen Daly. 2002. "An 'Essamplaire Essai' on the Rhetoricity of Needlework Sampler-Making: A Contribution to Theorizing and Historicizing Rhetorical Praxis." *Rhetoric Review* 21 (4): 309–38.

Goldmith, Oliver. 1896. *An Abridgement of the History of England; from the Invasion of Julius Caesar to the Death of George the Second.* 11th ed. Philadelphia: M. Carey.

Goodsell, Woodystine. 1931. *Pioneers of Women's Education in the United States: Emma Willard, Catharine Beecher, Mary Lyon.* New York: McGraw-Hill.

Gordon, Edward E., and Elaine H. Gordon. 2003. *Literacy in America: Historic Journey and Contemporary Solutions.* Westport, Conn.: Praeger.

Graff, Harvey J. 1967. *The Legacies of Literacy: Continuities and Contradictions in Western Culture and Society.* Bloomington: Indiana University Press.

———. 1979. *The Literacy Myth: Literacy and Social Structure in the Nineteenth-Century City.* New York: Academic Press.

———. 2010. "The Literacy Myth at Thirty." *Journal of Social History* 43 (3): 635–61.

Grant, Zilpah. 1820. To Mary Lyon. 5 February. Zilpah Grant Bannister Papers, Series A: Correspondence, Sub-series 1: Letters by Bannister, 1823–1874, Mount Holyoke College Archives, South Hadley, Mass.

Green, Elizabeth Alden. 1979. *Mary Lyon and Mount Holyoke: Opening the Gates.* Hanover, N.H.: University Press of New England.

Greene, Jamie Candelaria. 1994. "Misperspectives on Literacy: A Critique of an Anglocentric Bias in Histories of American Literacy." *Written Communication* 11 (2): 251–69.

Greenly, Albert H. 1955. *A Bibliography of Father Richard's Press in Detroit.* Ann Arbor: University of Michigan Press.

Greenwell, Berenice. 1933. "Nazareth's Contribution to Education 1812–1933." PhD diss., New York University.

Greer, Allan. 1978. "The Pattern of Literacy in Quebec, 1745–1899." *Histoire Sociale, Social History* 11:295–335.

———. 2000. *The Jesuit Relations: Natives and Missionaries in Seventeenth-Century North America.* Boston: Bedford/St. Martin's.

Grimké, Angelina. (1836) 1989. *Appeal to the Christian Women of the South.* In *The Public Years of Sarah and Angelina Grimké: Selected Writings, 1835–1839,* edited by Larry Ceplair, 36–79. New York: Columbia University Press.

WORKS CITED

Grimké, Sarah. (1836) 1989. *An Epistle to the Clergy of the Southern States.* In *The Public Years of Sarah and Angelina Grimké: Selected Writings, 1835–1839*, edited by Larry Ceplair, 90–115. New York: Columbia University Press.

Grimshaw, William. 1819. *History of England from the First Invasion of Julius Caesar, to the Peace of Ghent; Comprising Every Political Event Worthy of Remembrance, a Progressive View.* Philadelphia: Benjamin Warner.

Guilday, Peter. 1969. *The Life and Times of John England.* 2 vols. New York: Arno Press and the New York Times.

Guthrie, William. 1794. *A New System of Modern Geography: or, A Geographical, Historical, and Commercial Grammar; and Present State of the Several Nations of the World.* Philadelphia: [Matthew Carey]. Early American Imprints, Series 1.

———. 1809. *A New Geographical, Historical, and Commercial Grammar, and Present State of the Several Kingdoms of the World.* Philadelphia: Johnson and Warner.

Hale, Sarah Josepha. 1834a. "Convents Are Increasing: Conditions of Females in the East[;] What Should Be Done?" *Ladies Repository* 7 (12): 560–64.

———. 1834b. "How to Prevent the Increase of Convents." *Ladies Repository* 7 (11): 517–21.

———. 1856. *Woman's Record, or Sketches of All Distinguished Women: From the Creation to A.D. 1854.* New York: Harper.

———. 1860. "Troy Female Seminary." *Godey's Lady's Book*, 4 October, 369. American Periodicals.

Harriet, Sister. 1822. To Sister Clare. 28 July. *Early Annals, 1812–1842*, 64. ASCN.

Harris, Benjamin. 1685. *The Protestant Tutor for Children.* Boston: Samuel Green. Early American Imprints, Series 1.

Heaney, Jean Frances. 1992. *A Century of Pioneering: A History of the Ursuline Nuns in New Orleans (1727–1827).* Edited by Mary Ethel Booker Stefken. New Orleans: Ursuline Sisters of New Orleans.

Hennesey, James. 1983. *American Catholics: A History of the Roman Catholic Community in the United States.* New York: Oxford University Press.

Henry, J. Q. A. N.d. *Rome's Substitute for Marriage.* Milan, Ill.: Rail Splitter Press. UNDA: Pant 5/01, Anti-Catholicism n.d.

Hitchcock, Edward. 1851. *The Power of Christian Benevolence: Illustrated in the Life and Labors of Mary Lyon.* Northampton, Mass.: Hopkins, Bridgman.

Howlett, William J. 1906. *Historical Tribute to St. Thomas' Seminary at Poplar Neck: Near Bardstown, Kentucky.* St. Louis: B. Herder.

———. 1915. *Life of Rev. Charles Nerinckx: Pioneer Missionary of Kentucky and Founder of the Sisters of Loretto at the Foot of the Cross.* Techny, Ill.: Mission Press S.V.D.

WORKS CITED

Hume, David. 1810. *The History of England: From the Invasion of Julius Caesar to the Revolution of 1688.* 7 vols. Boston: Thomas L. Plowman. Early American Imprints, Series 2.

"Hume and Smollet [sic] Abridged." 1824. *United States Literary Gazette* (Boston), 15 October, 1. American Periodicals.

Irvine, Leigh. 1886. "Biographical Sketch." In *The Poet Scout: A Book of Song and Story*, edited by Jack Crawford, ix–xi. New York: Funk and Wagnalls.

Jacobi, Bonnie Schaffhauser. 2001. "Music in Higher Education for Females in Nineteenth-Century America." *Journal of Historical Research in Music Education* 23 (1): 46–59.

Janvrin, Mary W. 1863. "Little Miss Stoddard." *Godey's Lady's Book*, April. Accessible Archives.

Jones, Charles Colcock. 1842. *The Religious Instruction of the Negroes in the United States.* Savannah: Thomas Purse. Google Books.

———. 1852. *A Catechism of Scripture Doctrine and Practice for Families and Sabbath Schools: Designed Also for the Oral Instruction of Coloured People.* Philadelphia: Presbyterian Board of Publications. Google Books.

Keach, Benjamin. 1695. *Instructions for Children: or, The Child's and Youth's Delight, Teaching an Easier Way to Spell and Read TRUE ENGLISH.* New York: Will. Bradford at the Bible in New-York. Early American Imprints, Series 1.

Keenan, Mary Ellen. 1934. "French Teaching Communities and Early Convent Education in the United States, 1727–1850." PhD diss., Catholic University, Washington, D.C.

Kelley, Mary. 2006. *Learning to Stand and Speak: Women, Education, and Public Life in America's Republic.* Chapel Hill: University of North Caroline Press.

Kelly, Ellin M., ed. 1981. *Numerous Choirs: A Chronicle of Elizabeth Bayley Seton and Her Spiritual Daughters.* Vol. 1, *The Seton Years, 1774–1821.* Evansville, Ind.: Mater Dei Provinciate.

Kelly, Theodosia. N.d. "Memoirs." ASL.

Kenrick, Francis. 1834. To Paul Cullen. In *The Life and Times of John England*, 2 vols., edited by Peter Guilday, 1:532. New York: Arno Press and the New York Times.

Kerber, Linda K. 1986. *Women of the Republic: Intellect and Ideology in Revolutionary America.* New York: W. W. Norton.

Kersey, Shirley Nelson. 1981. *Classics in the Education of Girls and Women.* Metuchen, N.J.: Scarecrow Press.

Kolmer, Elizabeth. 1978. "Catholic Women Religious and Women's History: A Survey of the Literature." *American Quarterly* 30 (5): 639–49.

Lambert, Frank. 2003. *The Founding Fathers and the Place of Religion in America.* Princeton: Princeton University Press.

Lansing, Mary Florence. 1937. *Mary Lyon through Her Letters*. Boston: Books Inc.

Lerner, Gerda. 1997. *Why History Matters: Life and Thought*. New York: Oxford University Press.

Leslie, Bruce. 2001. "Where Have All the Academies Gone?" *History of Education Quarterly* 41:262–70.

Livermore, Mary Ashton. 1887. *My Story of the War: A Woman's Narrative of Four Years Personal Experience as Nurse in the Union Army*. Hartford: A. D. Worthington.

Lockridge, Kenneth A. 1974. *Literacy in Colonial New England: An Inquiry into the Social Context of Literacy in the Early Modern West*. New York: Norton.

"Loretto Deaf Academy." 1840. In *The Metropolitan Catholic Almanac and Laity's Directory*, 416. Baltimore: Fielding Lucas Jr.

"Loretto Female Academy." 1840. In *The Metropolitan Catholic Almanac and Laity's Directory*, 415. Baltimore: Fielding Lucas Jr.

"Loretto Literary and Benevolent Academy." 1838. In *The Metropolitan Catholic Almanac and Laity's Directory*, 231. Baltimore: Fielding Lucas Jr.

Lovejoy, Joseph C., Owen Lovejoy, and John Quincy Adams. 1838. *Memoir of the Rev. Elijah P. Lovejoy: Who Was Murdered in Defence of the Liberty of the Press, at Alton, Illinois, Nov. 7, 1837*. New York: J. S. Taylor.

Lyon, Mary. 1837. *General View of the Principles and Design of the Mount Holyoke Female Seminary*. Boston: Perkins and Marvin.

———. N.d. *The Inception of Mount Holyoke College*. Springfield, Mass.: Springfield Printing and Binding.

Lyon, Mary, and Marion Florence Lansing. 1937. *Mary Lyon through Her Letters*. Boston: Books, Inc.

Maes, Camillus P. 1880. *The Life of Rev. Charles Nerinckx, with a Chapter on the Early Catholic Missions of Kentucky; Copious Notes on the Progress of Catholicity in the United States of America, from 1800 to 1828; an Account of the Establishment of the Society of Jesus in Missouri; and an Historical Sketch of the Sisterhood of Loretto in Kentucky, Missouri, New Mexico, etc*. Cincinnati: R. Clarke.

Maher, Mary Denis. 1999. *To Bind Up the Wounds: Catholic Sister Nurses in the U.S. Civil War*. Baton Rouge: Louisiana State University Press.

Mann, Horace. (1848) 1957. "Twelfth Annual Report." In *The Republic and the School: Horace Mann on the Education of Free Men*, edited by Lawrence A. Cremin, 79–112. New York: Teachers College, Columbia University.

Mann, Mary Peabody. 1937. *Life of Horace Mann*. Washington, D.C.: National Education Association.

Mannard, Joseph Gerald. 1986. "Maternity . . . of the Spirit: Nuns and Domesticity in Antebellum America." *U.S. Catholic Historian* 5 (3–4): 305–24.

———. 1989. "'Maternity of the Spirit': Women Religious in the Archdiocese of Baltimore, 1790–1860." PhD diss., University of Maryland College Park.
Margaret George. 1849. To Mother Catherine Spalding, 26 August. ASCN.
Martin, Marie de Saint Jean. 1946. *Ursuline Method of Education*. Rahway, N.J.: Quinn and Boden.
Mather, Cotton. 1706. *The Negro Christianized: An Essay to Excite and Assist the Good Work, the Instruction of the Negro-Servants in Christianity*. Boston: B. Green.
———. 1707. *The Fall of Babylon: A Short and Plain Catechism, Which Detects and Confutes the Principles of Popery: and Arms the* PROTESTANT *from the Tower of David, for the Defence of His Holy Religion*. Boston: B. Green.
Mattingly, Carol. 2005. "How Erasure Came for the Archbishop (Fénelon): Reexamining the French Connection." Paper presented at the Conference on College Composition and Communication, San Francisco, 19 March.
———. 2006. "Uncovering Forgotten Habits: Anti-Catholic Rhetoric and Nineteenth-Century American Women's Literacy." *CCC* 58 (2): 160–81.
"Mayor's Office." 1832. *American Mercury*, 17 September, 2. Early American Newspapers.
McCluskey, Neil G. 1964. "America and the Catholic Schools." In *Catholic Education in America: A Documentary History*, edited by Neil G. McCluskey, 1–44. New York: Teachers College.
McEntee, Mary Bernard. 1972. *The Valley: A Narrative of the Founding and Development of Saint Joseph Academy, High School, College, and Alumnae Association, Emmitsburg, MD 1809–1972*. N.p.: St. Joseph College Alumnae Association. ASJPH.
McGann, Agnes Geraldine. 1978. "Sisters of Charity of Nazareth: Random Sketches from the Archives." ASCN.
McGann, Mary Agnes. 1917. *The History of Mother Seton's Daughters, the Sisters of Charity of Cincinnati Ohio, 1809–1917*. New York: Longmans, Green. ASCN.
McGill, Anna Blanche. 1917. *The Sisters of Charity of Nazareth Kentucky*. New York: Encyclopedia Press.
McGreevy, John T. 2003. *Catholicism and American Freedom*. New York: W. W. Norton.
McNeil, Betty Ann. 1996. "Elizabeth Seton—Mission of Education, Faith and Willingness to Risk." *Vincentian Heritage* 17 (3): 185–200.
Menard, Marie. Undated manuscript. OLB-9, 90, ASCN.
"Merry's Monthly Chat." 1869. *Merry's Museum for Boys and Girls*. September, 268.
The Metropolitan Catholic Almanac and Laity's Directory. 1838. Baltimore: Fielding Lucas Jr.

———. 1839. Baltimore: Fielding Lucas Jr.

———. 1840. Baltimore: Fielding Lucas Jr.

———. 1844. Baltimore: Fielding Lucas Jr.

Metz, Judith. 1996. "The Sisters of Charity in Cincinnati, 1829–1852." *Vincentian Heritage* 17 (3): 201–44.

Metz, Judith, and Virginia Wiltse. 1989. "Sister Margaret Cecilia George: A Biography." Sisters of Charity of Cincinnati. ASJPH.

Meyers, Robert Manson. 1972. *The Children of Pride: A True Story of Georgia and the Civil War.* New Haven, Conn.: Yale University Press.

Minogue, Anna C. 1921. *Pages from a Hundred Years of Dominican History: The Story of the Congregation of Saint Catharine of Sienna.* New York: Frederick Pustet.

Misner, Barbara. 1988. *"Highly Respectable and Accomplished Ladies": Catholic Women Religious in America, 1790–1850.* New York: Garland.

Mobberley, Joseph P. 1813. To Mathew Carey. 8 December. "Selections from the Correspondence of the Deceased Mathew Carey." *Records of the American Catholic Historical Society of Philadelphia,* 10:225. Philadelphia: American Catholic Historical Society of Philadelphia.

Monaghan, E. Jennifer. 1988. "Literacy Instruction and Gender in Colonial New England." *American Quarterly* 40:18–41.

———. 2005. *Learning to Read and Write in Colonial America.* Amherst: University of Massachusetts Press.

Monica, M. 1927. *Angela Merici and Her Teaching Ideas.* New York: Longmans, Green.

Monk, Maria. 1836. *Awful Disclosures, by Maria Monk, of the Hotel Dieu Nunnery of Montreal.* New York: Maria Monk.

Morrow, Diane Batts. 2002. *Persons of Color and Religious at the Same Time: The Oblate Sisters of Providence, 1828–1860.* Chapel Hill: University of North Caroline Press.

Morse, Jedidiah. 1784. *Geography Made Easy.* New Haven: Meigs, Bowen, and Dana. Early American Imprints, Series 1.

———. 1801 *The American Universal Geography, or, a View of the Present State of All the Kingdoms, States, and Colonies in the Known World.* Boston: Isaiah Thomas and Ebenezer T. Andrews. Early American Imprints, Series 2.

———. 1812. *American Universal Geography; or, A View of the Present State of All the Kingdoms, States, and Colonies in the Known World.* Boston: Thomas and Andrews. Early American Imprints, Series 2.

Morse, Samuel Finley Breese. 1835. *Foreign Conspiracy against the Liberties of the United States.* New York: Leavitt, Lord and Co.

Mother Frances Gardiner: Sister of Charity of Nazareth, 1800–1878. 1972. Nazareth, Ky.: Nazareth Motherhouse. ASCN.

WORKS CITED

Murphy, M. Benedict. 1958. "Pioneer Roman Catholic Girls' Academies; Their Growth, Character, and Contribution to American Education: A Study of Roman Catholic Education for Girls from Colonial Times to the First Plenary Council of 1852." PhD diss., Columbia University.

Murray, Lindley. 1795. *English Grammar, Adapted to the Different Classes of Learners.* New York: Wilson, Spence, and Mawman.

———. 1800. *The English Reader: Or, Pieces in Prose and Poetry, Selected from the Best Writers.* Philadelphia: J. Ormrod.

———. 1810. *Key to the Exercises Adapted to Murray's English Grammar.* Philadelphia: W. M'Culloch. Early American Imprints, Series 2.

———. 1817. *English Grammar, Adapted to the Different Classes of Learners.* Philadelphia: A. Walker.

Nasaw, David. 1981. *Schooled to Order: A Social History of Public Schooling in the United States.* Oxford: Oxford University Press.

Nash, Margaret A. 2001. "'Cultivating the Powers of Human Beings': Gendered Perspectives on Curricula and Pedagogy in the Academies of the New Republic." *History of Education Quarterly* 41:239–50.

"Nazareth Female Academy." 1840. In *The Metropolitan Catholic Almanac and Laity's Directory*, 93. Baltimore: Fielding Lucas Jr.

Nerinckx, Charles. 1823. To Louis DuBourg. In *St. Louis Catholic Historical Review*, April 1919, 161.

The New-England Primer, Improved, or, An Easy and Pleasant Guide to the Art of Reading. 1795. Boston: Nathaniel Coverly.

Nichols, F. 1809. *A Compend of Geography Containing a Concise Description of the Different Countries of the Earth.* Philadelphia: F. Nichols. Early American Imprints, Series 2.

Nietz, John A. 1961. *Old Textbooks: Spelling, Grammar, Reading, Arithmetic, Geography, American History, Civil Government, Physiology, Penmanship, Art, Music—as Taught in the Common Schools from Colonial Days to 1900.* Pittsburgh: University of Pittsburgh Press.

Noonan, Paschala. 1997. *Signadou: History of the Kentucky Dominican Sisters.* Manhasset, N.Y.: Brookville Books.

Norton, Mary Beth. 1980. *Liberty's Daughters: The Revolutionary Experience of American Women, 1790–1800.* Ithaca: Cornell University Press.

Oates, Mary J. 1994. "Catholic Female Academies on the Frontier." *U.S. Catholic Historian* 12:121–36.

O'Connell, Ellen. N.d. "Tropes and Other Figures of Rhetoric Illustrated." ASCN.

O'Daniel, V. F. 1932. *A Light of the Church in Kentucky; or, The Life, Labors, and Character of the Very Rev. Samuel Thomas Wilson, O.P.S.T.M., Pioneer Educator and the First Provincial of a Religious Order in the United States.* Washington, D.C.: Dominicana.

O'Leary, Mary. 1936. *Education with a Tradition: An Account of the Educational Work of the Society of the Sacred Heart*. New York: Longman, Green.

"Original Rule and Constitutions of the Oblate Sisters of Providence." 1829. Box 41, AOSP.

Paine, Thomas. 2001. *Common Sense and Related Writings*. Edited by Thomas P. Slaughter. Boston: Bedford/St. Martin's.

"Papacy in the United States." 1834. *American Quarterly Register* 7 (1): 57. APS Online.

Park, Edwards A., ed. 1845. *The Preacher and Pastor by Fenelon, Herbert, Baxter, Campbell*. Andover, N.Y.: Mark H. Newmar. Archives of the Maryland Province of the Society of Jesus, Woodstock Library, Georgetown University, Washington, D.C.

Parton, James. 1868. "Our Roman Catholic Brethren." *Atlantic Monthly*, April, 432–52.

Partridge, Frances M. 1839. *Nunneries as They Are*. New York: Burnett and Pollard.

Perko, F. Michael. 1988. *Enlightening the Next Generation: Catholics and Their Schools, 1830–1980*. New York: Garland.

Pinkerton, John. 1804. *Modern Geography, a Description of the Empires, Kingdoms, States and Colonies, with the Oceans, Seas, and Isles, in All Parts of the World*. Philadelphia: J. Conrad and Co. Early American Imprints, Series 2.

———. 1805. *John Pinkerton's Geography Epitomised for the Use of Schools by David Doyle*. Philadelphia: Samuel F. Bradford. Early American Imprints, Series 2.

"Plan of the Institute." 1890. *Constitutions and Rules of the Society of the Sacred Heart of Jesus*. N.p.: Rochampton. ASSH.

"Poetry from the Baltimore Chronicle." 1832. *The Torch Light and Public Advertiser*, 13 September, 1. Early American Periodicals.

Porterfield, Amanda. 1992. *Female Piety in Puritan New England*. New York: Oxford University Press.

———. 1997. *Mary Lyon and the Mount Holyoke Missionaries*. New York: Oxford University Press.

Powell, Anna. 2012. "'Lessons and Exercises in Polite Literature': The Pedagogy and Literature Curriculum of Mother Columba Carroll, a Sister of Charity of Nazareth." MA thesis, University of Louisville.

"Preparatory School." 1840. In *The Metropolitan Catholic Almanac and Laity's Directory*, 143. Baltimore: Fielding Lucas Jr.

"Preparatory School of Gethsemani." 1838. *Catholic Advocate* 3 (29): 231. ASCN.

"The Prison-Hospital." 1852. *New York Daily Times*, 29 December, 6.

"Prospectus, St. Joseph's Academy." 1831. ASJPH.

WORKS CITED

A Protestant's Resolution: Shewing His Reasons Why He Will Not Be a Papist. Digested into So Plain a Method of Question and Answer, That an Ordinary Capacity May Be Able to Defend the Protestant Religion against the Most Cunning Jesuit, or Popish Priest. 1746. Boston: Printed for D. Gookin. Early American Imprints, Series 1.

Raboteau, Albert J. 2004. *Slave Religion: The "Invisible Institution" in the Antebellum South.* New York: Oxford University Press.

Rapley, Elizabeth. 1990. *The Devotes: Women and Church in Seventeenth-Century France:* Montreal: McGill-Queen's University Press.

Règlements des Religieuses Ursulines de la Congrégation de Paris. 1705. Paris. Google Books.

Regulations of the School of St. Joseph. 1812. In *Elizabeth Bayley Seton: Collected Writings* (1812) 2006, edited by Regina Bechtle and Judith Metz, 3b:124–26. Hyde Park, N.Y.: New City Press.

"Reprinted from *Providence Journal,* 'Sisters of Charity.'" 1832. *Portland (Maine) Eastern Argus,* 5 December, 2. Early American Newspapers.

Resnick, Daniel P., and Lauren B. Resnick. 1977. "The Nature of Literacy: A Historical Exploration." *Harvard Educational Review* 47:370–85.

Ringer, Jeffrey. 2013. "The Dogma of Inquiry: Composition and the Primacy of Faith." *Rhetoric Review* 32 (3): 345–69.

Rippa, S. Alexander, ed. 1969. *Educational Ideas in America: A Documentary History.* New York: David McKay.

Roman Catholic Female Schools: A Letter of an American Mother to an American Mother. N.d. In *Tracts on Romanism.* New York. American Tract Society.

Rosenberg, Charles F. 1962. *The Cholera Years: The United States in 1832, 1849, and 1866.* Chicago: University of Chicago Press.

Rousey, Dennis C. 2006. "Catholics in the Old South: Their Population, Institutional Development and Relations with Protestants." *U.S. Catholic Historian* 24 (4): 1–21.

Royster, Jacqueline Jones. 2000. *Traces of a Stream: Literacy and Social Change among African American Women.* Pittsburgh: University of Pittsburgh Press.

Rudolph, Frederick. 1962. *The American College and University, a History.* New York: Alfred A. Knopf.

Rules of the Society and School of Loretto, Kentucky. 1820. London: Keating and Brown. ASL.

Russell, William F. 1914. "The Entrance of History into the Curriculum of the Secondary School." *History Teacher's Magazine* 5:311–318.

Savage, Mary Lucinda. 1923. *The Congregation of Saint Joseph of Carondelet: A Brief Account of Its Origin and Its Work in the United States (1650–1922).* St. Louis: Congregation of St. Joseph of Carondelet.

Saye, Albert Berry. 1948. *A Constitutional History of Georgia, 1732–1945.* Athens: University of Georgia Press.

"The School Girl in France." 1844. *United States Catholic Magazine and Monthly*, May, 285–97. APS Online.

Schultz, Stanley K. 1973. *The Culture Factory: Boston Public School, 1789–1860.* New York: Oxford University Press.

Scott, Anne Firor. 1978. "What, Then, Is the American: This New Woman?" *Journal of American History* 65 (3): 679–703.

Seabrook, Whitemarsh B. 1834. *An Essay on the Management of Slaves, and Especially, on Their Religious Instruction; Read before the Agriculture Society of St. John's Colleton.* Charleston: A. E. Miller.

The Secretary's Guide, or, Young Man's Companion, in Four Parts. 1729. New York: William Bradford. Early American Imprints, Series 1.

Semple, Henry Churchill. 1925. *The Ursulines in New Orleans and Our Lady of Prompt Succor: A Record of Two Centuries, 1727–1925.* New York: P. J. Kennedy and Sons.

Seton, Elizabeth Bayley. 2000–2006. *Elizabeth Bayley Seton: Collected Writings.* 3 vols. Edited by Regina Bechtle and Judith Metz. Hyde Park, N.Y.: New City Press.

Silcox, Claris Edwin, and Galen M. Fisher. 1934. *Catholics, Jews and Protestants: A Study of Relationships in the United States and Canada.* New York: Harper and Brothers.

"Sisters of Charity." 1828. *Daily National Journal*, 16 April, 3. Early American Newspapers.

"Sisters of Charity." 1832a. *Niles Weekly Register* (Baltimore), 27 October, 144. American Periodicals.

"The Sisters of Charity." 1832b. *Vidalia Whig and Illinois Intelligencer*, 28 November, 1091. Early American Newspapers.

"The Sisters of Charity and the Cholera." 1833. *Philadelphia Times*, 14 November, 2. Early American Newspapers.

"Sisters of Mercy." N.d. *Cincinnati Daily Commercial.* Folder: Early Nineteenth-Century Clippings, Archives, Sisters of Mercy–Cincinnati, Ohio.

"Sister Stanislaus Jones." N.d. *Biographical Sketches.* Archives, Georgetown Visitation Convent, Washington, D.C.

Sizer, Theodore R. 1964. *The Age of the Academies.* New York: Columbia University Press.

Sizer, Theodore R., Nancy Sizer, Sally Schwager, Lynne Templeton Brickley, and Glee Krueger. 1993. *To Ornament Their Minds: Sarah Pierce's Litchfield Female Academy, 1792–1833.* Litchfield, Conn.: Litchfield Historical Society.

"Sketches from Life School, Number Three: Blackwell's Island—The Lunatic Asylum." 1852. *New York Daily Times*, 27 September, 2. Early American Newspapers.

"Sketch of the Catholic Lecture; from the New-York Truth Teller." 1831. *United States Catholic Miscellany*, 18 June, 404. American Periodicals.

Sklar, Kathryn Kish. 1973. *Catharine Beecher: A Study in American Domesticity*. New Haven: Yale University Press.

———. 1993. "The Schooling of Girls and Changing Community Values in Massachusetts Towns, 1750–1820." *History of Education Quarterly* 33: 511–42.

Smith, B. B. N.d. To Bishop Flaget. Flaget Letters, FHS.

Smith, Timothy L. 1967. "Protestant Schooling and American Nationality, 1800–1850." *Journal of American History* 53 (4): 679–95.

"SMS Faculty Minutes Book." July 1791–October 1910. RG 1, box 21, ASMSU.

Soltow, Lee, and Edward Stevens. 1981. *The Rise of Literacy and the Common School in the United States: A Socioeconomic Analysis to 1870*. Chicago: University of Chicago Press.

Spalding, Catherine. 1834. To Louisville City Council. 10 February. DLB, Original Letters of Mother Catherine Spalding.

———. 1841. To Bishop Joseph Flaget. 6 July. DLB, Original Letters of Mother Catherine Spalding.

———. 1844. To Claudia Elliot. 10 August. DLB, Original Letters of Mother Catherine Spalding.

Spalding, Martin J. 1844. *Sketches of the Early Catholic Missions of Kentucky; from Their Commencement in 1787, to the Jubilee of 1826–27*. Louisville: R. J. Webb and Brothers.

"Spread of Catholics in the United States: No. 11: Female Religious Orders." 1836. *Christian Register and Boston Observer*, 28 May, 1. Early American Newspapers.

"Spread of Catholics in the United States: No. 12: Female Religious Orders." 1836. *Christian Register and Boston Observer*, 4 June, 1. Early American Newspapers.

Starr, Harris Elwood. 1930. "Timothy Dwight." In *Dictionary of American Biography*, edited by Allen Johnson and Dumas Malone, 5:573–77. New York: Charles Scribner's Sons.

"Statistics of Popery in the United States." 1835. *Western Christian Advocate*, 6 March, 1. APS Online.

Stern, Andrew. 2007. "Protestant-Catholic Relations in the Antebellum South." *Religion and American Culture: A Journal of Interpretation* 17 (2): 165–95.

Stone, Lawrence. 1969. "Literacy and Education in England, 1640–1900." *Past and Present* 42:14–159.

Stow, Sarah D. (Locke). 1887. *History of Mount Holyoke Seminary during Its First Half Century, 1837–1887*. Springfield, Mass.: Springfield Printing.

Sullivan, Eleonore C. 1975. *Georgetown Visitation since 1799*. Washington: Sullivan.

Sullivan, Mary Christina. 1940. "Some Non-permanent Foundations of Religious Orders and Foundations in the United States, 1793–1850." *Catholic Historical Records and Studies* 31:7–118.

Szpila, Kathleen. 2012. "Lest We Forget: Ellen Ryan Jolly and the Nuns of the Battlefield Monument." *American Catholic Studies* 123 (4): 23–43.

Tebbel, John William. 1972. *A History of Book Publishing in the United States.* Vol. 1. New York: R. R. Bowker.

Thompson, Margaret Susan. 1987. "To Serve the People of God: Nineteenth-Century Sisters and the Creation of an American Religious Life." Working Paper Series: Charles and Margaret Hall Cushwa Center for the Study of American Catholicism at the University of Notre Dame. Series 18.2.

Thwaites, Reuben Gold. (1896) 1925. "Introduction." In *The Jesuit Relations and Allied Documents: Travels and Explorations of the Jesuit Missionaries in North America 1610–1791,* edited by Reuben Gold Thwaites and Edna Kenton, 1:xix–liv. New York: Albert and Charles Boni.

Tolley, Kim. 1996. "Science for Ladies, Classics for Gentlemen: A Comparative Analysis of Scientific Subjects in the Curricula of Boys' and Girls' Secondary Schools in the United States, 1794–1650." *History of Education Quarterly* 26 (2): 129–53.

———. 2001. "The Rise of the Academies: Continuity or Change?" *History of Education Quarterly* 41: 225–38.

Tolley, Kim, and Nancy Beadie. 2001. "Introduction: Reappraisals of the Academy Movement." *History of Education Quarterly* 41: 216–24.

"To the Sisters of Charity." 1834. *American* (New York), 4 October, 2. Early American Newspapers.

Tyack, David. 1966. "The Kingdom of God and the Common School: Protestant Ministers and the Educational Awakening in the West." *Harvard Educational Review* 36 (4): 447–69.

The United States Catholic Almanac; or Laity's Directory for the Year 1833. 1833. Baltimore: James Myres. ASCN.

The United States Catholic Almanac; or Laity's Directory for the Year 1836. 1836. Baltimore: James Myres. ASCN.

The United States Catholic Almanac; or Laity's Directory for the Year 1837. 1837. Baltimore: James Myres. ASCN.

The United States Catholic Almanac; or Laity's Directory for the Year 1860. 1860. Baltimore: F. Lucas. ASCN.

U.S. Department of Education. 1871. *Special Report of the Commissioner of Education on the Condition and Improvement of Public Schools in the District of Columbia.* Washington: Government Printing Office.

Vanderpoel, Emily Noyes, and Elizabeth C. Barney Buel. 1903. *Chronicles of a Pioneer School from 1792 to 1833, Being the History of Miss Sarah Pierce and Her Litchfield School.* Cambridge: Cambridge University Press.

Van Tassel, David D. 1960. *Recording America's Past: An Interpretation of the Development of Historical Studies in America, 1607–1884*. Chicago: University of Chicago Press.

Walch, Timothy. 1988. "Catholic School Books and American Values: The Nineteenth Century Experience." In *Enlightening the Next Generation: Catholics and Their Schools, 1830–1980*, edited by F. Michael Perko, 267–76. New York: Garland.

Walker, Peter F. 1978. *Moral Choices: Memory, Desire, and Imagination in Nineteenth-Century American Abolition*. Baton Rouge: Louisiana State University.

Wand, Augustin C., and M. Lilliana Owens, eds. 1972. *Documents: Nerincks—Kentucky—Loretto 1804–1851 in Archives Propaganda Fide Rome*. St. Louis: Mary Loretto Press.

Ware, Ann Patrick. 1999. *Glimpses of Early Loretto Life: 1838–1840*. Nerinx, Ky.: Hardin Creek Press.

Webb, Benedict Joseph. 1884. *The Centenary of Catholicity in Kentucky*. Louisville: C. A. Rogers.

Webster, Noah. 1787. *An American Selection of Lessons in Reading and Speaking. Calculated to Improve the Minds and Refine the Tastes of Youth*. Philadelphia: Young and McCulluch. Early American Imprints, Series 1.

"What the Bible Can Do for Catholics." 1833. *New York Observer and Chronicle*, 31 August, 1.

Whelpley, Samuel. 1806. *An Historical Compend Containing a Brief Survey of the Great Line of History from the Earliest Times to the Present Day*. Morristown, N.J.: Henry P. Russell.

Whittelsey, A. G. 1835. "Catholic Schools." *Mother's Magazine*, March, 76–77.

Willard, Emma. (1819) 1918. *A Plan for Improving Female Education*. Middlebury, Vt.: Middlebury College.

———. (1835) 1850. *Universal History in Perspective*. 10th ed. New York: A. S. Barnes.

———. 1838. *Letter Addressed as a Circular to the Members of the Willard Association for the Mutual Improvement of Female Teachers*. Troy, N.Y.: Elias Gates.

———. 1853. *Last Leaves of American History: Embracing a Separate History of California*. New York: A. S. Barnes and Co.

———. 1854. *Universal History, in Perspective*. 12th ed. New York: A. S. Barnes and Co.

Willigman, M. Theresa Catherine. N.d. "First Foundress of the Oblates." AOSP.

Wittenberg, Patricia. 1994. *The Rise and Fall of Catholic Religious Orders: A Social Movement Perspective*. New York: State University of New York Press.

WORKS CITED

Wolff, Florence. 1982. *From Generation to Generation: The Sisters of Loretto, Their Constitutions and Devotions, 1812—Vatican II*. Louisville: General Printing Company. ASL.

Woodbridge, William Channing, and Emma Willard. 1827. *A System of Universal Geography*. Hartford: Oliver D. Cooke. Google Books.

Woodford, Frank B., and Albert Hyma. 1958. *Gabriel Richard*. Detroit: Wayne State University.

Woodham-Smith, Cecil. 1989. *The Great Hunger: Ireland, 1845–1849*. New York: Old Town Books.

Woodhouselee, Lord Alexander Fraser Tytler. 1809. *The Elements of General History, Ancient and Modern to Which Are Added, a Table of Chronology, and a Comparative View of Ancient and Modern Geography*. Philadelphia: T. and G. Palmer for F. Nichols. Early American Imprints, Series 2.

Woodson, Carter Godwin. 1919. *The Education of the Negro Prior to 1861: A History of the Education of the Colored People of the United States from the Beginning of Slavery to the Civil War*. Washington: Associated Publishers.

Woody, Thomas. 1929. *A History of Women's Education in the United States*. New York: Science Press.

Worcester, Joseph Emerson. 1826. *Elements of History, Ancient and Modern*. Boston: Timothy Swan. Early American Imprints, Series 1.

Workman, Benjamin. 1801. *Elements of Geography, Designed for Young Students in That Science*. Philadelphia: John M'Cullough. Early American Imprints, Series 2.

Wright, Elizabethada. 2013. "'God Sees Me': Surveillance and Oratorical Training at Nineteenth-Century St. Mary-of-the-Woods in Indiana." In *Rhetoric, History, and Oratorical Education: America Women Learn to Speak*, edited by David Gold and Catherine L. Hobbs, 116–33. New York: Routledge.

The Young Gentleman and Lady's Monitor, and English Teacher's Assistant. 1795. Hudson, N.Y.: Stoddard, Ashbel. Early American Imprints, Series 1.

Zagarri, Rosemarie. 2007. *Revolutionary Backlash: Women and Politics in the Early American Republic*. Philadelphia: University of Pennsylvania Press.

Zboray, Ronald J. 1993. *A Fictive People: Antebellum Economic Development and the American Reading Public*. New York: Oxford University Press.

INDEX

abolitionist movement, 194–96. *See also* African Americans
academies, scholarship perspectives, 12. *See also* convent academies
Academy of St. Mary Magdalen, 86
Adams, John Quincy, 226n11
Adams Academy, 51, 52
Adolphus, Christina, 66–67
African Americans: abolitionist movement, 194–96; in convent communities, 190–94, 231nn16–17; literacy restriction, 156, 186–88, 196, 231n18; religious instruction approach, 186, 188–89. *See also* Oblate Sisters of Providence community
Alexandria Gazette, 168
Alfieri, Vittorio, 107
Algonquin language, 9
alphabetic instruction, 20, 21, 22, 23
American Bible Society, 47
American Home Missionary Society, 199
The American Preceptor (Bigham), 27
American Quarterly Register, 59
An American Selection of Lessons . . . (Webster), 27–28
American Tract Society, 70
Ancient History (Rollin), 104
Andrew, James A., 232n22
Anglican Church, Virginia, 80, 225n1
anti-Catholicism, overviews: imagery, 117–20; laws, 4–5, 21–22, 47, 80–81, 219n6; sisters' impact, 165–66, 180–83, 220n8, 229n1; slavery comparisons, 194–95. *See also specific topics, e.g.*, Beecher, Catharine; schoolbooks
Appeal to the Coloured Citizens of the World (Walker), 187
arithmetic sections, spellers, 23–24
arts instruction, 149–50
astronomy textbook, 35–36
Atkinson, George, 199
Atlanta Daily Register, 178
Atlantic Monthly, 182
Aubert, Jean-Baptiste, 136–37
Audé, Eugenie, 139, 154–55
Austen, Jane, 106
Austria, in Willard's geography, 65
Awful Disclosures (Monk), 54–55

Babade, Pierre, 114
Balas, Marie, 87, 89, 210
Baltimore, cholera epidemic, 170, 229n4
Bancroft, George, 75
Baptists, 46, 232n22
Barat, Louis, 150–51
Barat, Madeleine Sophie: classroom materials shipment, 154; Duchesne's Indian mission, 162; portrait of, 129; society founding, 209; teacher recruitment challenge, 135. *See also* Duchesne, Rose Philippine (correspondence topics)
Barber, Jerusha, 87
Bardstown, Kentucky, 83, 85. *See also* Sisters of Charity of Nazareth community, Kentucky

259

INDEX

Barry, Teresa, 210
Battle of New Orleans, 176
Baudier, Roger, 192
Baym, Nina, 66, 76
Beady, Nancy, 12
Beaven, Mary, 209
Bechtle, Regina, 88
Beecher, Catharine: anti-Catholic rhetoric, 15; classroom materials, 48; conversion mission, 51; fund-raising rhetoric, 62–65; school opening, 201; school structure proposal, 74–75
Beecher, Edward, 77
Beecher, Henry Ward, 77
Beecher, Lyman, 47, 56–57, 77, 78, 194
Beecher, Mary, 48, 201
Beecher, Roxanne Foote, 73
Bennett, James Gordon, 55
Bernard, Mary, 232n1
Bethlehem Academy, Kentucky, 92
Bible: in Beecher's fund-raising rhetoric, 62; distribution in Irish schools, 44–45; Mann's sectarian argument, 231n13; for religious instruction, 51; as schoolbook, 21, 23, 27, 34, 187
Bigham, Caleb, 27
Billington, Ray Allen, 195
Bizzell, Patricia, 1
black population. *See* African Americans
Bloody Monday, 72
boarding schools, 9, 72–76, 89, 95, 101–3
Bodine-Reed, Cheryl A., 147–48
Boegue, Rose/Rosanne, 128, 210
Boston Daily Atlas and Bee, 194
Boyle, Elizabeth, 216
Brazil, in geographies, 42
Brereton, John, 14
Britain/British influence: anti-Catholic actions, 4–5, 219n6; in geographies, 29, 42; in histories, 32, 33, 66; scholarship opportunities, 201–2

Bruckner, Martin, 28
Bruté, Simon, 7, 93, 105, 107
Buchanan, James, 226n11
Buel, Elizabeth C. Barney, 50
Burke, Edmund, 219n6
Burke, Mary Elizabeth, 210
Burns, J. A., 35, 37, 212
Butler, Benjamin, 177
Butler, Frederick W., 32–33
Butler, James P., 38
Butler, Mary Ann, 208
Button, H. Warren, 12
Byrne, Catherine, 210
Byrne, Patricia, 150
Byrne, William, 86
Byron, Lord, 106–7

Cahokia, Illinois, 135, 156
calendars, in spellers, 23
Callan, Louise, 138, 146, 160
Callcott, George H., 31
Campau, Angelique, 211–12
Campbell, George, 203–4
Canada, in geographies, 42. *See also* Ursuline communities, Quebec
Capers, William, 188
Carey, Mathew, 35, 37, 41–42, 43, 45, 105
Carmelites, 207, 225n3, 232n1
Carondelet, Missouri. *See* Sisters of St. Joseph communities
Carpenter, Charles, 33
Carr, Jean Ferguson, 21
Carr, Stephen L., 21
Carrico, Mary, 209
Carrico, Teresa, 209
Carroll, Columba, 90–91, 101–4, 105–6, 110–11
Carroll, John, 7, 41, 105, 114, 196
Catechetical Compend of General History . . . (Butler), 32–33
A Catechism, or Short Abridgement of Christian Doctrine . . ., 36–37

INDEX

Catechism for the Use of Methodist Missions (Capers), 188
The Catechism of Preservation (Jamison), 143
catechisms, 22, 23, 24–25, 36–38, 186
Cathechism Scripture Doctrine (Jones), 188–89
Catholic colleges, French influence, 203–4
The Catholick Christian Instructed in the Sacraments . . . (Challoner), 37–38
celibacy, 25, 38, 53–55, 58, 75
Challoner, Richard, 37–38
Chalmers, Thomas, 105
Charleston, Massachusetts. *See* Ursuline community, Charleston, Massachusetts
Child, Lydia Maria, 106, 187
The Child's Spelling Book . . . (Richard), 43
Chiniquy, Charles, 54
Chittenden, Lucius E., 177–78
cholera epidemic, 167–74, 229n4
Christian Party, 230n5
Christian Register and Boston Observer, 167
Christoph, Julie Nelson, 14
Cincinnati, 57, 112–13, 174–75
Cincinnati Chronicle and Literary Gazette, 174
Cincinnati Daily Commercial, 174–75
Cincinnati Journal, 57, 167
Civil War, religious community service, 176–85
Clark, Emily, 10–11, 13, 151, 163, 231n16
Clarke, Mary Frances, 210
classroom materials, 86–87, 104–10, 154–55, 229n7. *See also* curriculum offerings; schoolbooks
class structure perspectives, 96–97, 151–53
Clay, Henry, 78, 226n11
Clerc, Laurent, 157

Clinton, Catherine, 89, 221n15
Cloriviere, Joseph, 86, 87
Clossy/Clossey, Susan, 208, 216
clothing, 110, 114–15, 134–35
Coburn, Carol K., 13, 177
Cogswell, Joseph, 75
commandments, 22, 46
common schools, 3, 64, 84, 199, 226nn4–5
A Compend of Geography . . ., 29
confession, 53–54, 119
Congregationalists, 24–25, 35, 71, 77, 80, 225n1
Connecticut, 47, 186–87, 225n2
Constitution, U.S., 7, 26, 81
convent academies: boarding practices, 9, 72–76, 89, 95, 101–3; classroom materials, 86–87, 104–10, 154–55, 229n7; literature review, 12–14; numbers of, 15–16, 199–200; promotional materials, 98–99; as proprietary school incentive, 14–15, 58–61; quality education reputation, 69–71, 74–75, 78–79; religious instruction, 143–47; rules and schedules, 99, 110–11, 213–17. *See also* curriculum offerings; Sisters *entries*; Visitation Academy, Georgetown
convent communities: African American members, 191–93, 231nn16–17; during cholera epidemic, 167–73, 229n4; chronological summary, 207–12; class structure perspectives, 96–97, 151–53; conflicts with ecclesiastical superiors, 111–15, 162–63; education missions, 6–8, 81–82, 220n8; entrant literacy levels, 82–85; French influence, 131–33; geographic patterns, 133–34, 135, 136, 225n2, 228n2; impact on anti-Catholic sentiment, 165–67, 180–83, 229n1; Jesuit influence, 136–38; lifestyle advantages,

261

convent communities (*continued*) 115–16, 163; mutual support networks, 189–90, 192; opposition themes, 52–58, 120; orphanages, 97–98, 174, 184; post–Civil War appreciation, 181–85; role model expectations, 110–11; and slavery system, 190–91, 194–97; teacher training, 85–92, 105–7, 190; transition hardships summarized, 134–36, 159–63; wartime service, 176–82. *See also* Oblate Sisters of Providence community; Sisters *entries*; Ursuline *entries*
convent escape narratives, 27, 54–55
convent schools. *See* convent academies
conversion mission, 49–52, 155–56
Coton, Pierre, 137
Cott, Nancy, 198
Cotton, John, 22
Crandall, Prudence, 186–87
Crawford, Jack Wallace, 180, 230n10
Cremin, Lawrence, 187
Crimean War, 230n6
Crittenden, Anne Mary, 72
Crittenden, John J., 72
Cromwell, Oliver, 31
Crumlish, John Mary, 98
Cumming, Kate, 179
curriculum offerings: convent academies, 69–71, 92–95, 100–101, 138–43, 147–51; day schools, 96–97; proprietor schools, 49–52; for teacher training, 85–89
Curtis, Sarah A., 18, 116, 132

Les Dames de la Retraite, Charleston, South Carolina, 150, 193, 211, 228n2
Daniell, Beth, 189
Datty, Julia, 89, 210
Daughters of Charity communities, 113, 130, 177, 181, 208. *See also* Sisters of Charity *entries*

David, Jean Baptiste: conflicts with Seton, 114; convent community founding, 209; on prejudice reduction, 166; recruitment of O'Connell, 88; schoolbooks search, 37, 39, 105; teacher training, 83, 85–86, 226n7
Davies, Benjamin, 30
Davis, Henry, 77
Davis, Jefferson, 78, 226n11
day schools, 93–97, 153, 189
decorative arts instruction, 149–50
Decount, Augustine, 87
de l'Épée, Abbé, 156–58
Deloul, Louis, 113, 115, 192
DePalma, Michael-John, 14
Derry, New Hampshire, 51–52
Detroit, Michigan, 43–44, 211–12, 219n3, 232n2
Dickerson, Clare Joseph, 207
Dickinson, Emily, 71–72
dictionary-type spellers, 23
Dilhet, John, 211–12
disease epidemics, 167–74, 229n4
Dixon, Henry, 23
domestic skills, instruction, 16, 221n13
Dominican Sisters of St. Rose, 84, 113, 209
Donaghoe, Terence James, 210
Donaldson, Louisiana, 177
Don Juan (Alfieri), 107
Donohue, Francis J., 36, 44
Douay Bible, 23, 41, 45
Doyle, Mary Ellen, 13, 209, 231n16
Druilhet, Julien, 137
Dubois, Jean, 211
Dubourg, Louis, 83, 111, 114, 160, 162–63, 231n18
Duchemin, Almaide, 210
Duchemin, Marie Therese, 89, 128
Duchesne, Rose Philippine: language difficulties, 160, 192; leadership role summarized, 209; portrait of, 129

Duchesne, Rose Philippine (correspondence topics): African Americans, 192–93, 231n18; anti-Catholicism, 134; classroom materials, 154–55; Detroit teaching community, 232–33; domestic help problem, 159–60; education instructions, 139; English language, 150–51; funding problem, 162–63; Jesuit influence, 136–37, 138; moral conduct dismay, 161–62; novices, 133, 143; religious knowledge concerns, 160–61; slaves, 191

Duffy, John, 14

Du Jarday, Hery, 211

Dwight, Nathaniel, 30, 47

Dwight, Timothy, 47–48

Eastman, Caroline, 13

The Education of the Southern Belle (Farnham), 221n14

Edwards, Jonathan, 47, 71, 77

Elder, A. J., 169–70

Elements of Geography (Workman), 30

Elements of History . . . (Worcester), 33

Elizabeth, Queen, 27

Elkins, Stanley, 204

Ellis, John Tracy, 7, 80

Elson, Ruth Miller, 26

Ely, Ezra Stiles, 172, 230n5

Emerson, Joseph, 56–57, 68, 78

Emerson, Ralph, 56–57

Emmitsburg, Maryland. *See* Sisters of Charity of St. Joseph community, Emmitsburg

England. *See* Britain/British influence

England, John, 37, 114, 151–52, 166, 208, 210

English Grammar (Murray), 34

The English Reader (Murray), 27

Entich's New Spelling Dictionary, 23

An Epistle to the Clergy . . . (Grimké), 194

Essay on the Management of Slaves, . . . (Seabrook), 188

etiquette instruction, 142–43

Eucharist, catechism explanation, 38

The Evils Suffered by American Women and . . . (Beecher), 62–63, 74–75

Ewens, Mary, 132, 177, 229n1

The Fall of Babylon (Mather), 24–25

Farnham, Christie Anne, 110, 221n14

Fénelon, François, 202–3

Fennings, Daniel, 23

Fenwick, Edward, 45

Fern, Fanny, 182

First Amendment, 26, 81

First Provincial Council, 39

Fiske, Fidelia, 68, 71, 73

Fitzgerald, Oscar Penn, 171–72

Flaget, Benedict Joseph: authority conflicts, 113, 233; Detroit teaching community, 233; teacher training, 85

Flaget, Benedict Joseph (correspondence topics): African American women, 192; anti-Catholicism reduction, 166, 184; dress of sisters, 115; student challenges, 83; taxation, 228n5

Fletcher, William, 180–81

Fontbonne, St. John, 211

Foreign Conspiracy against the Liberties . . . (Morse), 195, 232n21

Foster, John, 105

Fouché, Simon, 85

Fournier, Julie, 228n4

Foxe's Book of Martyrs, 22

France/French influence: convent communities characterized, 131–33; explorers/settlers, 2–3, 219n3; in histories, 33; language instruction, 189; scholarship opportunities, 201–3; women's literacy in American colonies, 9–11, 220nn9–10

INDEX

Franchot, Jenny, 54
Franciscans, 2, 6
French influence. *See* France/French influence
funding, foreign, 76–77
Further Disclosures (Monk), 55

Gallaudet, Thomas Hopkins, 157
Galveston News, 181–82
Gannett, Cinthia, 14
Gardiner, Frances, 91
Gardiner, Harriet, 209
Garrison, William Lloyd, 187
Gartland, Jane Frances, 216
Gaston, William Joseph, 114
Gautland, Jan Frances, 107
Gawthrop, Richard, 3
General View of . . . Holyoke Female Seminary (Lyon), 61–62
geographies, 28–30, 35–36, 39, 105
George, Margaret, 90, 115, 174, 217
Georgetown. *See* Visitation Academy, Georgetown
Germany, in Willard's geography, 65
Gethsemani academy, Kentucky, 93–94
Gettysburg, 177
Gilgannon, Mary McAuley, 230n6
Girard, Abbé, 203
Godey's Lady's Book, 183
"God Sees Me" (Wright), 14
Goldblatt, Eli, 14
Goldsmith, Oliver, 40, 48
Gontery, John, 137
Graff, Harvey, 1, 4, 17, 21
Graff, Nelson, 14
grammars, schoolbook, 34–35
Grant, Ulysses S., 178, 226n11
Grant, Zilpah, 51, 52, 60–61, 68, 71, 77–78
Gray, Lady Jane, 27
Greek instruction, 189
Green, Elizabeth Alden, 52

Greene, Jamie Candelaria, 2
Greer, Allan, 10, 220n10
Gregory XVI, 196
Grimké, Angela, 194
Grimké, Sarah, 194
Grimshaw, William, 40
Groulx, Lionel, 220n10
Guilday, Peter, 211
Gunpowder Plot, in histories, 40–41
Guthrie, William, 41–42, 105
Guyart, Marie, 136, 228n3
Gwynn, Mary, 209

Hachard, Jacques, 228n3
Hachard, Marie Madeleine, 13, 163, 228n3
Hale, David, 232n20
Hale, Nathan, 232n20
Hale, Sarah Josepha, 15, 58–59, 69
Hallock, Gerard, 232n20
Hamilton, Regis, 159–60
Harris, Benjamin, 24
Havern, Ann, 208
hearing-impaired instruction, 135–36, 156–59, 228n4
hedge schools, 219n6
Hemans, Felicia, 106, 107
Hennesey, James, 193
Henni, Martin, 172
Henry, J. Q. A., 53–54
Herzberg, Bruce, 1
history instruction, 28, 30–34, 39–40, 50–51, 66–67, 104, 141–42
History in the United States (Callcott), 31
The History of England . . . (Hume and Smollett), 33–34
History of England (Hume), 31
History of the Popes (Ranke), 63
history sections, spellers, 23–24
homoerotic attractions, Carroll's guidelines, 102–3
hornbooks, 20

264

INDEX

hospitals, 176, 199, 232n1. *See also* disease epidemics
Howe, Jemima, 27
Hughes, Antonia, 208
Hughes, John, 46, 69
Hume, David, 27, 31, 33–34
Huron language, 9
Hyma, Albert, 43

Ignatius Loyola, 63
immigration, 45–46, 62, 74. *See also* anti-Catholicism, overviews
Indians, American, 9, 155–56, 162, 220n9
Instructions for Children (Keach), 23
invocations, hornbooks, 20
Iowa, 210, 228n2
Ipswich Academy, 52
Ireland: Bible distributions, 44–45; Britain's anti-Catholic laws, 4–5; in schoolbooks, 29–30, 31, 42, 65
Ireton, Henry, 31
Irish Ursulines. *See* Ursuline communities; Ursuline community, Boston
Italy, in geographies, 29, 30, 65

Jackson, Andrew, 226n11
Jacquenot, Bartholomew, 137
Jamison, Francis B., 143
Jefferson, Thomas, 81
Jesuit Relations, 136
Jesuits, 2, 6, 63, 136–38, 203, 219n3
Jones, Charles Coldcock, 188–89, 231n14
Jones, Stanislaus, 87
Jordan, Fanny, 216, 217
Joubert, James H., 210

Keach, Benjamin, 23
Keenan, Mary Ellen, 153
Kelley, Mary, 12–13, 69, 202
Kelly, Eliza, 210
Kenrick, Francis, 35

Kentucky, 63, 84, 226nn4–5. *See also* Sisters of Charity of Nazareth community, Kentucky; Sisters of Loretto community
Kerber, Linda, 49, 55
Ketchum, Hiram, 187
Key to the Exercises Adapted to . . . (Murray), 34–35
King James Bible, 23
Knecht, Sharon, 89
Know-Nothing Party, 195

Labadie, Monique, 211–12
La Fourche, Louisiana, 95, 112, 114
Lalor, Alice, 207
Lambert, Frank, 81
Lange, Elizabeth, 87, 89, 127, 210
language instruction, 9, 150–51, 189, 192
Last Leaves of American History (Willard), 66
Latin instruction, 189
Learning to Stand and Speak (Kelley), 12–13
Legacies of Literacy (Graff), 4
Lerner, Gerda, 13–14
Leslie, Eliza, 106
Litchfield Female Academy, Pierce's: advocacy themes, 15; Beecher's influence, 78; boarding school element, 225n13; opening of, 201; pioneer reputation, 12, 14; religious agenda, 49, 50–51, 224n8
Literacy, Economy, and Power (Duffy et al.), 14
Literacy Myth (Graff), 4
literacy narratives, overviews: Catholicism's activity, 6–8; Protestantism myth, 1–6; scholarship opportunity, 16–18; women's education, 9–16, 196–97. *See also specific topics*, e.g., schoolbooks; Ursuline community, New Orleans

265

INDEX

Livermore, Mary Ashton, 178–79
Locke, John, 20
Lockridge, Kenneth, 1, 10
Logan, Shirley, 201
Loretto Academy. *See* Sisters of Loretto community
Loriquet, Nicolas, 137
Louisville Journal, 72
Lovejoy, Elijah P., 57, 196
Lucas, Fielding, 35–36
Luther, Martin, 3
Lyon, Lucy, 68
Lyon, Mary. *See* Mount Holyoke, Lyon's
Lyons, Elizabeth, 211–12

Madison, James, 81
Maher, Mary Denis, 176–77
Maine, convent communities, 225n2
Maintenon, Madame de, 202
Mallet, Shepton, 97
Maloney, M. Charles, 208
Manifest Destiny, in Willard's history, 66
Mann, Horace, 19–20, 187
Mann, Margaret, 210
Mannard, Gerald, 83, 84, 92
Mapping Christian Rhetorics (DePalma and Ringer), 14
Maria Clara, Sister, 177
Marillac, Louise de, 190
marriage: in anti-Catholic rhetoric, 25, 53, 55; C. Beecher's condemnation, 75; register signatures, 10–11, 16, 220n10, 221n12
Martin, Marie de Saint Jean, 137
martyr stories, 22, 24
Mary, Queen, 33, 274?
Mary Augustine, Sister, 87
Maryland: anti-Catholic law, 5, 22, 80; Catholic population, 25; Congregational Church establishment, 225n1. *See also* Sisters of Charity of St. Joseph community, Emmitsburg

Mary Martha, Sister, 92
Mary of the Incarnation, 9
Massachusetts: school taxes, 19–20; state-based religion, 47, 225n2. *See also* Ursuline community, Boston
mathematics textbook, 35
Mather, Cotton, 24–25, 186
Mathevon, Lucille, 135
Matthews, Bernardina, 207
Mayo Clinic, 232n1
McCarthy, Borgia, 208
McDermott, Maria, 207
McEntee, Mary Bernard, 88, 96
McMan, Judith, 209
mentally ill, care for, 175
Merici, Angela, 6, 207
Merrill, Horatio, 77
Merry's Museum for Boys and Girls, 183
Methodist Church, 232n22
Metz, Judith, 88
Mexico, in schoolbooks, 30, 66
Miles, Pius, 86
Milk for Babes (Cotton), 22
Misner, Barbara, 82–83, 96
Mobberley, Joseph P., 37, 105
Modern Geography (Pinkerton), 10
Molyneux, Robert, 35, 37
Monaghan, E. Jennifer, 1, 23
Monk, Maria, 54–55
Montgomery, Alabama, 178
monument, 183, 230n11
morality-literacy connections, overview, 19–21, 49–52. *See also specific topics, e.g.*, curriculum offerings; schoolbooks
Mordecai, Jacob, 12
Morrow, Diane Batts, 13, 89, 193, 226n10
Morse, Jedidiah, 29, 47
Morse, Samuel F. B., 195, 232n21
Mortensen, Peter, 189
mother houses, 63, 125
Mother's Magazine, 59

266

INDEX

Mount Benedict Academy. *See* Ursuline community, Boston
Mount Holyoke, Lyon's: anti-Catholic rhetoric, 15, 61–62, 74; boarding practices, 73; conversion mission, 51, 52, 68, 71–72; fund-raising appeals, 60–61; influences on, 77–78; teacher compensation, 75–76; tuition, 75, 76
Mullen, Kitty, 216
Murphy, Anna, 139
Murphy, John, 39
Murphy, Maria, 208
Murray, Lindley, 27, 34

Nantucket Massachusetts Inquirer, 169
Nash, Margaret A., 12, 68–69
A Nation of Speechifiers (Eastman), 13
Neale, Leonard, 207
The Negro Christianized (Mather), 186
Nerinckx, Charles: African American members, 192, 231n17; convent community initiation, 208; on growth of convent, 92; on reduction of anti-Catholicism, 166; teacher training, 83, 86, 156
Netherlands, in Davies' geography, 29–30
New-England Primer, 22
New England Tract Society, 47
A New Geographical, Historical, and Commercial Grammar (Guthrie), 41
New Hampshire, 51–52, 225n2
New Orleans, marriage register signatures, 10–11. *See also* Ursuline community, New Orleans
New Orleans Whig, 172
A New System of Geography (Davies), 30
New System of Modern Geography (Guthrie), 41–42
New York: anti-Catholic law, 21–22; school funding conflict, 46; Ursuline community, 208, 228n2; Willard's address to legislature, 50

New York Daily Times, 230n9
New York Herald, 55
New York Journal of Commerce, 195, 232n21
New York Times, 179–80, 182
New York Truth Teller, 45
Nietz, John A., 26
Nightingale, Florence, 230n6
Niles Weekly Register, 168–69
Noonan, Paschala, 84, 86, 159
Norton, Mary Beth, 12
Novia Scotia, 4–5
Nowacek, Rebecca S., 14
Nuns of the Battlefield, 183, 230n11

Oates, Mary J., 12
Oblate Sisters of Providence community: overview, 210; in convent support network, 192; curriculum offerings, 100; education mission, 82; funding, 226n10, 227n13; history scholarship about, 13; member education levels, 87, 89, 92; member portraits, 127; in slavery system, 191; success of, 193; teacher training, 86, 90
O'Connell, Anthony, 177
O'Connell, Ellen, 88–89, 91, 107–9
O'Connor, Ann, 88–89
O'Conway, Cecilia, 208, 216, 217
O'Gorman, Honora, 210
O'Gorman, Mary, 210
O'Leary, Mary, 143
On Education Book 1st (Carroll), 101
Open Convents . . . (Dwight), 47
Oratorians, 6
Order of the Visitation of the Blessed Lady, 207. *See also* Visitation Academy, Georgetown
Oregon, school models, 199
orphanages, 97–98, 174, 184
O'Toole, Rose, 210

INDEX

Pakenham, Edward, 176
Park, Edwards A., 203–4
Parton, James, 182
penance, catechism explanation, 36
Pennsylvania, 46–47, 80
Perkins, Justin, 68
Persons of Color and Religious. . . . (Morrow), 13
Phelps, Austin, 14
Philadelphia, cholera epidemic, 170–71, 229n4
Phillips, Wendell, 195
Pierce, James, 50–51
Pierce, Sarah. *See* Litchfield Female Academy, Pierce's
Pinkerton, John, 10
Pioneer Spirit (Doyle), 13
Pious Ladies, 207
A Plea for the West (Beecher), 57
Poland, in geographies, 29, 65
Polk, James K., 226n11
Pomey, François, 104
Pommerel, Celestine, 228n4
Poor Clares, 162, 190, 207, 228n2, 232n1
poor-oriented works, 174–75
population statistics, 7
Porterfield, Amanda, 53, 60, 68, 71
Portugal, in geographies, 29, 30, 42, 65
prayers in schoolbooks, 20, 36
Prentice, George D., 72
Presbyterian Church, 232n22
primers, 5–6, 20–21, 22–23, 35
property loss, convent communities, 112–13, 228n21, n23
proprietor schools: advocacy rhetoric, 15, 58–65, 74; conversion mission, 49–52, 71–72, 76; pioneer reputation, 11, 14. *See also* Beecher, Catharine; Litchfield Female Academy, Pierce's; Mount Holyoke, Lyon's
Protestantism myth. *See* literacy narratives, overviews

A Protestant's Resolution, 25–26
The Protestant Tutor for Children (Harris), 24
Provenzo, Eugene F., 12
psalters, 21
purgatory, catechism explanation, 36

Quebec Act, 27–28
Quinn, Martina, 216

Raboteau, Albert J., 188
Radcliffe, Ann, 106
Raikes, Robert, 61
Ralle, Sebastien, 33
Ranke, Leopold von, 63
readers, schoolbook, 26–28
Rebel Private, Front and Rear (Fletcher), 180–81
Recollects, 219n3
Reed, Lucy Ann (later Woodbridge), 48
Reeve, James E., 232n22
Règlements: etiquette guidelines, 142–43; instruction guidelines, 139, 140, 145–46; Jesuit influence, 137; schedule guidelines, 218; student monitor responsibilities, 153. *See also* Ursuline *entries*
relics, catechism explanation, 37
The Religious Instruction of the Negroes . . . (Jones), 188
Religious Intelligencer, 44
retirement, teachers, 103–4
Revolutionary Backlash (Zagarri), 13
rhetoric instruction, 202–3
rhetoric scholarship, literature review, 14
Rhodes, Mary, 84, 87, 208
Richard, Gabriel, 43–44, 211–12, 219n3, 232n2
Ringer, Jeffrey, 14
Robinson, John, 33–34
Rogers, John, 22, 24

INDEX

Rollin, Charles, 39–40, 104
Roman Catholic Female Schools (American Tract Society), 70
Roman Catholic Primer, 35
"Rome's Substitute for Marriage" (Henry), 53–54
Rosati, Joseph, 112, 114, 156, 163
Rosenberg, Charles F., 167–68
Round Hill, Massachusetts, 75
Rourke, Mary Ann, 147
Royster, Jacqueline Jones, 17, 201
Rudolph, Frederick, 65
Rules of the Society and School of Loretto, Kentucky, 81–82, 140, 165–66, 220n8
Russia, in Willard's geography, 65

sacraments, 22
saints, catechism explanation, 37
Sansbury, Mariah, 209
Satterlee Military Hospital, 130, 230n10
schoolbooks: catechisms, 24–25, 36–38; Catholic-oriented publishers, 35–38; Congregationalist influences, 46–48; Detroit-based publishers, 43–44; for European-based communities, 154–55; geographies, 28–30, 39, 41–42; grammars, 34–35; histories, 30–34, 39–41; Indian language, 9; readers, 26–28; reform interest, 44–46, 48; spellers, 23–24; themes summarized, 5–6, 19–23, 26
Schultz, Lucille M., 21
Schultz, Stanley, 56
science instruction, 87, 93, 148–49, 164
Scott, Julia, 84, 115
Seabrook, Whitemarsh B., 188
The Secretary's Guide, 23
Sedgwick, Catharine Maria, 106
Seton, Elizabeth: African American students, 193; background, 83, 87, 88, 208; children's education, 115; ecclesiastical authority conflict, 114; image of, 126; on reading materials, 227n19; on teaching, 84; writing instructions, 109–10
Seton, Josephine, 107
Seward, William, 46
Sharpe, Sister Ignatia, 87
Sharpe, Ursula, 207
Shelley, Mary, 106
Short but Comprehensive System of the Geography . . . (Dwight), 30, 47
signature evidence, literacy levels, 10, 16, 83, 221n12
Sigourney, Lydia, 106
Sisters of Charity of Nazareth community, Kentucky: overview, 7, 209; African American students, 193; in Beecher's speech, 63; during cholera epidemic, 172–73, 174; classroom materials, 39, 105–9; in convent support network, 136; curriculum offerings, 98, 148; ecclesiastical authority conflicts, 115; enrollment patterns, 72, 78, 98, 226n11; impact on anti-Catholicism, 166; painting of buildings, 124; property loss, 112, 228n21; Protestant students, 72, 78, 226n11; teacher training, 85, 88, 90–91; tuition, 95
Sisters of Charity of Our Lady of Mercy, South Carolina. *See* Sisters of Mercy community, Charleston, South Carolina
Sisters of Charity of St. Joseph community, Emmitsburg: overview, 208; African American students, 193; classroom exercises, 109–10; in convent support network, 89, 190; curriculum offerings, 93, 96, 149; ecclesiastical authority conflicts, 113–14; education mission, 96; enrollment patterns, 73, 98, 115; impact on anti-Catholicism,

INDEX

Sisters of Charity of St. Joseph community (*continued*) 183–84; member demographics, 83–84; painting of buildings, 123; property loss, 112; religion tolerance, 99; teacher training, 90, 91–92, 192; tuition, 227n13; wartime service, 177

Sisters of Charity of the Blessed Virgin, Iowa, 210, 228n2

Sisters of Loretto community: overview, 208; African American students, 193; classroom materials, 104, 154; in convent support network, 190; curriculum offerings, 93–95, 100–101, 110, 140, 148, 149; ecclesiastical authority conflicts, 113, 114; member numbers, 7–8, 92; mission statements, 165–66; promotion themes, 98, 99; property loss, 112, 228n23; school rules, 99, 213–15; in slavery system, 191; subordinate role expectations, 111; teacher training, 85, 86, 90; tuition, 94–95

Sisters of Mercy community, Charleston, South Carolina: overview, 210; African American students, 156, 193; class structure perspectives, 151–52; curriculum offerings, 100; Datty's leadership, 89; in slavery system, 191

Sisters of Mercy community, Cincinnati, 112–13, 174–75

Sisters of St. Joseph communities: overview, 211; African American students, 156; buildings, 125; continued learning mission, 131, 228n4; curriculum offerings, 138–39, 140, 145–46, 149–50; deaf community instruction, 156, 157, 159; establishment of, 135, 156; history scholarship, 13; in slavery system, 191–92; support of, 135–36, 190; travel clothing, 134–35

Sisters of the Good Shepherd, 190

Sisters of the Holy Cross, 190

Sisters of the Holy Family, 192

Sisters of the Sacred Heart community: overview, 132, 209; classroom materials, 154–55, 229n7; class structure perspective, 152; conflicts with ecclesiastical superiors, 114; curriculum approach, 139, 141–42, 147–48, 150–51, 164; founding mission, 144, 145; Jesuit influence, 137–38, 209; religious studies, 143; in slavery system, 191; Ursuline support of, 190. *See also* Duchesne *entries*

Sizer, Theodore, 51, 71

Sklar, Kathryn Kish, 75

slavery system, 190–97

Smith, B. B., 226n5

Smith, Martha, 13, 177

Smith, Timothy, 46

Smollett, Tobias, 33–34

Society of the Sacred Heart. *See* Sisters of the Sacred Heart community

Soltow, Lee, 10

Spain, in geographies, 29, 65

Spalding, Catherine: conflicts with ecclesiastical superiors, 114; Doyle's biography of, 13; leadership role summarized, 209; orphanage founding, 174; portrait of, 127; on service during cholera epidemic, 173; slavery perspective, 231n16; teacher training, 91, 92

Spalding, Martin J., 228n21

Spanish conquistadors, 2

Speed, James, 226n6

spelling instruction, 23–24, 141, 231n12

Spelling Primer for Children . . . (Molyneux), 35

Spirited Lives (Coburn and Smith), 13

St. Charles, Missouri, 162

St. Cyr school, 202, 232n2

St. Francis Academy. *See* Oblate Sisters of Providence community

INDEX

St. Joseph Academy. *See* Sisters of Charity of St. Joseph community, Emmitsburg
St. Joseph College, 85, 98, 226n6
St. Joseph Institute for the Deaf, 156
St. Louis Observer, 196
St. Louis Sacred Heart Academy, 149
St. Magdalen's Convent, 63
St. Mary's College, 85, 98
St. Mary's Hospital, 232n1
St. Michael School and Convent, 124
St. Peter's Orphan Asylum, 174
St. Pierre, Mother, 181
St. Thomas Seminary, 85
St. Vincent Academy, 69–70
Stern, Andrew, 194
Stevens, Edward, 10
Stone, Lawrence, 1
Stow, Sarah D. Locke, 51, 52, 60–61
Strauss, Gerald, 3
Stuart, Christina, 208
Sullivan, Mary Christina, 193
Sulpicians, 6, 35, 115, 203
Sweden, in Willard's history, 66–67
Swisshelm, Jane Grey, 194
syllabic instruction, 20, 21, 22, 23
A System of Universal Geography (Willard and Woodbridge), 65

Tappan, Arthur, 195–96
Tappan, Lewis, 195
Tarleton, Severly, 209
taxation, 19–20, 226n5
Taylor, Zachary, 78, 226n11
teacher training: convent communities, 83, 85–92, 105–7, 190, 192, 226n7; proprietary schools, 75–76
Tebbel, John, 41
textbooks. *See* schoolbooks
Thompson, Margaret Susan, 151
Tolley, Kim, 12, 87, 200–201
Tooke, Andrew, 104

Took's Patheon of the . . . Illustrious Heroes, 104
Tour, Charles de la, 137
Trabold, Bryan, 14
Traditions of Eloquence (Gannett Brereton), 14
Tranchepain, Marie, 228n3
Trappistines, 232n1
Treatise on the Education of Girls (Fénelon), 202
Trollope, Frances, 106
Troy Female Seminary, 69
Tudor, Mary, 27
tuition, 75, 76, 89, 93, 94–95, 136, 227n13
Tyler, John, 226n11
Tynack, David, 199

Unitarians, 71, 72, 167
Universal History in Perspective (Willard), 66–67
Universal Spelling-Book (Fennings), 23
University of Michigan, 43
Ursuline communities: overview, 207–8; etiquette guidelines, 142–43; founding mission, 6–7, 144–45; instruction approach, 139, 140, 144–46, 229n8; Jesuit influence, 137; in New York, 208, 228n2; in South Carolina, 100, 151–52, 166; student schedule requirement, 218; wartime service impact, 181–82
Ursuline communities, Quebec: buildings, 121–22; founding of, 2; French support, 134; Indian students, 9, 156, 220n9; literacy evidence, 10, 220n10
Ursuline community, Boston: boarding school promotion, 73; curriculum offerings, 148, 149; destruction of, 132; establishment of, 132, 208; Protestant students, 71; tuition costs, 95

INDEX

Ursuline community, Charleston, Massachusetts: classroom materials, 104, 155; curriculum offerings, 148, 155; destruction of, 47, 132; founding of, 58; opposition themes, 47, 56–57, 58

Ursuline community, New Orleans: African American students, 156; buildings, 122; class structure perspective, 151; in convent support network, 190; curriculum offerings, 148; founding of, 2–3, 9, 126; history scholarship about, 13; literacy evidence, 10–11; living conditions, 134; political elites, 72; in slavery system, 191; wartime service, 176

Vanderpoel, Emily Noyes, 50
Vidalia Whig and Illinois Intelligencer, 169–70
Virginia, 80, 81, 225n1
Visitation Academy, Georgetown: classroom materials, 86–87, 104, 105; curriculum offerings, 93, 97, 98, 100, 148; education impact numbers, 92; establishment of, 207, 225n3; facility description, 73; painting of, 123; political elites, 70, 79, 226n11; tuition, 227n13

Walch, Timothy, 35
Walker, David, 187
Walker, Peter, 194
wartime service, religious communities, 176–85, 230n6
Webb, Ben J., 88
Webster, Noah, 27–28, 231n12

Wells, Elizabeth, 209
Western Female Institute, 62–63, 76. *See also* Willard, Emma
Westminster Shorter Catechism, 22
Whall, Thomas, 46
Wheeler, Michael, 86–87
White, Rose Landry, 115, 208
White, Thomas, 61
Whitfield, James, 166
Whittelsey, Mrs. A. G., 59
Wiget, Bernardine, 46
Willard, Emma, 33, 50, 65–68, 72, 76, 77
Williams, Elizabeth, 211–12
Wilson, Samuel Thomas, 86, 209
women's literacy, overviews: early nineteenth-century U.S., 11–16, 200–201; French American colonies, 9–11; religious competition effects, 198–99; scholarship opportunities, 196–97, 201–2. *See also specific topics, e.g.,* convent academies; Oblate Sisters of Providence community; schoolbooks
Woodbridge, William C., 47–48, 65–66
Woodford, Frank B., 43
Woodson, Carter, 89
Woody, Thomas, 12, 52, 68–69
Worcester, Joseph Emerson, 33
Workman, Benjamin, 30
Wright, Elizabethada, 14
writing instruction, 109–10, 140–42

The Young Gentlemen and Lady's Monitor . . . , 35

Zagarri, Rosemarie, 13, 200
Zboray, Ronald, 36

CAROL MATTINGLY, a specialist in nineteenth-century rhetoric and composition, is a professor emerita at the University of Louisville and the author or editor of four books, including *Appropriate[ing] Dress: Women's Rhetorical Style in Nineteenth-Century America* and *Well-Tempered Women: Nineteenth-Century Temperance Rhetoric*.